The Gamekeeper
at Home

===

The Amateur
Poacher

RICHARD JEFFERIES

Born at Coate Farm, near Swindon

6 November 1848

Died at Goring, Sussex

14 August 1887

The Gamekeeper at Home *was first published
in the* Pall Mall Gazette *at irregular intervals
between 4 January and 24 April 1878 and in
volume form, revised, in the same year.* The
Amateur Poacher *was also serialized in the*
Pall Mall Gazette *between 1 March and 25 June
1879 and issued in volume form, revised, in that
year. Both books were first published anonymously.*

RICHARD JEFFERIES

The Gamekeeper
at Home

The Amateur
Poacher

With an Introduction by
RICHARD FITTER

OXFORD   NEW YORK   TORONTO   MELBOURNE
OXFORD UNIVERSITY PRESS

Oxford University Press, Walton Street, Oxford OX2 6DP

OXFORD LONDON GLASGOW
NEW YORK TORONTO MELBOURNE WELLINGTON
IBADAN NAIROBI DAR ES SALAAM CAPE TOWN
KUALA LUMPUR SINGAPORE JAKARTA HONG KONG TOKYO
DELHI BOMBAY CALCUTTA MADRAS KARACHI

Text first published in The World's Classics series, 1948. This
edition first published as an Oxford University Press paperback, 1978
Reprinted 1979

British Library Cataloguing in Publication Data

Jefferies, Richard
   The gamekeeper at home; &, The amateur poacher.
   1. Game protection – England – Wiltshire
   2. Poaching – England – Wiltshire
   I. Title II. Jefferies, Richard. The amateur poacher
   639'.95'0924   SK353   77–30722
   ISBN 0–19–281240–8

Printed in Great Britain by
Fletcher & Son Ltd, Norwich

CONTENTS

vi   *Contents*

INTRODUCTION

In many ways the world of Richard Jefferies is more remote from late twentieth-century England than it was from that of the Saxons who first settled in north Wiltshire more than a thousand years before. If you stand by Coate Water today, and can remember it as it was even thirty years ago, when I first visited it, you will be appalled. Between what Jefferies so often refers to as the lake or the shallow mere and the precipitous wooded slopes a mile or so to the south, runs the incessant roar of the M4, whose concrete ribbon slashes the Jefferies country in half. It is as if the District Railway ran slap through the nave of St. Paul's Cathedral. This fact alone sunders us from the mid-Victorian world that Jefferies so vividly evokes in *The Gamekeeper at Home* and *The Amateur Poacher*.

Jefferies, the son of a farmer, was born in 1848, at Coate Farm, now swallowed up in what we are no longer even allowed to call Swindon (itself a product of the high noon of Victorian economic success), but Thamesdown, a bastard invention of the bureaucrats who have with another pen thrown a motorway between the Thames and the downs. He was endowed with a temperament more usually associated with literary intellectuals than with farmers' sons, and although, as these two books amply show, he enjoyed most of the normal sporting pursuits of a country boy, he later developed an introspective way of mooning around on the downs that his family and neighbours clearly regarded as most unsatisfactory.

'Our Dick' baffled them, and indeed he was something of a phenomenon. His abilities put him into a very small category of highly talented writers on the countryside, alongside Arthur Young, William Cobbett, George Sturt, W. H. Hudson, and Edward Thomas. He was not an agrarian like Young, or a politician like Cobbett, or even a poet like Thomas. He was an observer of the ways of the human and animal inhabitants of the countryside, and an observer of the highest order. He had a most remarkable capacity for bringing the social life of Victorian Wiltshire—and, one cannot doubt, most of Victorian rural England too—into the sharpest relief. Open *The Gamekeeper at Home* at random and the first paragraph you light upon will show what I mean:

The book-learning of the keeper's boy is rather limited, for he was taught by the parish clerk and schoolmaster before the Education Acts were formulated. Still, he can read, and pores over the weekly paper of rural sports, &c., taken for the guests at the great house and when out of date sent down to the keeper's cottage. In fact, he shows a little too much interest in the turf columns to be quite satisfactory to his father, who is somewhat anxious about his acquaintance with the jockeys from the training-stables on the downs hard by—an acquaintance he discourages as tending to no good. Like his father, he is never seen abroad without a pair of leathern gaiters, and, if not a gun, a stout gnarled ground-ash stick in his hand.

Every line of this paragraph shows how keenly he has observed, and how retentively he has remembered, those little touches about the days before the Education Act of 1870 ('we must educate our masters')

and about the weekly papers (was it *The Field* or perhaps *Land and Water* or *The Country Gentleman?*) taken for the guests at the great house and later sent down to the keeper. Even that last 'down' evokes the whole apparatus of Victorian class gradations.

Most of the later writings are as much concerned with the wildlife of the countryside as with its human inhabitants. He soon moved away from his beloved Wiltshire, even up to Cobbett's hated Wen ('the great Wen of all' was what he called it), and from the social matrix he had so closely observed from his median vantage point, halfway between the Olympian inhabitants of the great house and the landless labourers at the bottom of the heap. But the wildlife he could observe wherever he went, whether at Coate, at a still almost rural Surbiton in London-ward Surrey, or eventually at Goring on the Sussex coastal plain. By a curious coincidence I have lived not more than twenty miles and sometimes only two miles from all three, and can testify that his Surbiton and Goring countrysides have been obliterated with even greater thoroughness than the district around Coate. But in his time the wildlife was there and he recorded what he saw, accurately and unsentimentally, thus avoiding the greatest pitfall of the nature writer, the 'fluffy bunny' syndrome. Here is how he deals with rabbits:

The grass conceals the body of the animal, and nothing is visible beyond the tips of the ears; and at thirty yards distance one pair of ears is very like another pair. The developed ear is, however, less pointed than the other; and in the rabbit of a proper size they are or seem to be wider apart. The eye is also guided by the grass itself and the elevation of the rabbit's head above it when lifted in alarm at a chance sound: if the animal is full grown of course the head stands higher. In motion the difference is at once seen; the larger animal's back and flanks show boldly, while the lesser seems to slip through the grass. By these signs, and by a kind of instinct which grows upon one when always in the field, it is possible to distinguish between them even in tall grass and in the gloaming.

It might be thought that in a gamekeeping context he would be unsentimental, but let himself go at other times. But not a bit of it. Here he is again on rabbits in *Wild Life in a Southern County*:

In the evening, as the shadows deepen and a hush falls upon the meads, they come out and chase and romp with each other. When a couple are at play one will rush ten or a dozen yards away and begin to nibble as if totally unconscious of the other. The second meanwhile nibbles too, but all the while stealthily moves forward, not direct, but sideways, towards the first, demurely feeding. Suddenly the second makes a spring; the first, who has been watching out of the corner of his eye all the time, is off like the wind. Or sometimes he will turn and face the other, and jump clean over, a foot high. Sometimes both leap up together in the exuberance of their mirth.

Jefferies's observations are by no means confined to the natural features of the countryside. They also throw a flood of light on contemporary social habits, and make one realise that with human behaviour there is nothing new under the sun. We think of today as being a time of especial social violence, but through the interstices of Jefferies's prose we catch glimpses of an equally violent society a hundred years ago. Does not this have quite a modern ring?

Intoxicated louts think it fine fun to unhinge gates, and
let cattle and horses stray abroad, to tear down rails, and
especially to push the coping-stones off the parapets of
bridges which span small streams. They consider it clever
to heave these over with a splash into the water, or to
throw down half a dozen yards of 'dry wall' . . . Much
more serious offences than these are sometimes committed,
as cutting horses with knives, and other mutilations.

The only acts that do not occur almost daily today
are the horse mutilations. Such is the change in
public opinion on cruelty to animals that the one
thing guaranteed to provoke a public outcry nowadays would be the discovery of someone treating a
horse in this way.

Jefferies's career was brief, for he died at the early
age of 39, but once he decided to earn his living by
writing he was doomed to write at pressure for the
rest of his days, like Edward Thomas a generation
later. The remarkable thing is that his country
writings are so good, despite the overwork. But that
is partly because a naturalist, even in a town, never
runs out of material. However much he observes the
same thing year after year, it is never quite the same.
One year the first brimstone butterflies emerge in
early March, in another not until Easter. One year
the beech leaves colour and fall in late October, in
another not until well after Martinmas. One pair of
cock blackbirds will spar and fight for their territory
on the lawn all day; another will respect each other's
boundaries with hardly more than a token flourish
of the tail. In fact, just as human reactions to the
same situation are infinite in their variety—though

sometimes appearing to have a horrid sameness—so
it is in the countryside. So long as a country writer
is not confined to his bed, he can always find something to write about, without going to the lengths of
James Barrie's journalist who could write for any
journal he chose on the subject of his walking-stick
alone.

Jefferies began, like so many other writers, as a
journalist on his local paper, the *North Wilts Herald*.
But unlike the others he proved to be a writer
rather than a journalist, so his way forward lay not
into the crowded corridors of Fleet Street, but to the
lonely uplands of freelancing. His first breakthrough
came in November 1872 with a series of percipient
letters to *The Times* on the Wiltshire agricultural
labourer, 'usually strong built, broad-shouldered and
massive in frame, but . . . spoilt by the clumsiness of
his walk and the want of grace in his appearance',
just when public interest had been aroused by Joseph
Arch and his Farm Labourers' Union. From that
good start he established his position with *The Gamekeeper at Home* six years later, in which he showed as
deep a knowledge of the ways of the keeper, and his
enemies the poachers, as the letters had revealed of
the farm worker. The success of *The Amateur Poacher*,
following in the next year, enabled him to abandon
the writing of his rather futile novels. He must have
come to realize that if he wrote about what he knew,
he succeeded, but if he tried to imagine the feelings
of people in other walks of life he failed. So for the
rest of his life he poured out books of countryside
observations, at first written as books, like *Wild Life*

in a Southern County (1879) and *Round about a Great Estate* (1880), but later, after he had moved to Surbiton, to be nearer his markets, often largely composed of articles that had appeared elsewhere: *Nature Near London* (1883), *The Life of the Fields* (1885), *The Open Air* (1889). In between he managed at last to write two successful novels, both almost wholly autobiographical, *Bevis, the Story of a Boy* (1882) and *Amaryllis at the Fair* (1887), and one actual autobiography, *The Story of my Heart* (1883), which is one of the more remarkable self-portraits to come out of the nineteenth century. It is an intimate record, not of his career, but of his mental development, such as few other writers have even attempted. No wonder most readers find it rather tough going. So they do the writings of the great mystics, and this is perhaps the only work of mystical genius to come out of the English countryside.

The Jefferies country is still, despite Thamesdown and the M4, a rather special corner of southern England. There is nothing very unusual about Coate Water, now officially devoted to the recreation of the citizens of Thamesdown, except that in this part of England, unlike Cheshire, Shropshire, and East Anglia, shallow meres without concrete banks are distinctly unusual. Even though Coate Water is artificial, resulting from the damming of a small brook, it looks a great deal more natural than most other stretches of fresh water south of the Thames. The farmland between Coate and the downs is also not out of the way, but looks nowadays a great deal pleasanter as seen from the M4 than when looking towards that motorway—which it is difficult to avoid doing. But when you get to the escarpment of the downs, the scene changes completely. Steep cliff-like slopes and ravines cut into the scarp and are thickly wooded. I know of nowhere else quite like this corner of the southern chalklands. There are other steep slopes—my own village of Chinnor in the Oxfordshire Chilterns owes its name to lying below one—and some of them are wooded. There are other ravines, and some of these are wooded too, though some like the famous Devil's Dyke in the South Downs of Sussex, are not. But to find a similar combination of wooded cliffs and ravines you would have to go, not anywhere on the chalk, except perhaps around Petersfield in Hampshire, but to the carboniferous limestone, in the Mendips or the Brecon Beacons. Beyond the scarp still lie the downs, stretching southward, almost unbuilt on, for several miles, and with only a few interruptions right to the southern rim of Salisbury Plain. Here is one of the larger stretches in southern England of perhaps not unspoilt, for the stutter of the tractor has long replaced the tinkle of the sheep bell, but open and gloriously windswept country. There are fewer thyme-scented banks than when Jefferies lay and dreamed on Liddington Castle and conceived *The Story of My Heart*—the tractor has seen to that—but here, as elsewhere on the wide chalklands of Wessex, a man can still come to seek his gods and not hear engines droning *all* the time.

November 1977   RICHARD FITTER

The Gamekeeper
at Home

SKETCHES OF NATURAL HISTORY
AND RURAL LIFE

———

When shaws beene sheene, and shradds full fayre,
And leaves both large and longe,
It is merrye walking in the fayre forrest,
To hear the small birdes songe.

BALLAD OF GUY OF GISBORNE

PREFACE

THOSE who delight in roaming about amongst the fields and lanes, or have spent any time in a country house, can hardly have failed to notice the custodian of the woods and covers, or to observe that he is often something of a 'character.' The Gamekeeper forms, indeed, so prominent a figure in rural life as almost to demand some biographical record of his work and ways. From the man to the territories over which he bears sway—the meadows, woods, and streams—and to his subjects, their furred and feathered inhabitants, is a natural transition. The enemies against whom he wages incessant warfare—vermin, poachers, and trespassers—must, of course, be included in such a survey.

Although, for ease and convenience of illustration, the character of a particular Keeper has been used as a nucleus about which to arrange materials that would otherwise have lacked a connecting link, the facts here collected are really entirely derived from original observation.

R. J.

CHAPTER I

THE keeper's cottage stands in a sheltered 'coombe', or narrow hollow of the woodlands, overshadowed by a mighty Spanish chestnut, bare now of leaves, but in summer a noble tree. The ash wood covers the slope at the rear; on one side is a garden, and on the other a long strip of meadow with elms. In front, and somewhat lower, a streamlet winds, fringing the sward, and across it the fir plantations begin, their dark sombre foliage hanging over the water. A dead willow trunk thrown from bank to bank forms a rude bridge; the tree, not even squared, gives little surface for the foot, and in frosty weather a slip is easy. From this primitive contrivance a path, out of which others fork, leads into the intricacies of the covers, and from the garden a wicket-gate opens on the ash wood. The elms in the meadow are full of rooks' nests, and in the spring the coombe will resound with their cawing; these black bandits, who do not touch it at other times, will then ravage the garden to feed their hungry young, despite ingenious scarecrows. A row of kennels, tenanted by a dozen dogs, extends behind the cottage: lean retrievers yet unbroken, yelping spaniels, pointers, and perhaps a few greyhounds or fancy breeds, if 'young master' has a taste that way.

Beside the kennels is a shed ornamented with rows upon rows of dead and dried vermin, furred and feathered, impaled for their misdeeds; and over the door a couple of horseshoes nailed for luck—a superstition yet lingering in the by-ways of the woods and hills. Within are the ferret hutches, warm and dry; for the ferret is a shivery creature, and likes nothing so well as to nozzle down in a coat-pocket with a little hay. Here are spades and billhooks, twine and rabbit nets, traps, and other odds and ends scattered about with the wires and poacher's implements impounded from time to time.

In a dark corner there lies a singular-looking piece of mechanism, a relic of the olden times, which when dragged into the light turns out to be a man-trap. These terrible engines have long since been disused—being illegal, like spring-guns—and the rust has gathered thickly on the metal. But, old though it be, it still acts perfectly, and can be 'set' as well now as when in bygone days poachers and thieves used to prod the ground and the long grass, before they stepped among it, with a stick, for fear of mutilation.

The trap is almost precisely similar to the common rat-trap or gin still employed to destroy vermin, but greatly exaggerated in size, so that if stood on end it reaches to the waist, or above. The jaws of this iron wolf are horrible to contemplate—rows of serrated projections, which fit into each other when closed, alternating with spikes a couple of inches long, like tusks. To set the trap you have to stand on the spring —the weight of a man is about sufficient to press it down; and, to avoid danger to the person preparing this little surprise, a band of iron can be pushed forward to hold the spring while the catch is put into position, and the machine itself is hidden among the bushes or covered with dead leaves. Now touch the pan with a stout walking-stick—the jaws cut it in two in the twinkling of an eye. They seem to snap together with a vicious energy, powerful enough to break the bone of the leg; and assuredly no man ever got free whose foot was once caught by these terrible teeth.

The keeper will tell you that it used to be set up in the corner of the gardens and orchard belonging to the great house, and which in the pre-policemen days were almost nightly robbed. He thinks there were quite as many such traps set in the gardens just outside the towns as ever there were in the woods and preserves of the country proper. He recollects but one old man (a mole-catcher) who actually had experienced in his youth the sensation of being caught; he went lame on one foot, the sinews having been cut or divided. The trap could be chained to its place if desired; but, as a matter of fact, a chain was unnecessary, for no man could possibly drag this torturing clog along.

Another outhouse attached to the cottage contains a copper for preparing the food for both quadrupeds and birds. Some poultry run about the mead, and perhaps with them are feeding the fancy foreign ducks which in summer swim in the lake before the hall.

The cottage is thatched and oddly gabled—built before 'improvements' came into fashion—yet cosy; with walls three feet thick, which keep out the cold of winter and the heat of summer. This is not solid masonry; there are two shells, as it were, filled up between with rubble and mortar rammed down hard.

Inside the door the floor of brick is a step below the level of the ground. Sometimes a peculiar but not altogether unpleasant odour fills the low-pitched sitting room—it is emitted by the roots burning upon the fire, hissing as the sap exudes and boils in the fierce heat. When the annual fall of timber takes place the butts of the trees are often left in the earth, to be afterwards grubbed and split for firewood, which goes to the great house or is sold. There still remain the roots, which are cut into useful lengths and divided among the upper employés. From elm and oak and ash, and the crude turpentine of the fir, this aromatic odour, the scent of the earth in which they grew, is exhaled as they burn.

The ceiling is low and crossed by one huge square beam of oak, darkened by smoke and age. The keeper's double-barrelled gun is suspended from this beam: there are several other guns in the house, but this, the favourite, alone hangs where it did before he had children—so strong is habit; the rest are yet more out of danger. It has been a noble weapon, though now showing signs of age—the interior of the breech worn larger than the rest of the barrel from constant use; so much so that, before it was converted to a breech-loader, the wad when the ramrod pushed it down would slip the last six inches, so loosely fitting as to barely answer its purpose of retaining the shot; so that when cleaned out, before the smoke fouled it again, he had to load with paper. This in a measure anticipated the 'choke-bore', and his gun was always famous for its killing power. The varnish is worn from the stock by incessant friction against his coat, showing the real grain of the walnut-wood, and the trigger-guard with the polish of the sleeve shines like silver. It has been his companion for so many years that it is not strange he should feel an affection for it; no other ever fitted the shoulder so well, or came with such delicate precision to the 'present' position. So accustomed is he to its balance and 'hang' in the hand that he never thinks of aiming; he simply looks at the object, still or moving, throws the gun up

from the hollow of his arm, and instantly pulls the
trigger, staying not a second to glance along the
barrel. It has become almost a portion of his body,
answering like a limb to the volition of will without
the intervention of reflection. The hammers are
chased and elegantly shaped—perfectly matching:
when once the screw came loose, and the jar of a shot
jerked one off among the dead leaves apparently beyond hope of recovery, he never rested night or day
till by continuous search and sifting the artistic piece
of metal was found. Nothing destroys the symmetry
of a gun so much as hammers which are not pairs;
and well he knew that he should never get a smith to
replace that delicate piece of workmanship, for this
gun came originally from the hands of a famous
maker, who got fifty, or perhaps even seventy guineas
for it years ago. It did not shoot to please the purchaser—guns of the very best character sometimes
take use to get into thorough order—and was thrown
aside, and so the gun became the keeper's.

These fine old guns often have a romance clinging
to them, and sometimes the history is a sad one. Upstairs he still keeps the old copper powder-flask
curiously chased and engraved, yet strong enough to
bear the weight of the bearer, if by chance he sat
down upon it while in his pocket, together with the
shot-belt and punch for cutting out the wads from
cardboard or an old felt hat. These the modern
system of loading at the breech has cast aside. Here,
also, is the apparatus for filling empty cartridge-cases
—a work which in the season occupies him many
hours.

Being an artist in his way, he takes a pride in the
shine and polish of his master's guns, which are not

always here, but come down at intervals to be cleaned and attended to. And woe be to the first kid gloves that touch them afterwards; for a gun, like a sardine, should be kept in fine oil, not thickly encrusting it, but, as it were, rubbed into and oozing from the pores of the metal and wood. Paraffin is an abomination in his eyes (for preserving from rust), and no modern patent oil, he thinks, can compare with a drop of gin for the locks—the spirit never congeals in cold weather, and the hammer comes up with a clear, sharp snick. He has two or three small screwdrivers and gunsmith's implements to take the locks to pieces; for gentlemen are sometimes careless and throw their guns down on the wet grass, and if a single drop of water should by chance penetrate under the plate it will play mischief with the works, if the first speck of rust be not forthwith removed.

His dog-whistle hangs at his buttonhole. His pocket-knife is a basket of tools in itself, most probably a present from some youthful sportsman who was placed under his care to learn how to handle a gun. The corkscrew it contains has seen much service at luncheon-time, when under a sturdy oak, or in a sheltered nook of the lane, where the hawthorn hedge and the fern broke the force of the wind, a merry shooting party sat down to a well-packed hamper and wanted someone to draw the corks. Not but what the back of the larger blade has not artistically tapped off the neck of many a bottle, hitting it gently upwards against the rim. Nor must his keys be forgotten. The paths through the preserves, where they debouch on a public lane or road, are closed with high-sparred wicket gates, well pitched to stand the weather, and carefully locked, and of course he has a key. His watch, made on purpose for those who walk by night, tells him the time in the densest darkness of the woods. On pressing a spring and holding it near the ear, it strikes the hour last past, then the quarters which have since elapsed; so that even when he cannot see an inch before his face he knows the time within fifteen minutes at the outside, which is near enough for practical purposes.

In personal appearance he would be a tall man were it not that he has contracted a slight stoop in the passage of the years, not from weakness or decay of nature, but because men who walk much lean forward somewhat, which has a tendency to round the shoulders. The weight of the gun, and often of a heavy game-bag dragging downwards, has increased this defect of his figure, and, as is usual after a certain age, even with those who lead a temperate life, he begins to show signs of corpulency. But these short-comings only slightly detract from the manliness of his appearance, and in youth it is easy to see that he must have been an athlete. There is still plenty of power in the long sinewy arms, brown hands, and bull-neck, and intense vital energy in the bright blue eye. He is an ash-tree man, as a certain famous writer would say; hard, tough, unconquerable by wind or weather, fearless of his fellows, yielding but by slow and imperceptible degrees to the work of time. His neck has become the colour of mahogany, sun and tempest have left their indelible marks upon his face; and he speaks from the depths of his broad chest, as men do who talk much in the open air, shouting across the fields and through the copses. There is a solidity in his very footstep, and he stands like an oak. He meets your eye full and unshirkingly, yet without insolence; not as the labourers do, who either stare with sullen ill-will or look on the earth. In brief, freedom and constant contact with nature have made him every inch a man; and here in this nineteenth century of civilised effeminacy may be seen some relic of what men were in the old feudal days when they dwelt practically in the woods. The shoulder of his coat is worn a little where the gun rubs, and so is his sleeve; otherwise he is fairly well dressed.

Perfectly civil to everyone, and with a willing manner towards his master and his master's guests, he has a wonderful knack of getting his own way. Whatever the great house may propose in the shooting line, the keeper is pretty certain to dispose of in the end as he pleases; for he has a voluble 'silver' tongue, and is full of objections, reasons, excuses, suggestions, all delivered with a deprecatory air of superior knowledge which he hardly likes to intrude upon his betters, much as he would regret to see them go wrong. So he really takes the lead, and in nine cases in ten the result proves he is right, as minute local knowledge naturally must be when intelligently applied.

Not only in such matters as the best course for the shooting party to follow, or in advice bearing upon the preserves, but in concerns of a wider scope, his influence is felt. A keen, shrewd judge of horseflesh— (how is it that if a man understands one animal he seems to instinctively see through all?)—his master in a careless way often asks his opinion before concluding a bargain. Of course the question is not put direct, but 'By-the-by, when the hounds were here you saw so-and-so's mare; what do you think of her?' The keeper blurts out his answer, not always flattering or very delicately expressed; and his view is not forgotten. For when a trusted servant like this accompanies his master often in solitary rambles for hours together, dignity must unbend now and then, however great the social difference between them; and thus a man of strong individuality and a really valuable gift of observation insensibly guides his master.

Passing across the turnips, the landlord, who perhaps never sees his farms save when thus crossing them with a gun, remarks that they look clean and free from weeds; whereupon the keeper, walking respectfully a little in the rear, replies that so-and-so, the tenant, is a capital farmer, a preserver of foxes and game, but has suffered from the floods—a reply that leads to inquiries, and perhaps a welcome reduction of rent. On the other hand, the owner's attention is thus often called to abuses. In this way an evilly-disposed keeper may, it is true, do great wrongs, having access to the owner and, in familiar phrase, 'his ear'. I am at present delineating the upright keeper, such as are in existence still, notwithstanding the abuse lavished upon them as a class—often, it is to be feared, too well deserved. It is not difficult to see how in this way a man whose position is lowly may in an indirect way exercise a powerful influence upon a large estate.

He is very 'great' on dogs (and, indeed, on all other animals); his opinion is listened to and taken by everybody round about who has a dog, and sometimes he has three or four under treatment for divers ills. By this knowledge many 'tips' are gained, and occasionally he makes a good thing by selling a pup at a high price. He may even be seen, with his velveteen jacket carefully brushed, his ground-ash stick under his arm, and hat in hand, treading daintily for fear of soiling the carpet with his shoe, in the ante-room, gravely prescribing for the ailing pug in which the ladies are interested.

At the farm-houses he is invited to sit down and take a glass, being welcome for his gossip of the great house, and because, having in the course of years been thrown into the society of all classes, he has gradually acquired a certain tact and power of accommodating himself to his listener. For the keeper, when he fulfils his duty in a quiet way as a man of experience does, is by no means an unpopular character. It is the too officious man who creates a feeling among the tenants against himself and the whole question of game. But the quiet experienced hand, with a shrewd knowledge of men as well as the technicalities of his profession, grows to be liked by the tenantry, and becomes a local authority on animal life.

Proud, and not without reason, of his vigour and strength, he will tell you that though between fifty and sixty he can still step briskly through a heavy field-day, despite the weight of reserve ammunition he carries. He can keep on his feet without fatigue from morn till eve, and goes his rounds without abating one inch of the distance. In one thing alone he feels his years—*i.e.* in pace; and when 'young master,' who is a disciple of the modern athletic school, comes out, it is about as much as ever he can do to keep up with him over the stubble. Never once for the last thirty years has he tossed on a bed of sickness; never once has he failed to rise from his slumber refreshed and ready for his labour. His secret is—but let him tell it in his own words:

'It's indoors, sir, as kills half the people; being in-

doors three parts of the day, and next to that taking
too much drink and vittals. Eating's as bad as drinking; and there ain't nothing like fresh air and the
smell of the woods. You should come out here in the
spring, when the oak timber is throwed (because, you
see, the sap be rising, and the bark strips then), and
just sit down on a stick fresh peeled—I means a trunk,
you know—and sniff up the scent of that there oak
bark. It goes right down your throat, and preserves
your lungs as the tan do leather. And I've heard say
as folk who work in the tan-yards never have no illness. There's always a smell from trees, dead or living
—I could tell what wood a log was in the dark by my
nose; and the air is better where the woods be. The
ladies up in the great house sometimes goes out into
the fir plantations—the turpentine scents strong, you
see—and they say it's good for the chest; but, bless
you, you must live in it. People go abroad, I'm told,
to live in the pine forests to cure 'em: I say these here
oaks have got every bit as much good in that way. I
never eat but two meals a day—breakfast and supper:
what you would call dinner—and maybe in the
middle of the day a hunch of dry bread and an apple.
I take a deal for breakfast, and I'm rather lear [hun-
gry] at supper; but you may lay your oath that's why
I'm what I am in the way of health. People stuffs
theirselves, and by consequence it breaks out, you see.
It's the same with cattle; they're overfed, tied up in
stalls and stuffed, and never no exercise, and mostly
oily food too. It stands to reason they must get bad:
and that's the real cause of these here rinderpests and
pleuro-pneumonia and what-nots. At least that's my
notion. I'm in the woods all day, and never comes
home till supper—'cept, of course, in breeding-time,

to fetch the meal and stuff for the birds—so I gets the fresh air, you see; and the fresh air is the life, sir. There's the smell of the earth, too—'specially just as the plough turns it up—which is a fine thing; and the hedges and the grass are as sweet as sugar after a shower. Anything with a green leaf is the thing, depend upon it, if you want to live healthy. I never signed no pledge; and if a man asks me to take a glass of ale, I never says him no. But I ain't got no barrel at home; and all the time I've been in this here place, I've never been to a public. Gentlemen give me tips—of course they does; and much obliged I be; but I takes it to my missus. Many's the time they've axed me to have a glass of champagne or brandy when we've had lunch under the hedge; but I says no, and would like a glass of beer best, which I gets, of course. No; when I drinks, I drinks ale: but most in general I drinks no strong liquor. Great coat!—cold weather! I never put no great coat on this thirty year. These here woods be as good as a topcoat in cold weather. Come off the open field with the east wind cutting into you, and get inside they firs and you'll feel warm in a minute. If you goes into the ash wood you must go in farther, because the wind comes more between the poles.' Fresh air, exercise, frugal food and drink, the odour of the earth and the trees—these have given him, as he nears his sixtieth year, the strength and vitality of early manhood.

He has his faults: notably, a hastiness of temper towards his undermen, and towards labourers and wood-cutters who transgress his rules. He is apt to use his ground-ash stick rather freely without thought of consequences, and has got into trouble more than once in that way. When he takes a dislike or suspicion of a man, nothing will remove it; he is stubbornly inimical and unforgiving, totally incapable of comprehending the idea of loving an enemy. He hates cordially in the true pagan fashion of old. He is full of prejudices, and has some ideas which almost amount to superstitions; and, though he fears nothing, has a vague feeling that sometimes there is 'summat' inexplicable in the dark and desolate places. Such is this modern man of the woods.

The impressions of youth are always strongest with us, and so it is that recollecting the scenes in which he passed his earlier days he looks with some contempt upon the style of agriculture followed in the locality; for he was born in the north, where the farms are sometimes of a great area, though perhaps not so rich in soil, and he cannot forgive the tenants here because they have not got herds of three or four hundred horned cattle. Before he settled down in the south he had many changes of situation, and was thus brought in contact with a wonderful number of gentlemen, titled or otherwise distinguished, whose peculiarities of speech or appearance he loves to dwell upon. If the valet sees the hero or the statesman too closely, so sometimes does the gamekeeper. A great man must have moments when it is a relief to fling off the constant posturing necessary before the world; and there is freshness in the gamekeeper's unstudied conversation. The keeper thinks that nothing reveals a gentleman's character so much as his 'tips'.

'Gentlemen is very curious in tips,' he says, 'and there ain't nothing so difficult as to know what's coming. Most in general them as be the biggest guns, and what you would think would come out handsome, chucks you a crown and no more; and them as you

knows ain't much go in the way of money slips a sove-
reign into your fist. There's a deal in the way of giving it too, as perhaps you wouldn't think. Some gents
does it as much as to say they're much obliged to you
for kindly taking it. Some does it as if they were
chucking a bone to a dog. One place where I was,
the governor were the haughtiest man as ever you see.
When the shooting was done—after a great party, you
never knowed whether he were pleased or not—he
never took no more notice of you than if you were a
tree. But I found him out arter a time or two. You
had to walk close behind him, as if you were a
spaniel; and by-and-by he would slip his hand round
behind his back—without a word, mind—and you
had to take what was in it, and never touch your hat
or so much as "Thank you, sir." It were always a five-
pound note if the shooting had been good; but it never
seemed to come so sweet as if he'd done it to your
face.'

The keeper gets a goodly number of tips in the
course of the year, from visitors at the great house,
from naturalists who come now and then, from the
sportsmen, and regularly from the masters of three
packs of hounds; not to mention odd moneys at
intervals in various ways, as when he goes round to
deliver presents of game to the chief tenants on the
estate or to the owner's private friends. Gentlemen
who take an interest in such things come out every
spring to see the young broods of pheasants—which,
indeed, are a pretty sight—and they always leave
something behind them. In the summer a few picnic
parties come from the town or the country round
about, having permission to enter the grounds. In the
winter half a dozen young gentlemen have a turn at

the ferreting; a great burrow is chosen, three or four ferrets put in at once without any nets, so that the rabbits may bolt freely, and then the shooting is like volleys of musketry fire. For sport like this the young gentlemen tip freely. After the rook-shooting party in the spring from the great house, with their rook-rifles and sometimes crossbows, have had the pick of the young birds, some few of the tenants are admitted to shoot the remainder—a task that spreads perhaps over two or even three days, and there is a good deal of liquor and silver going about. Then gentlemen come to fish in the mere, having got the necessary permission, and they want bait and some attention, which the keeper's lad, being an adept himself, can render better than anyone else; and so he too gets his share. Besides which, being swift of foot, and with a shrewd idea which way the fox will run when the hunt is up, he is to the fore when a lady or some timid gentleman wants a gate opened—a service not performed in vain. For breaking-in dogs also the keeper is often paid well; and, in short he is one of those fortunate individuals whom all the world tips.

CHAPTER II

HIS FAMILY AND CASTE

THE interior of the cottage is exquisitely clean; it has that bright pleasant appearance which is only possible when the housewife feels a pride in her duties, and goes about them with a cheerful heart. Not a speck of dust can be seen upon the furniture, amongst which is a large old-fashioned sofa: the window panes are clear and transparent—a certain sign of loving care expended on the place, as on the other hand dirty windows are an indication of neglect, so much so that the character of the cottager may almost be guessed from a glance at her glass. The keeper's wife is a buxom vivacious dame, whose manners from occasional contact with the upper ranks—the ladies from the great house sometimes look in for a few minutes to chat with so old a servant of the family —are above what are usually found in her station. She receives her callers—and they are many—with a quiet, respectful dignity: desirous of pleasing, yet quite at her ease.

Across the back of the sofa there lies a rug of some beautiful fur which catches the eye, but which at first the visitor cannot identify. Its stripes are familiar, and not unlike the tiger's, but the colour is not that of the forest tyrant. She explains that this rug comes within her special sphere. It is a carriage-rug of cat-skin; the skins carefully selected to match exactly, and cured and prepared in the same way as other more famous furs. They have only just been sewn together, and the rug is now spread on the sofa to dry. She has made rugs, she will tell you, entirely of black cat skins, and very handsome they looked; but not equal to this, which is wholly of the tabby. Certainly the gloss and stripe, the soft warmth and feel to the hand, seem to rival many foreign and costly importations. Besides carriage-rugs, the gamekeeper's wife has made others for the feet—some many-coloured, like Joseph's coat.

All the cats to which these skins belonged were shot or caught in the traps set for vermin by her husband and his assistants. The majority were wild—that is, had taken up their residence in the woods, reverting to their natural state, and causing great havoc among the game. Feasting like this and in the joys of freedom, many had grown to a truly enormous size, not in fat, as the domestic animal does, but in length of back and limb. These afforded the best skins; perhaps out of eight or nine killed but two would be available or worth preserving.

This gives an idea of the extraordinary number of cats which stray abroad and get their living by poaching. They invariably gravitate towards the woods. The instance in point is taken from an outlying district far from a town, where the nuisance is comparatively small; but in the preserves say from ten to twenty miles round London the cats thus killed must be counted by thousands. Families change their homes, the cat is driven away by the new comer and takes to the field. In one little copse not more than two acres in extent, and about twelve miles from Hyde Park Corner, fifteen cats were shot in six weeks, and nearly all in one spot—their favourite haunt. When two or three wild or homeless animals take up their abode in a wood, they speedily attract half a dozen hitherto tame ones; and, if they were not destroyed, it would be impossible to keep either game or rabbits.

She has her own receipts for preserving furs and feathers, and long practice has rendered her an adept. Here are squirrels' skins also prepared; some with the bushy tail attached, and some without. They vary in size and the colour of the tail, which is often nearly white, in others more deeply tinged with red. The fur is used to line cloaks, and the tail is sometimes placed in ladies' hats. Now and then she gets a badger-skin, which old country folk used to have made into waistcoats, said to form an efficacious protection for weak chests. She has made rugs of several sewn together, but not often.

In the store-room upstairs there are a few splendid fox-skins, some with the tails tipped with white, others tipped with black. These are used for ladies' muffs, and look very handsome; the tail being occasionally curled round the muff. This sounds a delicate matter, and dangerously near the deadly sin of vulpecide. But it is not so. In these extensive woods, with their broad fringes of furze and heath, the foxes now and then become inconveniently numerous, and even cub-hunting will not kill them off sufficiently, especially if a great 'head' of game is kept up, for it attracts every species of beast of prey.

Besides the damage to game, the concentration of too many foxes in one district is opposed to the interest of the hunt—first, because the attendant destruction of neighbouring poultry causes an unpleasant feeling; next, because when the meet takes place the plethora of foxes spoils the sport. The day is wasted in 'chopping' them at every corner; the pack breaks up into several sections, despite whip, horn, and voice; and a good run across country cannot be obtained. So that once now and then a judicious thinning-out is necessary; and this is how the skins come into the hands of the keeper's wife. The heads go to ornament halls and staircases; so do the pads and occasionally the brush. The teeth make studs, set in gold; and no part of Reynard is thrown away, since the dogs eagerly snap up his body.

Once or twice she has made a moleskin waistcoat for a gentleman. This is a very tedious operation. Each little skin has to be separately prepared, and when finished hardly covers two square inches of surface. Consequently it requires several scores of skins, and the work is a year or more about. There is then the sewing together, which is not to be accomplished without much patience and skill. The fur is beautifully soft and glossy, with more resemblance to velvet than is possessed by any other natural substance, and very warm. Mittens for the wrists are also made of it, and skull-caps. Mole-skin waistcoats used to be thought a good deal of, but are now only met with occasionally as a curiosity.

The old wooden mole-trap is now almost extinct, superseded by the modern iron one, which anybody can set up. The ancient contrivance, a cylinder of wood, could only be placed in position by a practised hand, and from his experience in this the mole-catcher—locally called 'oont-catcher'—used to be an important personage in his way. He is now fast becoming extinct also—that is, as a distinct handicraftsman spending his whole time in such trapping. He was not unfrequently a man who had once occupied a subordinate place under a keeper, and when grown too feeble for harder labour, supported himself in this manner: contracting with the farmers to clear their fields by the season.

Neither stoats' nor weasels' skins are preserved, except now and then for stuffing to put under a glass case, though the stoat is closely allied to the genuine ermine. Polecats, too, are sometimes saved for the same purpose; in many woods they seem now quite extinct. The otter skin is valuable, but does not often come under the care of the keeper's wife. The keeper now and then shoots a grebe in the mere where the streamlet widens out into a small lake, which again is bordered by water-meadows. This bird is uncommon, but not altogether rare; sometimes two or three are killed in the year in this southern inland haunt. He also shoots her some jays, whose wings—as likewise the black-and-white magpie—are used for the same decorative purposes. Certain feathers from the jay are sought by the gentlemen who visit the great house, to make artificial flies for salmon-fishing. Of kingfishers she preserves a considerable number for ladies' hats, and some for glass cases. Once or twice she has been asked to prepare the woodpecker, whose plumage and harsh cry entitle him to the position of the parrot of our woods. Gentlemen interested in natural history often commission her husband to get them specimens of rare birds; and in the end he generally succeeds, though a long time may elapse before they cross his path. For them she has prepared some of the rare owls and hawks. She has a store of peacocks' feathers—every now and then people, especially ladies, call at the cottage and purchase these things. Country housewives still use the hare's 'pad' for several domestic purposes— was not the hare's foot once kept in the printing-offices?

The keeper's wife has nothing to do with rabbits,

but knows that their skins and fur are still bought in
large quantities. She has heard that geese were once
kept in large flocks almost entirely for their feathers,
which were plucked twice a year, she thinks; but this
is not practised now, at least not in the south. She has
had snakes' skins, or more properly sloughs, for the
curious. It is very difficult to get one entire; they are
fragile, and so twisted in the grass where the snake
leaves them as to be generally broken. Some country
folk put them in their hats to cure headache, which is
a very old superstition; but more in sport than earnest.
There are no deer now in the park. There used to be
a hundred years ago, and her husband has found
several cast antlers in the wood. The best are up at
the great house, but there is one on her staircase.
Will I take a few chestnuts? It is winter—the proper
time—and these are remarkably fine. No tree is
apparently so capricious in its yield as the chestnut
in English woods: the fruit of many is so small as to be
worthless, or else it does not reach maturity. But
these large ones are from a tree which bears a fine nut:
her husband has them saved every year. Here also
are half-a-dozen truffles if I will accept them: most
that are found go up to the great house; but of late
years they have not been sought for so carefully,
because coming in quantities from abroad. These
truffles are found, she believes, in the woods where the
soil is chalky. She used to gather many native herbs;
but tastes have changed, and new seasonings and
sauces have come into fashion.

Out of doors in his work the assistant upon whom
the gamekeeper places his chief reliance is his own
son—a lad hardly taller than the gun he carries, but
much older than would be supposed at first sight.

It is a curious physiological fact that although open-air life is so favourable to health, yet it has the apparent effect of stunting growth in early youth. Let two children be brought up together, one made to 'rough' it out of doors, and the other carefully tended and kept within; other things being equal, the boy of the drawing-room will be taller and to all appearance more developed than his companion. The labourer's children, for instance, who play in the lonely country roads and fields all day, whose parents lock their cottage doors when leaving for work in the morning so that their offspring shall not gain entrance and get into mischief, are almost invariably short for their age. In their case something may be justly attributed to coarse and scanty food; but the children of working farmers exhibit the same peculiarity, and although their food is not luxurious in quality, it is certainly not stinted in quantity. Some of the plough-boys and carters' lads seem scarcely fit to be put in charge of the huge cart-horses who obey their shouted orders, their heads being but a little way above the shafts—mere infants to look at. Yet they are fourteen or fifteen years of age. With these, and with the sons of farmers who in like manner work in the field, the period of development comes later than with town-bred boys. After sixteen or eighteen, after years of hesitation as it were, they suddenly shoot up, and become great, hulking, broad fellows, possessed of immense strength. So the keeper's boy is really much more a man than he appears, both in years and knowledge —meaning thereby that local intelligence, technical ability, and unwritten education which is the resultant of early practice and is quite distinct from book learning.

From his father he has imbibed the spirit of the woods and all the minutiæ of his art. First he learned to shoot; his highest ambition being satisfied in the beginning when permitted to carry the double-barrel home across the meadow. Then he was allowed occasionally to fire off the charges left in after the day's work, before the gun was hung against the beam. Next, from behind the fallen trunk of an oak he took aim at a sitting rabbit which had raised himself on his hind-quarters to listen suspiciously—resting the heavy barrels on the tree, and made nervous by the whispered instructions from the keeper kneeling on the grass out of sight behind, 'Aim at his shoulder, lad, if he be sitting sidelong; if a' be got his back to 'ee aim at his poll.' From this it was but a short step to be trusted with the single-barrel, and finally with the double; ultimately having one of his own and walking his own distinct rounds.

He is now a keen shot, even better than his father; for it is often observed that at a certain age young beginners in most manual arts reach an excellence which in later years fails them. Perhaps the muscles are more elastic, and respond instantaneously to the eye. This mere boy at snap-shooting in the 'rough' will beat crack sportsmen hollow. At the trap with pigeons he would probably fail; but in a narrow lane where the rabbits, driven out by the ferrets, just pop across barely a yard of open ground, where even a good shot may miss repeatedly, he is 'death' itself to the 'bunnies'. So, too, with a wood-hare—*i.e.* those hares that always lie in the woods as others do in the open fields and on the uplands. They are difficult to kill. They slip quietly out from the form in the rough grass under the ashstole, and all you have for guidance is the rustling and, perhaps, the tips of the ears, the body hidden by the tangled dead ferns and 'rowetty' stuff. When you try to aim the barrel knocks against the ashpoles, which are inconveniently near together, or the branches get in the way, and the hare dodges round a tree, and your cartridge simply barks a bough and cuts a tall dead thistle in twain. But the keeper's lad, who had waited for your fire, instantly follows, as it seems hardly lifting his gun to his shoulder, and the hare is stopped by the shot.

Rabbit-shooting, also, in an ash wood like this is trying to the temper; they double and dodge, and if you wait, thinking that the brown rascals must presently cross the partially open space yonder, lo! just at the very edge up go their white tails and they dive into the bowels of the earth, having made for hidden burrows. There is, of course, after all, nothing but a knack in these things. Still it is something to have acquired the knack. The lad, if you ask him, will proudly show off several gun tricks, as shooting left-handed, placing the butt at the left instead of the right shoulder and pulling the trigger with the left finger. He will knock over a running rabbit like this; and at short distances can shoot with tolerable certainty from under the arm without coming to the 'present,' or even holding the gun out like a pistol with one hand.

By slow degrees he has obtained an intimate acquaintance with every field on the place, and no little knowledge of natural history. He will decide at once, as if by a kind of instinct, where any particular bird or animal will be found at that hour.

He is more bitter than his father against poachers, and would like to see harder measures dealt out to them; but his chief use is in watching or checking the assistants, who act as beaters, ferreters, or keep up the banks and fences about the preserves, &c. Without a doubt these men are very untrustworthy, and practise many tricks. For instance, when they are set to ferret a bank, what is to prevent them, if the coast is clear, from hiding half a dozen dead rabbits in a burrow? Digging has frequently to be resorted to, and thus they can easily cast earth over and conceal the entrance to a hole. Many a wounded hare and pheasant that falls into the hands of the beaters never makes its appearance at the table of the sportsman; and doubtless they help themselves to the game captured in many a poacher's wire before giving notice of the discovery to the head man.

Some of these assistants wear waistcoats of calfskin with the hair on it. The hair is outside, and the roan-and-white colour has a curious appearance: the material is said to be very warm and durable. Such waistcoats were common years ago; but of late the looms and spindles of the manufacturing districts have reduced the most outlying of the provinces to a nearly dead uniformity of shoddy.

One pair of eyes cannot be everywhere at once; consequently the keeper, as his son grew up, found him a great help in this way: while he goes one road the lad goes the other, and the undermen never feel certain that someone is not about. Perhaps partly for this reason the lad is not a favourite in the village, and few if any of the other boys make friends with him. He is too loyal to permit of their playing trespass —he looks down on them as a little lower in the scale. Do they ever speak, even in the humblest way, to the proprietor of the place? In their turn they ostracize him after their fashion; so he becomes a silent, solitary youth, self-reliant, and old for his years.

He is a daring climber: as after the hawk's nest, generally made in the highest elms or pines—if that species of tree is to be found—taking the young birds to some farmhouse where the children delight in living creatures. Some who are not children, or are children of 'a larger growth', like to have a tame hawk in the garden, clipping the wings so that it shall not get away. Hawks have most amusing tricks, and in time become comparatively tame, at least to the person who feeds them. The beauty of the hawk's eye can hardly be surpassed: full, liquid, and piercing. In this way the keeper's boy often gets a stray shilling; also for young owls, which are still kept in some country houses, in the sheds or barns, to destroy the mice. When the corn was threshed with the flail, and was consequently exposed to the ravages of these creatures (if undisturbed they multiply in such numbers as would scarcely be credited) owls were almost domestic birds, being domiciled in every barn. Now they are more objects of curiosity, though still useful when large teams of horses are kept and require grain.

The keeper's boy sells, too, young squirrels from time to time, and the eggs of the rarer birds. In short, he has imbibed all the ways of the woods, and is an adept at everything, from 'harling' a rabbit upwards. By-the-bye, what is the etymology of 'harling', which seems to have the sense of entangling? It is done by passing the blade of the knife between the bone of the thigh and the great sinew—where there is nothing but skin—and then thrusting the other foot through the hole thus made. The rabbit or hare can then be conveniently carried by the loop thus formed, or slung on a stick or the gun-barrel across the shoulder. Of course the 'harling' is not done till the animal is dead.

The book-learning of the keeper's boy is rather limited, for he was taught by the parish clerk and schoolmaster before the Education Acts were formulated. Still, he can read, and pores over the weekly paper of rural sports, &c., taken for the guests at the great house and when out of date sent down to the keeper's cottage. In fact, he shows a little too much interest in the turf columns to be quite satisfactory to his father, who is somewhat anxious about his acquaintance with the jockeys from the training-stables on the downs hard by—an acquaintance he discourages as tending to no good. Like his father, he is never seen abroad without a pair of leathern gaiters, and, if not a gun, a stout gnarled ground-ash stick in his hand.

The gamekeeper's calling naturally tends to perpetuate itself and become hereditary in his family. The life is full of attraction to boys—the gun alone is hardly to be resisted; and, in addition, there are the animals and birds with which the office is associated, and the comparative freedom from restraint. Therefore one at least of his lads is sure to follow in his father's steps, and after a youth and early manhood spent out of doors in the woods it is next to impossible for him ever to quit the course he has taken. His children, again, must come within reach of similar influences, and thus for a lengthened period there must be a predisposition towards this special occupation.

Long service in one particular situation is not so common now as it used to be. Men move about from place to place, but wherever they are they still engage in the same capacity; and once a gamekeeper always a gamekeeper is pretty nearly true. Even in the present day instances of families holding the office for more than one or two generations on the same estate may be found; and years ago such was often the case. Occasionally the keeper's family has in this way by the slow passage of time become in a sense associated with that of his employer; many years of faithful service sensibly abridging the social gulf between master and servant. The contrary holds equally true; and so at the present day short terms of service and constant changes are accompanied by a sharp distinction separating employer and employé.

In such cases of long service the keeper holds a position more nearly resembling the retainer of the olden time than perhaps any other 'institution' of modern life. Pensioned off in his old age in the cottage where he was born, or which, at any rate, he first entered as a child, he potters about under his own vine and fig-tree—*i.e.* the pear and damson trees he planted forty years before—and is privileged now and then to give advice on matters arising out of the estate. He can watch the young broods of pheasants still, and superintend the mixing of their food: his trembling hand, upon the back of which the corded sinews are so strongly marked now the tissue has wasted, and over which the blue veins wander, can set a trap when the vermin become too venturesome.

He is yet a terror to evil-doers, and in no jot abates the dignity of more vigorous days; so that the superannuated ancients whose task it is to sweep the fallen leaves from the avenue and the walks near the great house, or to weed the gravel drive in feeble acknowledgement of the charitable dole they receive, fall to briskly when they see him coming with besom and rusty knife wherewith to 'uck' out the springing grass. He daily gossips with the head gardener (nominal), as old or older than himself; but his favourite haunt is a spot on the edge of a fir plantation where lies a fallen 'stick' of timber. Here, sheltered by the thick foliage of the fir and the hawthorn hedge at his back from the wind, he can sit on the log, and keep watch over a descending slope of meadow bounding the preserves and crossed by footpaths, along which loiterers may come. His sturdy son now sways the sceptre of ash over the old woods, and other descendants are employed about the place.

Sometimes in the great house there may be seen the counterfeit presentment of such a retainer limned fifty years ago, with dog and gun, and characteristic background of trees. His wife has perhaps survived till recently—strong and hale almost to the last; the most voluble gossip of the hamlet, full of traditions relating to the great house and its owners; a virago if crossed. It is recorded that upon one occasion in her prime she confronted a couple of poachers, and, by dint of tongue and threats of assistance close at hand, forced them to retire. It was at night that, her husband being from home and hearing shots in the wood, she sallied forth armed with a gun, faced the poachers, and actually drove them away, doubtless as much from fear of recognition as of bodily injury, though even that she was capable of inflicting, being totally fearless.

Nothing can be more natural than that when a man has shown an earnest desire to give satisfaction and proved himself honest and industrious, his employer should exhibit an interest in the welfare of his family. Now and then a small farm may be found in the hands of a man descended from or connected with a keeper. To successfully work a tenancy of such narrow limits it is necessary that the occupier should himself labour in the field from morn till dewy eve—the capacity to work being even more essential than capital; and so it happens that the smaller farms are occasionally held by men who have risen from the lower classes. The sons of keepers also become gentlemen's servants, as grooms, &c., in or out of the house.

A proposal was not long since made that gentlemen who had met with misfortune or were unable to obtain congenial employment should take service as gamekeepers—after the manner in which ladies were invited to become 'helps'. The idea does not appear to have received much practical support, nor does it seem feasible looking at the altered relations of society in these days. A gentleman 'out of luck', and with a taste for outdoor life and no objection to work, could surely do far better in the colonies, where he could shoot for his 'own hand', and in course of time achieve an independence, which he could never hope to attain as a gamekeeper.

In the olden times, no doubt, younger brothers did become, in fact, gamekeepers, head grooms, huntsmen, &c., to the head of the family. There was less of the sense of servitude and loss of dignity when the feeling of clanship was prevalent, when the great house was regarded as the natural and proper resource of every cadet of the family. But all this is changed. And for a man of education to descend to trapping vermin, filling cartridges, and feeding pheasants all his life would be a palpable absurdity with Australia open to him and the virgin soil of Central Africa eager for tillage.

Neither is every man's constitution capable of with-standing the wear and tear of a keeper's life. I have delineated the more favourable side already; but it has its shadows. Robust health, power of bearing fatigue, and above all of sustaining constant exposure in our most variable climate, are essential. No labourer is so exposed as the keeper: the labourer does not work in continued wet, and he is sure of his night's rest. The keeper is often about the best part of the night, and he cannot stay indoors because it rains.

The woods are lovely in the sunshine of summer; they are full of charm when the leaves are bursting forth in spring or turning brown with the early autumn frosts; but in wet weather in the winter they are the most wretched places conceivable in which to stroll about. The dead fern and the long grass are soaked with rain, and cling round the ankles with depressing tenacity. Every now and then the feet sink into soddened masses of decaying leaves—a good deal, too, of the soil itself is soft and peaty, being formed from the decomposed vegetation of years; while the boughs against which the passer-by must push fly back and send a cold shower down the neck. In fog as well as in rain the trees drip continuously; the boughs condense the mist and it falls in large drops —a puff of wind brings down a tropical shower.

In warm moist weather the damp steam that floats in the atmosphere is the reverse of pleasant. But a thaw is the worst of all, when the snow congealed on the branches and against the trunks on the windward side, slips and comes down in slushy, icy fragments, and the south-west or south-east wind, laden with chilling moisture, penetrates to the very marrow.

Even Robin Hood is recorded to have said that he could stand all kinds of weather with impunity, except the wind which accompanies a thaw. Wet grass has a special faculty for saturating leather. The very boots with which you may wade into a stream up to your ankles in perfect comfort are powerless to keep out the dew or raindrops on the grass-blades. The path of the keeper is by no means always strewn with flowers.

Probably the number of keepers has much increased of recent years, since the floodtide of commercial prosperity set in. Every successful merchant naturally purchases an estate in the country, and as naturally desires to see some game upon it. This necessitates a keeper and his staff. Then game itself—meaning live game—has become a marketable commodity, bought and sold very much as one might buy a standing crop of wheat.

Owners of land, whose properties are hardly extensive enough to enable them to live in the state which is understood by the expression 'country seat', frequently now resort to certain expedients to increase their incomes. They maintain a head of game large in comparison with the acreage: of course this must be attended to by a resident keeper; and they add to the original mansion various attractive extra buildings —*i.e.* a billiard-room, conservatories, and a range of modern stabling. The object, of course, is to let the house, the home farm, and the shooting for the season; including facilities for following the hunt. The proprietor is consequently only at home in the latter part of the spring and in the summer—sometimes not even then.

Again, there are large properties, copyhold, or held under long leases from corporate bodies, the tenants having the right to shoot. Instead of exercising the power themselves, they let the shooting. It consists mainly of partridges, hares, and rabbits; and one of their men looks after the game, combining the keeping a general watch with other duties. Professional men and gentlemen of independent income residing in county towns frequently take shooting of this kind. The farmers who farm their own land often make money of their game in the same way.

Gentlemen, too, combine and lease the shooting over wide areas, and of course find it necessary to employ keepers to look after their interests. The upper class of tradesmen in county and provincial towns where any facilities exist now sometimes form a private club or party and rent the shooting over several farms, having a joint-stock interest in one or more keepers. Poor land which used to be of very little value has, by the planting of covers and copses and the erection of a cottage for the keeper and a small 'box' for temporary occupation, in many cases been found to pay well if easily accessible from towns. Game, in short, was never so much sought after as at present; and the profession of gamekeeping is in no danger of falling into decay from lack of demand for the skill in woodcraft it implies.

CHAPTER III

IN THE FIELDS

Much other work besides preventing poaching falls upon the keeper, such as arranging for the battue, stopping fox 'earths' when the hounds are coming, feeding the young birds and often the old stock in severe weather, and even some labour of an agricultural character.

A successful battue requires no little *finesse* and patience exercised beforehand; weeks are spent in preparing for the amusement of a few hours. The pheasants are sometimes accustomed to leave the wood in a certain direction chosen as specially favourable for the sport—some copses at a little distance are used as feeding places, so that the birds naturally work that way. Much care is necessary to keep a good head of game together, not too much scattered about on the day fixed upon. The difficulty is to prevent them from wandering off in the early morning; and men are stationed like sentinels at the usual points of egress to drive them back. The beaters are usually men who have previously been employed in the woods and possess local knowledge of the ground, and are instructed in their duties long before: nothing must be left to the spur of the moment. Something of the skill of the general is wanted to organise a great battue: an instinctive insight into the best places to plant the guns, while the whole body of sportsmen, beaters, keepers with ammunition, should move in concert.

The gamekeeper finds his work fall upon him harder now than it used to do: first, sportsmen look for a heavier return of killed and wounded; next, they are seldom willing to take much personal trouble to find the game, but like it in a manner brought to them; and, lastly, he thinks the shooting season has grown shorter. Gentlemen used to reside at home the greater part of the winter and spread their shooting over many months. Now, the seaside season has moved on, and numbers are by the beach at the time when formerly they were in the woods. Then others go abroad; the country houses now advertised as 'to let' are almost innumerable. Time was when the local squire would have thought it derogatory to his dignity to make a commodity of his ancient mansion; now there seems quite a competition to let, and absenteeism is a reality of English as well as Irish country life. At least, such is the gamekeeper's idea, and he finds a confirmation of it in the sudden rush, as it were, made upon his preserves. Gentlemen who once spent weeks at the great house, and were out with him every day till he grew to understand the special kind of sport which pleased them most, and could consequently give them satisfaction, are now hardly arrived before they are gone again. With all his desire to find them game he is often puzzled, for game has its whims and fancies and will not accommodate itself to their convenience.

Then the keeper thinks that shooting does not begin so early as it once did. Partridges may be found in the market on the morning of the glorious First of September; but if you ask him how they get there, your reply is a nod and a wink. Nobody gets up early enough in the morning for that now: very often the first day passes by without a single shot being fired. The eagerness for the stubble and its joys is not so marked. This last season the late harvest interfered very much with shooting; you cannot walk through wheat or barley, and while the crops are standing the partridges have too much cover.

Many gentlemen again keep their pheasants till nearly Christmas: October goes by frequently without a bird being brought down in some preserves. Early in the new year, if the weather be mild, as it has been so often latterly, the birds begin to show signs of a disposition to pair off, and in consequence the guns are laid aside before the certificates expire. So that the keeper thinks the actual shooting season has grown shorter and the sport is more concentrated, and taken in rushes, as it were. This causes additional work and anxiety. If the family are away they still require a regular and sometimes a large supply of game for the table, which he has to keep up himself—assistants could hardly be trusted: the opportunity is too tempting.

Though a loyal and conscientious man, in his secret heart he does not like the hounds: and though of course he gets tipped for stopping the earths, yet it is a labour not exactly to his taste. The essence of game preserving is quiet, repose; the characteristic of the hunt is noise, horn, whoop, whip, the cry of the hounds, and the crash of the bushes as the field takes a jump. Students and bookworms like the quiet dust which settles in their favourite haunts—the housemaid's broom is fatal to retrospective thought: so the gamekeeper views the squadrons charging through his cherished copses, 'poaching' up the greensward of the winding 'drives', breaking down the fences, much as the artist views the sacrilegious broom 'putting his place to rights'. Pheasant, and hare, and rabbit all are sent helter-skelter anywhere, and take a day or two to settle down again.

Yet it is not so much the real genuine hunt that he dislikes: it is the loafers it brings together on foot. Roughs from the towns, idle fellows from the villages, cobblers, tinkers, gipsies, the nondescript 'residuum', all congregate in crowds, delighted at the chance of penetrating into the secret recesses of woods only thrown open two or three times a year. It is impossible to stay the inroad—the gates are wide open, the rails pulled down, and trespass is but a fiction for the hour. To see these gentry roaming at their ease in his woods is a bitter trial to the keeper, who grinds his teeth in silence as they pass him with a grin, perfectly aware of and enjoying his spleen. Somehow or other these fellows always manage to get in the way just where the fox was on the point of breaking cover; if he makes a clear start and heads for the meadows, before he has passed the first field a ragged jacket appears over the hedge, and then the language of the huntsman is not always good to listen to.

The work of rearing the young broods of pheasants is a trying and tedious one. The keeper has his own specific treatment, in which he has implicit faith, and laughs to scorn the pheasant-meals and feeding-stuffs advertised in the papers. He mixes it himself, and likes no one prying about to espy his secret, though in reality his success is due to watchful care and not to any particular nostrum. The most favourable spot for rearing is a small level meadow, if possible without furrows, which has been fed off close to the ground and is situated high and dry, and yet well sheltered with wood all round. Damp is a great enemy of the brood, and long grass wet with dew in the early morning sometimes proves fatal if the delicate young birds are allowed to drag themselves through it.

Besides the coops, here and there bushes, cut for the purpose, are piled in tolerably large heaps. The use of these is for the broods to run under if a hawk appears in the sky; and it is amusing to watch how soon the little creatures learn to appreciate this shelter. In the spring the greater part of the keeper's time is occupied in this way: he spends hours upon hours in the hundred and one minutiæ which ensure success. This breeding-time is *the* great anxiety of the year: on it all the shooting depends. He shakes his head if you hint that perhaps it would save trouble to purchase the pheasants ready for shooting from the dealers who now make a business of supplying them for the battue. He looks upon such a practice as the ruin of all true woodcraft, and a proof of the decay of the present generation.

In addition to the pheasants, the partridges, wild as they are, require some attention—the eggs have to be looked after. The mowers in the meadows frequently lay their nests bare beneath the sweep of the scythe: the old bird sometimes sits so close as to have her legs cut off by the sharp steel. Occasionally a rabbit, in the same way, is killed by the point of the blade as he lingers in his form. The mowers receive a small sum for every egg they bring, the eggs being placed under brood hens, kept for the purpose. But as a partridge's egg from one field is precisely like one from another field, the keeper may find, if he does not look pretty sharp after the mowers on the estate, that they have been bribed by a trifle extra to carry the eggs to another man at a distance. A

very unpleasant feeling often arises from suspicions
of this kind.

His agricultural labour consists in superintending
the cultivation of the small squares left for the growth
of grain in the centre of the copses, to feed and attract
the pheasants, and to keep them from wandering.
These have to be dug up with the spade—there would
be no room for using a plough—and spade-husbandry
is rather slow work. An eye has therefore to be kept
on the labourers thus employed lest they get into
mischief. The grain (on the straw) is sometimes given
to the birds laid across skeleton trestles, roughly
made of stout ash sticks, so as to raise it above the
ground and enable them to get at it better.

Ash woods are cut every year, or rather they are
mapped out into so many squares, the poles in which
come to maturity in succession—while one is down
another is growing up, and thus in a fixed course of
years the entire wood is thrown and renovated. A
certain time has, of course, to be allowed for purchasers to remove their property, and, as the roads
through the woods are often axle-deep in mud, in a
wet spring it has frequently to be extended. So many
men being about, the keeper has to be about also:
and then when at last the gates are nailed up, the
cattle turned out to grass in the adjacent fields often
break in and gnaw the young ash-shoots. In this way
a trespassing herd will throw back acres of wood for
a whole year, and destroy valuable produce. Properly
speaking, this should come under the attention of the
bailiff or steward of the demesne; but as the keeper
and his men are so much more likely to discover the
cattle first, they are expected to be on the watch.

After spending so many years of his life among trees,

it is natural that the keeper should feel a special interest, almost an affection for them. A branch ruthlessly torn down, a piece of bark stripped from the trunk with no possible object save destruction, a nail driven in—perhaps to break the teeth of the saw when at last the tree comes to be cut into planks—these things annoy him almost as much as if the living wood were human and could feel. For this reason, he too, like the members of the hunt, cordially detests the use of wire for fencing, now becoming so frequent. It cuts into the trees, and checks their growth and spoils their symmetry, if it does not actually kill them.

Sometimes the wire, which is stout and strong, is twisted right round the stem of a young oak, say a foot or more in diameter, which is thus made to play the part of a post. A firmer support could not be found; but as the tree swells with the rising sap, and expands year by year, the iron girdle circling about it does not 'give' or yield to this slow motion. It bites into the bark, which in time curls over and so actually buries the metal in the growing wood. Now this cannot but be injurious to the tree itself, and it is certainly unsightly.

One wire is seldom thought enough. Two or three are stretched along, and each of these causes an ugly scar. If allowed to remain long enough, the young wood will solidify and harden about the wire, which then cannot be withdrawn; and in consequence when taken finally to the sawpit, some three or four feet of the very 'butt' and best part of the trunk will be found useless. No sawyer will risk his implement —which requires some hours' work to sharpen—in wood which he suspects to contain concealed iron. So that, besides the injury to the appearance of the tree, there is a pecuniary loss. Even when the wires are not twisted round, but merely rub against one side of the bark, the same scars are caused there, though not to such an extent. Rough and strong as the bark seems to the touch, it speedily abrades under the constant pressure of the metal.

The keeper thinks that all those owners of property who take a pleasure in their trees should see to this and prevent it. There is nothing so detestable as this wire fencing in his idea. You cannot even sit upon it for rest, as you can on the old-fashioned post and rails. The convenient gaps which used to be found in every hedge at the corner are blocked now with an ugly rusty iron string stretched across, awkward to get over or under; while as for a horseman getting by, you cannot pull it down as you could 'draw' a wooden rail, and if you try to uncoil it from the blackthorn stem to which it is attached the jagged end is tolerably certain to scrape the skin from your fingers.

The keeper looks upon this simply as another sign of the idleness and dislike of taking trouble character-istic of the times. To set up a line of posts and rails requires some little skill; a man must know his business to stop a gap with a single rail or pole, fixing the ends firmly in among the underwood; even to fit thorn bushes in properly, so as to effectually bar the way, needs some judgement: but anybody can stretch a wire along and twist it round a tree. Hedge-carpen-tering was, in fact, a distinct business, followed by one or two men in every locality; but iron now sup-plants everything, and the hedges themselves are dis-appearing.

When the hedgers and ditchers were put to work to cut a hedge—the turn of every hedge comes round once in so many years—they used to be instructed, if they came across a sapling oak, ash, or elm, to spare it, and cut away the bushes to give it full play. But now they chop and slash away without remorse, and the young forest-tree rising up with a promise of future beauty falls before the billhook. In time the full-grown oaks and elms of the hedgerow decay, or are felled; and in consequence of this careless destruction of the saplings there is nothing to fill their place. The charm of English meadows consisted in no small degree in the stately trees, whose shadows lengthened with the declining sun and gave such pleasant shelter from the heat. Soon, however, if the rising generation of trees is thus cut down, they must become bare, open, and unlovely.

There is another mistake, often committed by owners of timber, who go to the other extreme, and in their intense admiration of trees refuse to permit the felling of a single one. Now in the forest or the woodlands, away from the park or pleasure-grounds, the old hollow trees are things of beauty, and to cut them down for firewood seems an act of vandalism. But it is quite another thing with an avenue or those groups which dot the surface of a park. Here, if a tree falls and there is no other to take its place, a gap is the result, which cannot be filled up, perhaps, under fifty or sixty years.

Let anyone stroll along beneath a stately avenue of elm or beech, such as are not difficult to find in rural districts, and are the pride and boast—and justly so—of this country, and, examining the trees with critical eye, what will he see? Three or four elms, I will say, are passed, and are evidently sound; but the fifth—a careless observer might go by it without remarking anything unusual—is really rotten to the centre. At the foot of the huge trunk, and growing out of it, is a bunch of sickly-looking fungi. Thrust your walking-stick sharply against the black wood there and it penetrates easily, and with a little pushing goes in a surprising distance; the tree seems undermined with rottenness. This decay really runs up the trunk perpendicularly: look, there are signs of it above at the knot-hole, thirty feet high, where more fungus is flourishing, as it always does in dead damp wood. The rain soaks in there, and filtrates slowly down the trunk, whose very heart as it were is eaten away, while outside all is fair enough.

Presently there arises a mighty wind, the tree snaps clean off twenty feet above the ground, and the upper part falls, a ponderous ruin, carrying with it one of the finest boughs of its nearest companion, and destroying its symmetry also. When examined, it appears that the trunk is totally useless as timber: this noble-seeming elm is fit for nothing but fuel. Or, perhaps, if there be water meadows on the estate, the farmers may be glad of it to act as a huge pipe to convey the fertilising stream across a ditch, or over a brook lying at a lower level. For this purpose, of course, the rotten part is scooped out: often the trunk is sawn down the middle, so as to make a double length.

But what a gap it has left in the great avenue! In a minute the growth of a century gone, the delight of generations swept away, and no living man, hardly the heir in his cradle, can hope to see that unsightly gap filled up.

The keeper does not hesitate to say that of the great trees in the avenues numbers stand in constant danger of such overthrow; and so it is that by slow degrees so many of the kings of the forest have disappeared without leaving successors. No care is taken to plant fresh saplings, no care is taken to select and remove the trees which have passed the meridian of their existence, and the final result is the extinction of the avenue or group. Perhaps the temper of the times is to blame for this neglect: men look only to the day and live fast. There is a sense of uncertainty in the atmosphere of the age: no one can be sure that the acorns he plants will be permitted to reach their prime, the hoofs of the 'iron horse' may trample them down as fresh populations grow. So the avenues die out, and the keeper mourns to think that in the days to come their place will be vacant.

Suddenly he pauses in his walk, stoops, and points out to me in the grass the white, smooth, round knob-like tops of several young mushrooms which are pushing their way up. He carefully covers these with some pieces of dead bark and desiccated dung, so that none of 'them lurching fellows as comes round shan't see 'em'—with a wink at his own cunning—so as to preserve them till they have grown larger. He advises me never to partake of mushrooms unless certain that they have not grown under oak trees: he will have it that even the true edible mushroom is hurtful if it springs beneath the shadow of the oak. And he is not singular in this belief.

Chatting about trees, he points out one or two oaks, not at all rotten, but split half-way up the trunk —the split is perfectly visible—yet they have not been struck by lightning; and he cannot explain it. Looking back upon the wood as we leave it with intense pride in his trees, he gives me a rough version of the old story: how a knight of ancient days, who had

done the king some great service, was rewarded with
a broad tract of land which he was to hold for three
crops. He sowed acorns, and thus secured himself and
descendants a tenure of almost 3,000 years, at least,
according to Dryden:—

> The monarch oak, the patriarch of trees,
> Shoots, rising up, and spreads by slow degrees;
> Three centuries he grows, and three he stays
> Supreme in state, and in three more decays.

The keeper wishes he had such an opportunity. The
knight, in his idea, reached the acme of wisdom with
his three crops of nearly a thousand years each.

His own kingdom may be said to begin with the
park, and the land 'in demesne' to quote the quaint
language of the Domesday Book: a record not without
its value as an outline picture of English scenery eight
centuries ago, telling us that near this village was a
wood, near that a stretch of meadow and a mill, here
again arable land and corn waving in the breeze, and
everywhere the park and domain of the feudal lords.
The beauty of the park consists in its 'breadth' as an
artist would say—the meadows with their green frames
of hedges are cabinet pictures, lovely, but small; this
is life size, a broad cartoon from the hand of Nature.
The sward rises and rolls along in undulations like the
slow heave of an ocean wave. Besides the elms there
is a noble avenue of limes, and great oaks scattered
here and there, under whose ample shade the cattle
repose in the heat of the day.

In summer from out the leafy chambers of the limes
there falls the pleasant sound of bees innumerable,
the voice of whose trembling wings lulls the listening
ear as the drowsy sunshine weighs the eyelid till I

walk the avenue in a dream. It leads out into the park—no formal gravel drive, simply a footpath on the sward between the flowering trees: a path that becomes less and less marked as I advance, and finally fades away, where the limes cease, in the broad level of the opening 'greeny field'. These honey-bees seem to fly higher and to exhibit much more activity than the great humble-bee: here in the limes they must be thirty feet above the ground. Wasps also frequently wing their way at a considerable elevation, and thus it is that the hive-bee and the wasp so commonly enter the upper windows of houses. When its load of honey is completed, the bee, too, returns home in a nearly straight line, high enough in the air to pass over hedges and such obstacles without the labour of rising up and sinking again.

The heavy humble-bee is generally seen close to the earth, and often goes down into the depths of the dry ditches, and may there be heard buzzing slowly along under the arch of briar and bramble. He seems to lose his way now and then in the tangled undergrowth of the woods; and if a footstep disturbs and alarms him, it is amusing to see his desperate efforts to free himself hastily from the interlacing grass-blades and ferns.

When the sap is rising, the bark of the smaller shoots of the lime-tree 'slips' easily—*i.e.* it can be peeled in hollow cylinders if judiciously tapped and loosened by gentle blows from the back of a knife. The plough-boys know this, and make whistles out of such branches, as they do also from the willow, and even the sycamore in the season when the sap comes up in its flood-tide.

It is difficult to decide at what time of the year the

park is in its glory. The may-flower on the great haw-thorn trees in spring may perhaps claim the pre-eminence, filling the soft breeze with exquisite odour. These here are trees, not bushes, standing separate, with thick gnarled stems so polished by the constant rubbing of cattle as almost to shine like varnish. The may-bloom, pure white in its full splendour, takes a dull reddish tinge as it fades, when a sudden shake will bring it down in showers. A flowering tree, I fancy, looks best when apart and not one of a row. In the latter case you can only see two sides and not all round it. Here tall horsechestnut trees stand single— one great silvery candelabrum of blossom. Wood-pigeons appear to have a liking for this tree. Nor must the humble crab-tree be forgotten; a crab-tree in bloom is a lovely sight.

The idea of a park is associated with peace and pleasure, yet even here there is one spot where the passions of men have left their mark. As previously hinted, the gamekeeper, like most persons with little book-learning and who take their impressions from nature, is somewhat superstitious, and regards this place as 'unkid'—*i.e.* weird, uncanny. One particu-lar green 'drive' into the wood opening on the park had always been believed to be a part of a military track used many ages ago, but long since ploughed up for the greater part of its length, and only pre-served here by the accident of passing through a wood. At last some labourers grubbing trees near the mouth of the drive came upon a number of human skeletons, close beneath the surface, and in their confused arrangement presenting every sign of hasty inter-ment, as if after battle. Since then the keeper avoids the spot; nor will he, hardy as he is, go near it at

night; not even in the summer moonlight, when the
night is merely a prolongation of the day.

There is nothing unusual in such a discovery: skeletons are found in all manner of places. I recollect seeing one dug out from the bank of a brook within two
feet of the stream. The place was perhaps in the olden
time covered with forest (traces of forest are to be
found everywhere, as in the names of hamlets), and
therefore more concealed than at present. Or, possibly, the stream, in the slow passage of centuries, may
have worn its way far from its original bed.

It is strange to think of, yet it is true enough, that,
beautiful as the country is, with its green meadows
and graceful trees, its streams and forests and peaceful
homesteads, it would be difficult to find an acre of
ground that has not been stained with blood. A
melancholy reflection this, that carries the mind backwards, while the thrush sings on the bough, through
the nameless skirmishes of the Civil War, the cruel
assassinations of the rival Roses, down to the axes of
the Saxons and the ghastly wounds they made. Everywhere under the flowers are the dead.

Not this park in particular, but others as well form
pages of history. The keeper, in fact, can claim an
ancient origin for his office, dating back to the forester
with a 'mark' a year and a suit of green as his wages,
and numbering in his predecessors Joscelin, the typical
keeper in Scott's novel of 'Woodstock', who aided the
escape of King Charles. Ever since the days of the
Norman King who loved the tall deer as if he were
their father—in the words of his contemporary—and
set store by the hares that they too should go free, the
keeper has not ceased out of the land.

There are always more small birds at the edge or

just outside a wood than inside it; so that after leaving
a meadow with blackbird, thrush, and finches merry
in the hedges, the wood seems quite silent and deserted
save by a solitary robin. This is speaking of the smaller
birds. The great missel-thrush especially delights in
the open space of the park dotted with groups of trees.
The missel-thrush is a lonely bird, and somehow seems
like an outlaw—as if, though not precisely dangerous,
he was looked upon with suspicion by the other birds,
which will frequently quit a bush or tree directly he
alights upon it. Yet he builds near houses, and year
after year in the same spot. I knew a large yew-tree
which stood almost in front and within a few yards of
a sitting-room window in which the missel-thrush had
regularly built its nest for twelve successive years.
These birds are singularly bold in defence of the nest,
flying round and chattering at those who would disturb it.

In the ha-ha wall of the park, which is made of
loose stones or without mortar, the tomtit, or titmouse,
has his nest. He creeps in between the stones, following the crannies for a surprising distance. Near here
the partridges roost on the ground; they like an open
space far from hedges, afraid, perhaps, of weasels and
rats. On the other side, where the wood comes up,
if you watch quietly, the pheasants step in lordly
pride out into the grass; so that there is no place
without its especial class of life.

Perhaps with the exception of our parks and hills,
there is scarcely any portion of southern England now
where a grand charge of cavalry could take place—
scarcely any open champaign country fit for operations of that kind with horse. In the Civil War even,
how constantly we read of 'lining the hedge with

match', and now with enclosures everywhere the difficulty would apparently be great, despite good roads.

Park-fed beef is thought by many to be superior because the cattle run free—almost wild—the entire year through, winter and summer, and have nothing but their natural food, grass and hay: in strong contrast with the bullocks shut up in stalls and forced forward with artificial food. A great number of parks have been curtailed in size as land became more valuable—the best ground being selected and hedged off for purely agricultural purposes; so that it not uncommonly happens that the actual park is the poorest soil in the district, having for that reason remained longest in a condition nearly resembling the original state of the country. So that when agitators of Communistic views lay stress upon the waste of land used for pleasure purposes they frequently declaim in utter ignorance of the facts, which are in exact opposition to their theories.

Like animals and birds, plants have their favourite haunts: violets love a bank with a southern aspect, especially if there be a hedge at the back for further shelter. Where you have by chance lighted upon a wild flower once you may generally reckon upon finding it again next year—such as the white variety of the bluebell or wild hyacinth, for which, unless you mark the place, you may search in vain amid the crowded blue bloom of the commoner sort. The orchis, with its purple flower and dark green spotted leaf, in the virtue of whose roots as a love-potion the old people still believe, the strange-looking adder's tongue, the modest wild strawberry, with its tiny but piquant flavoured fruit, all have their special resorts.

Even the cowslips have their ways: by brooks sometimes a larger variety grows; nor is there a sweeter
flower than its delicate yellow with small velvety
brown spots, like moles on beauty's cheek.

In autumn, when the leaves turn colour, the groups
of trees in the park are more effective in an artistic
point of view than those in the woods (unless overlooked from a hill close by, when it is like glancing
along a roof of gold), because they stand out clear, and
are not confused or lost in the general glow. But it
is evening now; and see—yonder the fox steals out
from the cover, wending his way down into the
meadows, where he will follow the furrows along their
course, mousing as he goes.

CHAPTER IV

HIS DOMINIONS:—THE WOODS—MEADOWS—AND WATER

THERE is a part of the wood where the bushes grow but thinly and the ash-stoles are scattered at some distance from each other. It is on a steep slope—almost cliff—where the white chalk comes to the surface. On the edge above rise tall beech trees with smooth round trunks, whose roots push and project through the wall of chalk, and bend downwards, sometimes dislodging lumps of rubble to roll head-long among the bushes below. A few small firs cling half-way up, and a tangled, matted mass of briar and bramble climbs nearly to them, with many a stout thistle flourishing vigorously.

To get up this cliff is a work of some little difficulty: it is done by planting the foot on the ledges of rubble, or in the holes which the rabbits have made, holding tight to roots which curl and twist in fantastic shapes, or to the woodbine hanging in festoons from branch to branch. The rubble under foot crumbles and slips, the roots tear up bodily from the thin soil, the branches bend, and the woodbine 'gives', and the wayfarer may readily descend much more rapidly than he desires. Not that serious consequences would ensue from a roll down forty feet of slope; but the bed of briar and bramble at the bottom is not so soft as it might be. The rabbits seem quite at home upon the steepest spot; they may be found upon much higher and more precipitous chalk cliffs than this, darting from point to point with ease.

Once at the summit under the beeches, and there a comfortable seat may be found upon the moss. The wood stretches away beneath for more than a mile in breadth, and beyond it winds the narrow mere glittering in the rays of the early spring sunshine. The bloom is on the blackthorn, but not yet on the may; the hedges are but just awakening from their long winter sleep, and the trees have hardly put forth a sign. But the rooks are busily engaged in the trees of the park, and away yonder at the distant colony in the elms of the meadows.

The wood is restless with life: every minute a pigeon rises, clattering his wings, and after him another; and so there is a constant fluttering and motion above the ash-poles. The number of wood-pigeons breeding here must be immense. Later on, if you walk among the ash, you may find a nest every half-dozen yards. It is formed of a few twigs making a slender platform, on which the glossy white egg is laid, and where the bird will sit till you literally thrust her off her nest with your walking-stick. Such slender platforms, if built in the hedgerow, so soon as the breeze comes would assuredly be dashed to pieces; but here the wind only touches the tops of the poles, and causes them to sway gently with a rattling noise, and the frail nest is not injured. When the pigeon or dove builds in the more exposed hedgerows the nest is stronger, and more twigs seem to be used, so that it is heavier.

Boys steal these eggs by scores, yet it makes no difference apparently to the endless numbers of these birds, who fill the wood with their peculiar hoarse notes, which some country people say resemble the words 'Take two cows, Taffy.' The same good folk

will have it that when the weather threatens rain the
pigeon's note changes to 'Joe's toe bleeds, Betty.'
The boys who steal the eggs have to swarm up the
ash-poles for the purpose, and in so doing often stain
their clothes with red marks. Upon the bark of the
ash are innumerable little excrescences which when
rubbed exude a small quantity of red juice.

The keeper detests this bird's-nesting; not that
he cares much about the pigeons, but because his
pheasants are frequently disturbed just at the season
when he wishes them to enjoy perfect quiet. It is
easy to tell from this post of vantage if anyone be
passing through the section of the wood within view,
though they may be hidden by the boughs. The
blackbirds utter a loud cry and scatter; the pigeons
rise and wheel about; a pheasant gets up with a
scream audible for a long distance, and goes with
swift flight skimming away just above the ash-poles;
a pair of jays jabber round the summit of a tall fir
tree, and thus the intruder's course is made known.
But the wind, though light, is still too cold and chilly
as it sweeps between the beech trunks to remain at
this elevation; it is warmer below in the wood.

At the foot of the cliff a natural hollow has been
further scooped out by labour of man, and shaped
into a small cave large enough for three or four to sit
in. It is partly supported by strong wooden pillars,
and at the mouth a hut of slabs, thickly covered by
furze-faggots, has been constructed, with a door, and
with roof thatched with reeds from the lake. A rude
bench runs round three sides; against the fourth some
digging tools recline—strong spades and grub-axes for
rooting out a lost ferret, left here temporarily for convenience. The place, rough as it is, gives shelter, and,

throwing the door open, there is a vista among the
ash-poles and the hazel bushes over-topped with great
fir trees and more distant oaks. In the later spring
this is a lovely spot, the ground all tinted with the
shimmering colour of the bluebells, and the hazel
musical with the voice of the nightingale.

Outside the wood, where the downland begins to
rise gradually there stretches a broad expanse of furze
growing luxuriantly on the thin barren soil, and a
mile or more in width. It has a beauty of its own when
in full yellow blossom—a yellow sea of flower, scenting
the air with an almost overpowering odour as of a
coarser pineapple, and full of the drowsy hum of the
bees busy in the interspersed thyme. It has another
beauty later on when the thick undergrowth of heath
is in bloom, and a pale purple carpet spreads around.
Here rabbits breed and sport, and hares hide, and the
curious furze-chats fly to and fro; and lastly, but not
leastly, my lord Reynard the Fox loves to take his
ease, till he finally meets his fate in the jaws of clamour-
ing hounds, or is assassinated with the aid of 'villanous
saltpetre'. He is not easily shot, and will stand a
charge fired broadside at a short distance without the
slightest injury or apparent notice, beyond a slight
quickening of his pace. His thick fur and tough skin
turn the pellets. Even when mortally wounded, life
will linger for hours.

The ordinary idea of the fox is that of a flying
frightened creature tearing away for bare existence;
he is really a bold and desperate animal. The keeper
will tell you that once when for some purpose he was
walking up a deep dry ditch his spaniel and retriever
suddenly 'chopped' a fox, and got him at bay in a
corner, when he turned, and in an instant laid the

spaniel helpless and dying and severely handled the retriever. Seeing his dogs so injured and the fox as it were under his feet, the keeper imprudently attempted to seize him, but could not retain his hold, and got the sharp white teeth clean through his hand.

Though but once actually bitten, he recollects being snapped at viciously by another fox, whom he found in broad daylight asleep in the hollow of a double mound with scarcely any shelter and within sixty yards of a house. Reynard was curled up on the ivy which in the hedges trails along the ground. The keeper crawled up on the bank and stopped, admiring the symmetry of the creature, when, purposely breaking a twig, the fox was up in a second, and snarled and snapped at his face, then slipped into the ditch and away. The fox is, in fact, quite as remarkable for boldness as for cunning. Last summer I met a fine fox on the turnpike road and close to a tollgate, in the middle of the day. He came at full speed with a young rabbit in his jaws, evidently but just captured, and did not perceive that he was observed till within twenty yards, when, with a single bound he cleared the sward beside the road, alighting with a crash in the bushes, carrying his prey with him.

Hares will sometimes, in like manner, come as it were to meet people on country roads. Is it that the eyes, being placed towards the side of the head, do not so readily catch sight of dangers in front as on the flanks, especially when the animal is absorbed in its purpose? Hares are peculiarly fond of limping at dusk along lonely roads.

Foxes, when they roam from the woods into the meadow-land, prefer to sleep during the day in those osier beds which are found in the narrow corners

formed by the meanderings of the brooks. Between
the willow-wands there shoots up a thick undergrowth
of sedges, long coarse grass, and reeds; and in these
the fox makes his bed, turning round and round till he
has smoothed a place and trampled down the grass;
then reclining, well sheltered from the wind. A dog
will turn round and round in the same way before he
lies down on the hearthrug.

These reeds sometimes grow to a great height, as
much as ten or twelve feet. Along the Thames they
are used, bound in bundles, to pitch the barges; when
the hull has been roughly coated with pitch, one end
of the bundle of reeds (thickest end preferred) is set
on fire and passed over it to make it melt and run
into the chinks. So, mayhap, the Saxon and Danish
rovers may have used them to pitch the bottoms of
their 'ceols' when worn from constantly grounding on
the shallows and eyots.

Here in the furze too is the haunt of the badger.
This animal becomes rarer year after year—the disuse
of the great rabbit-warrens being one cause; still he
lingers, and may be traced in the rabbit 'buries',
where he enlarges a hole for his habitation, sleeps
during the day, and comes forth in the gloaming. In
summer he digs up the wasps' nests, not, as has been
supposed, for the honey, but for the white larvae they
contain: the wasp secretes no honey at all, and her
nest is simply a series of cells in which the grubs
mature. Some credit the fox with a fondness for the
same food; and even the hornets' nest is said to be
similarly ravaged. It is the nest of the humble-bee
which the badger roots up for the honey. The humble-
bee uses a tiny hole in a dry bank, sometimes a crack
made by the heat in the earth, and really deposits true

honey in the comb. It is very sweet, like that of the hive bee, but a little darker in colour and much less in quantity. The haymakers search for these nests along the hedgerows in their dinner-hour, and eat the honey. There seem to be several sub-species of humble-bee, differing in size and habit. One has its nest as deep as possible in a hole; another makes a nest with scarcely any protection beyond the thick moss of the bank, almost on the surface of the ground. The badger's hole has before it a huge quantity of sand, which he has thrown out, and upon which the imprint of his foot will be found, a mark, perhaps, more like the spoor of the large game of tropical forests than that left by any other English animal. When seen it can ever afterwards be instantly identified by the most careless observer.

In the meadows lower down, bounding the wood, the hay is gone or is piled in summer ricks, which lean one one way and another the other, and upon whose roofs, sloping at an obtuse angle, the green snakes lie coiled in the sunshine. Often when the waggon comes, and the little rick is loaded, the 'pitch' of hay on the prong as it is flung up carries with it a snake whirling in the air. He falls on the sward and is instantly pounced upon by the farmer's dog, who worries him, seizes him by the middle and shakes him, while the snake twists and hisses in vain. Some dogs will not touch snakes, others seem to enjoy destroying them; but it is noticeable that a dog which previously has passed or avoided snakes, if once he kills one, never passes another without slaughtering it. A slime from the snake's skin froths over the dog's jaws, and the sight is very unpleasant.

I have often tried to discover how the snakes get

upon these summer ricks. Solomon could not understand the 'way of a serpent upon the rock', and the
way of a common snake up the summer rick seems
almost as inexplicable. Though the roof or 'top' is
often very much out of the proper conical shape, and
sometimes sinks down nearly to a level, the sides for
a height of three or four feet are generally perpendicular, affording no projection of any kind whatever;
hay is slippery, and the rick is, of course, too large for
the snake to encircle it. Yet there they are commonly
found to the intense alarm of the labouring women,
who never can get over their dislike of snakes, though
they see them so frequently. The only way I can
imagine by which they climb up is by means of the
holes, or galleries, used by field-mice. In summer
ricks there are sometimes many mice, and in pursuit
of these the snake may find its way up through their
'runs'. Toads are also occasionally found on these
ricks, and it is not exactly clear how they get there
either; but their object is plain—*i.e.* the insects which
swarm on the hay.

The thick hedgerows of these woodland meads are
full of trees, and others stand out in groups in the grass,
some of them hollow. Elms often become hollow,
and so do oaks; the latter have such large cavities
sometimes that one or more persons may easily crouch
therein. This is speaking of an ordinary-sized tree;
there are many instances of patriarchs of the forest
within whose capacious trunks a dozen might stand
upright.

These hollow trees, according to woodcraft, ought
to come down by the axe without further loss of time.
Yet it is fortunate that we are not all of us, even in
this prosaic age, imbued with the stern utilitarian

spirit; for a decaying tree is perhaps more interesting than one in full vigour of growth. The starlings make their nests in the upper knot-holes; or, lower down, the owl feeds her young; and if you chance to pass near, and are not aware of the ways of owls, you may fancy that a legion of serpents are in the bushes, so loud and threatening is the hissing noise made by the brood. The woodpecker comes for the insects that flourish on the dying giant; so does the curious little tree-climber, running up the trunk like a mouse; and in winter, when insect-life is scarce, it is amusing to watch there the busy tomtit. He hangs underneath a dead branch, head downwards, as if walking on a ceiling, and with his tiny but strong bill chips off a fragment of the loose dead bark. Under this bark, as he well knows, woodlice and all kinds of creeping things make their home. With the fragment he flies to an adjacent twig, small enough to be grasped by his claws and so give him a firm foothold. There he pecks his morsel into minute pieces and lunches on the living contents. Then, with a saucy chuckle of delight in his own cleverness, he returns to the larger bough for a fresh supply. As the bough decays the bark loosens, and is invaded by insects which when it was green could not touch it.

For the acorns the old oak still yields come rooks, pigeons, and stately pheasants, with their glossy feathers shining in the autumn sun. Thrushes carry wild hedge-fruit up on the broad platform formed by the trunk where the great limbs divide, and, pecking it to pieces, leave the seeds. These take root in the crevices which widen out underneath into a mass of soft decaying 'touchwood'; and so from the crown of the tree there presently stream downwards long trail-

ing briars, bearing in June the sweet wild roses and in
winter red oval fruit. Ivy comes creeping up, and
in its thick warm coverts nests are built. Below,
among the powdery 'touchwood' which lines the floor
of this living hut, great fungi push their coloured
heads up to the light. And here you may take shelter
when the rain comes unexpectedly pattering on the
leaves, and listen as it rises to a roar within the forest.
Sometimes wild bees take up their residence in the
hollow, slowly filling it with comb, buzzing busily to
and fro; and then it is not to be approached so care-
lessly, though so ready are all creatures to acknow-
ledge kindness that ere now I have even made friends
with the inhabitants of a wasp's nest.

A thick carpet of dark green moss grows upon one
side of the tree, and over it the tall brake fern rears
its yellow stem. In the evening the goat-sucker or
nightjar comes with a whirling phantom-like flight,
wheeling round and round: a strange bird, which will
roost all day on a rail, blinking or sleeping in the daylight, and seeming to prefer a rail or a branch without
leaves to one that affords cover. Here also the smaller
bats flit in the twilight, and, if you stand still, will
pursue their prey close to your head, wheeling about
it so that you may knock them down with your hand
if you wish. The labouring people call the bat 'bat-
mouse'. Here also come many beetles; and sometimes
on a summer's day the swallows will rest from their
endless flight on the dying upper branches, for they
too like a bough clear or nearly clear of leaves. All
the year through the hollow tree is haunted by every
kind of living creature, and therefore let us hope it
may yet be permitted to linger awhile safe from the
axe.

The lesser roots of the elm are porous like cane, and are sometimes smoked as cigars by the ploughboys. The leaf of the coltsfoot, which grows so luxuriously in many places and used to be regularly gathered and dried by the lower classes for the pipe, is now rarely used since the commoner tobaccos have become universally accessible.

Often and often, when standing in a meadow gateway partly hidden by the bushes, watching the woodpecker on the ant-hills, of whose eggs, too, the partridges are so fond (so that a good ant year, in which their nests are prolific, is also a good partridge year) you may, if you are still, hear a slight faint rustle in the hedge, and by-and-by a weasel will steal out. Seeing you he instantly pauses, elevates his head, and steadily gazes: move but your eyes and he is back in the hedge; remain quiet, still looking straight before you as if you saw nothing, and he will presently recover confidence, and actually cross the gateway almost under you.

This is the secret of observation: stillness, silence, and apparent indifference. In some instinctive way these wild creatures learn to distinguish when one is or is not intent upon them in a spirit of enmity; and if very near, it is always the eye they watch. So long as you observe them, as it were, from the corner of the eyeball, sideways, or look over their heads at something beyond, it is well. Turn your glance full upon them to get a better view, and they are gone.

When waiting in a dry ditch with a gun on a warm autumn afternoon for a rabbit to come out, sometimes a bunny will suddenly appear at the mouth of a hole which your knee nearly touches. He stops dead, as if petrified with astonishment, sitting on his haunches.

His full dark eye is on you with a gaze of intense curiosity; his nostrils work as if sniffing; his whiskers move; and every now and then he thumps with his hind legs upon the earth with a low dull thud. This is evidently a sign of great alarm, at the noise of which any other rabbit within hearing instantly disappears in the 'bury'. Yet there your friend sits and watches you as if spell-bound, so long as you have the patience neither to move hand or foot nor to turn your eye. Keep your glance on a frond of the fern just beyond him, and he will stay. The instant your eye meets his or a finger stirs, he plunges out of sight.

It is so also with birds. Walk across a meadow swinging a stick, even humming, and the rooks calmly continue their search for grubs within thirty yards; stop to look at them, and they rise on the wing directly. So, too, the finches in the trees by the roadside. Let the wayfarer pass beneath the bough on which they are singing, and they will sing on, if he moves without apparent interest; should he pause to listen, their wings glisten in the sun as they fly.

The meadows lead down to the shores of the mere, and the nearest fields melt almost insensibly into the green margin of the water, for at the edge it is so full of flags, and rushes, and weeds as at a distance to be barely distinguishable there from the sward. As we approach, the cuckoo sings passing over head; 'she cries as she flies' is the common country saying.

I used to imagine that the cuckoo was fond of an echo, having noticed that a particular clump of trees overhanging some water, the opposite bank of which sent back a clear reply, was a specially favourite resort of that bird. The reduplication of the liquid notes, as they travelled to and fro, was peculiarly pleasant: the water, perhaps, lending, like a sounding-board, a fullness and roundness to her song. She might possibly have fancied that another bird was answering; certainly she 'cried' much longer there than in other places. Morning after morning, and about the same time—eleven o'clock—a cuckoo sang in that group of trees, from noting which I was led to think that perhaps the cuckoo, though apparently wandering aimlessly about, really has more method and regularity in her habits than would seem.

Country people will have it that cuckoos are growing scarcer every year, and do not come in the numbers they formerly did; and, whether it be the chance of unfavourable seasons or other causes, it is certainly the fact in some localities. I recollect seeing as many as four at once in a tall elm—a tree they love—all crying and gurgling, as it were, in the throat together; this was some years since, and that district is now much less frequented by these birds.

There was a superstition that where or in whatever condition you happened to be when you heard the cuckoo the first time in the spring, so you would remain for the next twelvemonth; for which reason it was a misfortune to hear her first in bed, since it might mean a long illness. This, by-the-by, may have been a pleasant fable invented to get milkmaids up early of a morning.

The number of coarse fish in the brook which flows out of the shallow mere bounding one edge of the keeper's domain of woods has, he thinks, very much decreased of recent years. When he first came here the stream seemed full of fish, notwithstanding very little care had till then been taken with their preservation. They used to net it once now and then, and he has seen a full hundredweight of fair-sized jack, perch, tench, &c., taken out of the water in a very short time, besides quantities of smaller fry which were put back again. But although the brook, so far as his jurisdiction goes, has since been comparatively well preserved, yet he feels certain the fish have diminished.

There are no chemical works to account for this with the subtle poison of their waste, neither are there mills to prevent the fish coming up—perhaps it would be better if there were some mills, as they would stop the fish going down. I have noticed that where old water-wheels have ceased working the fish have almost disappeared. This, of course, may be but a purely local phenomenon, but it is certainly the case in some districts. Comparatively little wheat now is ground in rural places; the greater portion is carried away to the towns and turned into flour by steam. So that in walking up a brook you will now and then come upon an ancient mill whose business has departed: the fabric itself is tenanted by two or three cottage families, and their garden covers the site of the old mill-pond. In the depths of that pool there were formerly plenty of fish, with deep, dark spots in which to hide. Their natural increase was not swept away by floods; neither could they wander, because of the dam and grating. They were also under the eye of the miller, and so preserved. But when the dam was levelled and the stream allowed to follow its course, this resting-place, so to say, was abolished, and the fish dispersed were lost or captured.

Upon the particular brook which I have now in view there are no mills; but there used to be several large ponds—distinct from the stream, yet communicating by a narrow channel. These likewise sheltered the fish, and were favourable to their propagation. Improvements, however, have swept them away; they are filled up, every inch of ground having become valuable for agricultural purposes. Then there were vast ditches running up beside the hedgerows, and ending in the brook; perfect storehouses these of all aquatic life. Fish used to go up them for shelter (they were as deep or deeper than the brook itself, and it was a good jump for a man across) and to feed on the insects blown off the overhanging trees and bushes or brought down by the streamlet draining the field above. Wild duck made their nests among the rushes, sitting there while their beautiful consorts, the mallards, swam lonely in the mere. Moorhens were busy in the weeds, or came out to feed upon the sward.

Such great ditches are now filled up, and drains take their place. It is better so, no doubt, in a purely utilitarian sense, but the fish haunt the spot no more. Some of the reaches of the brook, where the ground was flat and boggy, used to resemble a long narrow lake, extremely shallow, with the deeper current running yards away from the shore: and here the snipe came in the winter. But the banks are now made up higher by artificial means, and the marsh is dry. All these changes diminish those aquatic nooks and corners in which fish love to linger.

Finally came the weed said to have been imported from America, pushing its way up stream, and filling it with an abominable mass of vegetable matter that no fish could enter. Hereabouts, however, this pest has of late shown signs of exhaustion—it does not grow with its former vigour, and its progress seems checked. The brook, after winding for several miles, the lower course being beyond the keeper's boundaries, empties itself into a canal; before the canal was made it ran much further, and itself increased in volume almost to a river. Now this canal is fished day and night by people on the tow-path: there is nominally a close time, but no one observes it, and the riparian owners, having discovered that they had a right so to do, net it mercilessly. The consequence is that the fish which go down the stream and enter the canal are speedily destroyed, while the canal on its part sends no fish to the upper waters. This is how the decrease of fish is accounted for, and it is the same with perhaps half a dozen other brooks in the same locality, all of which now fall into the canal, which is so incessantly plied with rod and net and nightline that little escapes.

CHAPTER V

SOME OF HIS SUBJECTS: DOGS, RABBITS, 'MICE,
AND SUCH SMALL DEER'

WHEN a dog, young and yet unskilled, follows his master across the meadows, it often happens that he meets with difficulties which sorely try the capacity of the inexperienced brain. The two come to a broad deep brook. The man glances at the opposite bank, and compares in his mind the distance to the other side with other distances he has previously leaped. The result is not quite satisfactory; somehow a latent doubt develops itself into a question of his ability to spring over. He cranes his neck, looks at the jump sideways to get an angular measurement, retires a few paces to run, shakes his head, deliberates, instinctively glances round as if for assistance or advice, and presently again advances to the edge. No; it will not do. He recalls to mind the division of space into yards, feet, and inches, and endeavours to apply it without a rule to the smooth surface of the water. He can judge a yard on the grass, because there is something to fix the eye on—the tall bennet or the buttercup yonder; but the water affords no data.

On second thoughts, yes—even the smooth flowing current has its marks. Here, not far from the steep bank, is a flag, bowed or broken, whose pennant-like tongue of green floats just beneath the surface, slowly vibrating to and fro, as you wave your hand in token of farewell. This is mark one—say three feet from the shore.

Somewhat farther there is a curl upon the water,

not constant, but coming every few seconds in obedience to the increase or decrease of the volume of the stream, which there meets with some slight obstacle out of sight. For, although the water appears level and unvarying, it really rises and sinks in ever so minute a degree with a rhythmic alternation. If you will lie down on the sward, you may sometimes see it by fixing a steady gaze upon the small circular cave where the gallery of a water-rat opens on this the Grand Canal of his Venice. Into it there rises now and again a gentle swell—barely perceptible—a faint pulse rising and falling. The stream is slightly fuller and stronger at one moment than another; and with each swell the curl, or tiny whirlpool, rotates above the hidden irregularity of the bottom. If you sit by the dam higher up the brook, and watch the arch of the cataract rolling over, it is perhaps more visible. Every now and then a check seems to stay the current momentarily: and at night, when it is perfectly still, listening to the murmur of the falling water from a distance, under the apple-trees in the garden it runs a scale—now up, then down; each variation of volume changing the musical note. This faint undulation is more visible in some brooks than others.

A third mark is where a branch, as it was carried along, grounded on a shallow spot; and one mast, as it were, of the wreck protruding upwards, catches the stray weeds as they swim down and holds them. Thus, step by step, the mind of the man measures the distance, and assures him that it is a little beyond what he has hitherto attempted; yet will not extra exertion clear it?—for having once approached the brink, shame and the dislike of giving up pull him forward. He walks hastily twenty yards up the brook,

then as many the other way, but discovers no more
favourable spot; hesitates again; next carefully ex-
amines the tripping place, lest the turf, undermined,
yield to the sudden pressure, as also the landing, for
fear of falling back. Finally he retires a few yards, and
pauses a second and runs. Even after the start, uncertain in mind and but half resolved, it is his own motion
which impels the will, and he arrives on the opposite
shore with a sense of surprise. Now comes the dog,
and note his actions; contrast the two, and say which
is instinct, which is mind.

The dog races to the bank—he has been hitherto
hunting in a hedge and suddenly misses his master—
and, like his lord, stops short on the brink. He has
had but little experience in jumping as yet; water is
not his natural element, and he pauses doubtfully. He
looks across earnestly, sniffs the air as if to smell the
distance, then whines in distress of mind. Presently he
makes a movement to spring, checks it, and turns
round as if looking for advice or encouragement.
Next he runs back a short way as if about to give it
up; returns, and cranes over the brink; after which he
follows the bank up and down, barking in excitement,
but always coming back to the original spot. The
lines of his face, the straining eye, the voice that seems
struggling to articulate in the throat, the attitude of
the body, all convey the idea of intense desire which
fear prevents him from translating into action. There
is indecision—uncertainty—in the nervous grasp of
the paws on the grass, in the quick short coursings to
and fro. Would infallible instinct hesitate? He has no
knowledge of yards, feet and inches—yet he is clearly
trying to judge the distance. Finally, just as his master
disappears through a gateway, the agony of his 'mind'

rises to the highest pitch. He advances to the very brink—he half springs, stays himself, his hinder paws slip down the steep bank, he partly loses his balance, and then makes a great leap, lights with a splash in mid-stream, and swims the remainder with ease. There is, at least, a singular coincidence in the outward actions of the two.

The gamekeeper, with dogs around him from morning till night, associated with them from childhood, has no doubts upon the matter whatever, but with characteristic decision is perfectly certain that they think and reason in the same way as human beings, though of course in a limited degree. Most of his class believe, likewise, in the reasoning power of the dog: so do shepherds; and so, too, the labourers who wait on and feed cattle are fully persuaded of their intelligence, which, however, in no way prevents them throwing the milking-stool at their heads when unruly. But the concession of reason is no guarantee against ill-usage, else the labourer's wife would escape.

The keeper, without thinking it perhaps, affords a strong illustration of his own firm faith in the mind of the dog. His are taught their proper business thoroughly; but there it ends. 'I never makes them learn no tricks,' says he, 'because I don't like to see 'em made fools of.' I have observed that almost all those whose labour lies in the field, and who go down to their business in the green meadows, admit the animal world to a share in the faculty of reason. It is the cabinet thinkers who construct a universe of automatons.

No better illustration of the two modes of observation can be found than in the scene of Goethe's 'Faust' where Faust and Wagner walking in the field are met by a strange dog. The first sees something more than a mere dog; he feels the presence of an intelligence within the outward semblance—in this case an evil intelligence, it is true, but still a something beyond mere tail and paws and ears. To Wagner it is a dog and nothing more—that will sit at the feet of his master and fawn on him if spoken to, who can be taught to fetch and carry or bring a stick; the end, however, proves different. So one mind sees the outside only; another projects itself into the mind of the creature, be it dog or horse or bird.

Experience certainly educates the dog as it does the man. After long acquaintance and practice in the field we learn the habits and ways of game—to know where it will or not be found. A young dog in the same way dashes swiftly up a hedge, and misses the rabbit that, hearing him coming, doubles back behind a tree or stole; an old dog leaves nothing behind him, searching every corner. This is acquired knowledge. Neither does all depend upon hereditary predisposition as exhibited in the various breeds—the setter, the pointer, the spaniel, or greyhound—and their especial drift of brain; their capacity is not wholly confined to one sphere. They possess an initiating power—what in man is called originality, invention, discovery: they make experiments.

I had a pointer that exhibited this faculty in a curious manner. She was weakly when young, and for that reason, together with other circumstances, was never properly trained: a fact that may perhaps have prevented her 'mind' from congealing into the stolidity of routine. She became an outdoor pet, and followed at heel everywhere. One day some ponds were netted, and of the fish taken a few chanced to be placed in a great stone trough from which cattle drank in the yard—a common thing in the country. Some time afterwards, the trough being foul, the fish —they were roach, tench, perch, and one small jack— were removed to a shallow tub while it was being cleansed. In this tub, being scarcely a foot deep though broad, the fish were of course distinctly visible, and at once became an object of the most intense interest to the pointer. She would not leave it; but stood watching every motion of the fish, with her head now on one side now on the other. There she must have remained some hours, and was found at last in the act of removing them one by one and laying them softly, quite unhurt, on the grass.

I put them back into the water, and waited to see the result. She took a good look, and then plunged her nose right under the surface and half-way up the neck completely submerging the head, and in that position groped about on the bottom till a fish came in contact with her mouth and was instantly snatched out. Her head must have been under water each time nearly a minute, feeling for the fish. One by one she drew them out and placed them on the ground, till only the jack remained. He puzzled her, darting away swift as an arrow and seeming to anticipate the enemy. But after a time he, too, was captured.

They were not injured—not the mark of a tooth was to be seen—and swam as freely as ever when restored to the water. So soon as they were put in again the pointer recommenced her fishing, and could hardly be got away by force. The fish were purposely left in the tub. The next day she returned to the amusement, and soon became so dexterous as to pull a fish out almost the instant her nose went under water.

The jack was always the most difficult to catch, but she managed to conquer him sooner or later. When returned to the trough, however, she was done—the water was too deep. Scarcely anything could be imagined apparently more opposite to the hereditary intelligence of a pointer than this; and certainly no one attempted to teach her, neither did she do it for food. It was an original motion of her own: to what can it be compared but mind proceeding by experiment? They can also adjust their conduct to circumstances, as when they take to hunting on their own account: they then generally work in couples.

If a spaniel, for instance, one of those allowed to lie loose about farmhouses, takes to hunting for herself, she is almost always found to meet a canine friend at a little distance from the homestead. It is said that spaniels when they go off like this never bark when on the heels of a rabbit, as they would do if a sportsman was with them and the chase legitimate. This suppression of what must be an almost uncontrollable inclination shows no little intelligence. If they gave tongue, they would be certainly detected, and as certainly thrashed. To watch the sneaking way in which a spaniel will come home after an unlawful expedition of this kind is most amusing. She makes her appearance on the road or footpath so as not to look as if coming from the hedges, and enters at the back; or if any movement be going on, as the driving of cattle, she will join in it, displaying extraordinary zeal in assisting: anything to throw off suspicion.

Of all sport, if a man desires to widen his chest, and gain some idea of the chase as it was in ancient days, let him take two good greyhounds and 'uncouple at the timorous flying hare', following himself on foot.

A race like this over the elastic turf of the downs, inhaling with expanded lungs air which acts on the blood as strong drink on the brain, stimulating the pulse, and strengthening every fibre of the frame, is equal to another year of life. Coursing for the coursing's sake is capital sport. A hare when sorely tried with the hot breath from the hounds' nostrils on his flanks, will sometimes puzzle them by dashing round and round a rick. Then in sweeping circles the trio strain their limbs, but the hare, having at the corners the inner side and less ground to cover, easily keeps just ahead. This game lasts several minutes, till presently one of the hounds is sharp enough to dodge back and meet the hare the opposite way. Even then his quick eye and ready turn often give him another short breathing space by rushing away at a tangent.

Rabbits, although of 'low degree' in comparison with the pheasant, really form an important item in the list of the keeper's charges. Shooting generally commences with picking out the young rabbits about the middle or towards the end of the hay harvest, according as the season is early or late. Some are shot by the farmers, who have the right to use a gun, earlier than this, while they still disport in the mowing grass. It requires experience and skill to select the young rabbit just fit for table from the old bucks, the does which may yet bring forth another litter, and those little bunnies that do not exceed the size of rats.

The grass conceals the body of the animal, and nothing is visible beyond the tips of the ears; and at thirty yards distance one pair of ears is very like another pair. The developed ear is, however, less pointed than the other; and in the rabbit of a proper size they are or seem to be wider apart. The eye is also guided by the grass itself and the elevation of the rabbit's head above it when lifted in alarm at a chance sound: if the animal is full grown of course the head stands higher. In motion the difference is at once seen; the larger animal's back and flanks show boldly, while the lesser seems to slip through the grass. By these signs, and by a kind of instinct which grows upon one when always in the field, it is possible to distinguish between them even in tall grass and in the gloaming.

This sort of shooting, if it does not afford the excitement of the pheasant battue, or require the alertness necessary in partridge killing, is not without its special pleasures. These are chiefly to be attributed to the genial warmth of the weather at that season, when the reapers have only just begun to put the tall corn to the edge of their crooked swords, and one can linger by the hedge-side without dread of wintry chills.

The aftermath in which the rabbits feed is not so tall as the mowing grass, and more easy and pleasant to walk through, though it is almost devoid of flowers. Neither does it give so much shelter; and you must walk close to the hedge, gliding gently from bush to bush, the slower the better. Rabbits feed several times during the day—*i.e.* in the very early morning, next about eleven o'clock, again at three or four, and again at six or seven. Not that every rabbit comes out to nibble at those hours, but about that time some will be seen moving outside the buries.

As you stroll beside the hedge, brushing the boughs, a rabbit feeding two hundred yards away will lift his head inquiringly from the grass. Then stop, and remain still as the elm tree hard by. In a minute or two, reassured, the ears perked up so sharply fall back,

and he feeds again. Another advance of ten or twenty
yards, and up go the ears—you are still till they drop
once more. The rabbit presently turns his back towards you, sniffing about for the tenderest blades;
this is an opportunity, and an advance of forty or
fifty paces perhaps is accomplished. Now, if you have
a rook-rifle you are near enough; if a smooth-bore,
the same system of stalking must be carried farther
yet. If you are patient enough to wait when he takes
alarm, and only to advance when he feeds, you are
pretty sure to 'bag' him.

Sometimes, when thus gliding with stealthy tread,
another rabbit will suddenly appear out of the ditch
within easy reach; it is so quiet he never suspected
the presence of an enemy. If you pause and keep
quite still, which is the secret of all stalking, he will
soon begin to feed, and the moment he turns his back
towards you up goes the gun; not before, because if
he sees your arm move he will be off to the ditch.
True, a snap-shot might be made as he runs, which at
first sight would appear more sportsmanlike than
'potting'; but it is not so, for it is ten chances to one
that you do not kill him dead on the spot in the short
distance he has to traverse. Perhaps the hind legs will
be broken; well, then he will drag them along behind
him, using the fore paws with astonishing rapidity and
power. Before the second barrel can be emptied he
will gain the shelter of the fern that grows on the edge
of the bank and dive into a burrow, there to die in
misery. So that it is much better to steadily 'pot' him.
Besides which, if a rabbit dies in a burrow all the other
animals in that particular burrow desert it till nature's
scavengers have done their work. A dog cannot well
be taken while stalking—not that dogs will not follow

quietly, but because a rabbit, catching sight of a dog, is generally stricken with panic even if a hundred yards away, and bolts immediately.

I have seen a rabbit whose back was broken by shot drag itself ten yards to the ditch. If the forelegs are broken, then he is helpless: all the kicks of the hind legs only tumble him over and over without giving him much progress. The effects of shot are very strange, and sometimes almost inexplicable: as when a hare which has received a pellet through the edge of the heart runs a quarter of a mile before dropping. It is noticed that hares and rabbits, hit in the vital organs about the heart, often run a considerable distance, and then, suddenly in the midst of their career, roll head over heels dead. Both hares and rabbits are occasionally killed with marks of old shot wounds, but not very often, and they are but of a slight character— the pellets are found just under the skin, with a kind of lump round them. Shot holes through the ears are frequently seen, of course doing no serious harm.

Now and then a rabbit hit in the head will run round and round in circles, making not the slightest attempt to escape. The first time I saw this, not understanding it, I gave the creature the second barrel; but next time I let the rabbit do as he would. He circled round and round, going at a rapid pace. I stood in his way, and he passed between my legs. After half a dozen circles the pace grew slower. Finally, he stopped, sat up quite still for a minute or so, and then drooped and died. The pellet had struck some portion of the brain.

I once, while looking for snipe with charges of small shot in the barrels, roused a fine hare, and fired without apparent effect. But after crossing about half of the field with a spaniel tearing behind, he began to slacken speed, and I immediately followed. The hare dodged the spaniel admirably, and it was with the utmost difficulty I secured him (refraining from firing the second barrel on purpose). He had been stopped by one single little pellet in the great sinew of the hind leg, which had partly cut it through. Had it been a rabbit he would certainly have escaped into a 'bury', and there, perhaps died, as shot wounds frequently fester: so that in stalking rabbits, or waiting for them behind a tree or bush, it is much better to take a steady aim at the head, and so avoid torturing the creature.

'Potting' is hardly sport, yet it has an advantage to those who take a pleasure in observing the ways of bird and animal. There is just sufficient interest to induce one to remain quiet and still, which is the prime condition of seeing anything; and in my own case the rabbits so patiently stalked have at last often gone free, either from their own amusing antics, or because the noise of the explosion would disturb something else under observation. In winter it is too cold; then you step quietly and yet briskly up to a fence or a gateway, and glance over, and shoot at once; or with the spaniels hunt the bunnies from the fern upon the banks, yourself one side of the hedge and the keeper the other.

In excavating his dwelling, the rabbit, thoughtless of science, constructs what may be called a natural auditorium singularly adapted for gathering the expiring vibrations of distant sound. His round tunnel bored in a sandy bank is largest at the opening, like the mouth of a trumpet, and contracts within—a form which focuses the undulations of the air. To obtain the full effect the ear should listen some short way within; but the sound, as it is thrown backwards after entering, is often sufficiently marked to be perceptible when you listen outside. The great deep ditches are dry in summer; and though shooting be not the object, yet a gun for knocking over casual vermin is a pleasant excuse for idling in a reclining position shoulder-high in fern, hidden like a skirmisher in such an entrenchment. A mighty root bulging from the slope of the bank forms a natural seat. There is a cushion of dark green moss to lean against, and the sand worked out from the burrows—one nearly on a level with the head and another lower down—has here filled up the ditch to some height, making a footstool.

In the ditch lie numbers of last year's oak leaves, which so sturdily resist decay. All the winter and spring they were soaked by the water from the 'land-springs'—as those which only run in wet weather are called—draining into it, and to that water they communicated a peculiar flavour, slightly astringent. Even moderate-sized streamlets become tainted in the latter part of the autumn by the mass of leaves they carry down, or filter through, in woodland districts. Often the cottagers draw their water from a small pool filled by such a ditch, and coated at the bottom with a thick layer of decomposing leaves. The taste of this water is strong enough to overcome the flavour of their weak tea, yet they would rather use such water than walk fifty yards to a brook. It must, however, be admitted that the brooks at that time are also tinctured with leaf, and there seems to be no harm in it.

Out from among these dead leaves in the ditch

protrudes a crooked branch fallen long since from the oak, and covered with grey lichen. On the right hand a tangled thicket of bramble with its uneven-shaped stems closes the spot in, and on the left a stole of hazel rises with the parasitical 'hardy fern' fringing it near the earth. The outer bark of the hazel is very thin; it is of a dark mottled hue; bruise it roughly, and the inner bark shows a bright green. The lowly ivy creeps over the bank—its leaves with five angles, and variegated with grey streaks. Through the hawthorn bushes above comes a faint but regular sound—it is the parting fibres of the grass-blades in the meadow on the other side as the cows tear them apart, steadily eating their way onwards. The odour of their breath floats heavy on the air. The sun is sinking, and there is a hush and silence.

But the rabbit-burrow here at my elbow is not silent; it seems to catch and heighten faint noises from a distance. A man is walking slowly home from his work up the lane yonder; the fall of his footsteps is distinctly rendered by the hole here. The dull thuds of a far-off mallet or 'bitel' (beetle) driving in a stake are plainly audible. The thump-thump of a horse's hoofs cantering on the sward by the roadside, though deadened by the turf, are reproduced or sharpened. Most distinct of all comes the regular sound of oars against the tholepins or rowlocks of a boat moving on the lake many fields away. So that in all probability to the rabbit his hole must be a perfect 'Ear of Dionysius', magnifying a whisper—unless, indeed, its turns and windings confuse the undulations of sound. It is observable that before the rabbit ventures forth he stays and listens just within the entrance of his burrow, where he cannot *see* any danger unless absolutely straight before him—a habit that may have unconsciously grown up from the apparent resonance of sound there.

Sitting thus silently on the root of the oak, presently I hear a slight rustling among the dead leaves at the bottom of the ditch. They heave up as if something was pushing underneath; and after a while, as he comes to the heap of sand thrown out by the rabbits, a mole emerges, and instantly with a shiver, as it were, of his skin throws off the particles of dust upon his fur as a dog fresh from the water sends a shower from his coat. The summer weather having dried the clay under the meadow turf and made it difficult to work, he has descended into the ditch, beneath which there is still a certain moistness, and where he can easily bore a tunnel.

It is rather rare to see a mole above ground; fortunately for him he is of diminutive size, or so glossy a fur would prove his ruin. As it is, every other old pollard willow tree along the hedge is hung with miserable moles, caught in traps, and after death suspended —like criminals swinging on a gibbet—from the end of slender willow boughs. Moles seem to breed in the woods: first perhaps because they are less disturbed there, next because under the trees the earth is usually softer, retains its moisture longer, and is easier to work. From the woods their tracks branch out, ramifying like the roads which lead from a city. They have in addition main arteries of traffic, king's highways, along which they will journey one after the other; so that the mole-catcher, if he can discover such a road, slaughters many in succession. The heaps they throw up are awkward in mowing grass, the scythe striking against them; and in consequence of complaints of their rapid multiplication in the woods the keeper has to employ men to reduce their numbers. It is curious to note how speedily the mole buries himself in the soil; it is as if he suddenly dived into the earth.

Another slight rustling—a pause, and it is repeated; this time on the bank, among the dry grass. It is mice; they have a nervous habit of progressing in sharp, short stages. They rush forward seven or eight inches with lightning-like celerity—a dun streak seems to pass before your eye; then they stop short a moment or two, and again make another dash. This renders it difficult to observe them, especially as a single dead brown leaf is sufficient to hide one. It is so silent that they grow bold, and play their antics freely, darting to and fro, round and under the stoles, chasing each other. Sometimes they climb the bushes, running along the upper surface of the boughs that chance to be nearly horizontal. Once on a hawthorn branch in a hedge I saw a mouse descending with an acorn; he was, perhaps, five feet from the ground, and how and from whence he had got his burden was rather puzzling at first. Probably the acorn, dropping from the tree, had been caught and held in the interlacing of the bush till observed by the keen, if tiny, eyes below.

Mice have a magical way of getting into strange places. In some farmhouses they still use the ancient, old-fashioned lanterns made of tin—huge machines intended for a tallow candle, and with plates of thin translucent horn instead of glass. They are not wholly despicable; since if set on the ground and kicked over by a recalcitrant cow in the sheds, the horn does not break as glass would. These lanterns, having a handle at the top, are by it hung up to the beam in the kitchen; and sometimes to the astonishment of the servants in the quiet of the evening, they are found to be animated by some motive power, swinging to and fro and partly turning round. A mouse has got in— for the grease; but how? that is the 'wonderment', as the rustic philosophers express it; for, being hung from the beam, eight or nine feet from the stone-flagged floor, there seems no way of approach for the mouse except by 'walking' on the ceiling or along and partly underneath the beam itself. If so, it would seem to be mainly by the propulsive power exerted previous to starting on the trip—just as a man can get a little way up the perpendicular side of a rick by running at it. Occasionally, no doubt, the mouse has entered when the lantern has been left opened while lighted on the ground, and so got shut in; but mice have been found in lanterns cobwebbed from long disuse.

Suddenly there peeps out from the lower rabbit-hole the stealthy reddish body of a weasel. I instinctively reach for the gun leaning against the bank, and immediately the spell is broken. The mice rush to their holes, the weasel darts back into the bowels of the earth, a rabbit that has quietly slipped out unseen into the grass bounds with eager haste to cover, and out of the oak overhead there rises, with a great clatter of wings, a wood-pigeon that had settled there.

When the pale winter sunshine falls upon the bare branches of an avenue of elms—such as so often ornament parks—they appear lit up with a faint rosy colour, which instantly vanishes on the approach of a shadow. This shimmering mirage in the boughs seems due to the myriads of lesser twigs, which at the extremities have a tinge of red, invisible at a distance till the sunbeams illuminate the trees. Beyond this

passing gleam of colour, nothing relieves the blackness of the January landscape, except here and there
the bright silvery bark of the birch.

For several seasons now in succession the thrush
has sung on the shortest days, as though it were spring;
a little later, in the early mornings, the blackbird
joins, filling the copse with a chorus at the dawn. But,
if the wind turns to east or north, the rooks perch on
the oaks in the hedgerows in the middle of the day,
puffing out their feathers and seeming to abandon all
search for food as if seized with uncontrollable melancholy. Hardy as these birds are, a long frost kills them
in numbers, principally by slow starvation. They die
during the night, dropping suddenly from their roosting-place on the highest boughs of the great beech-
trees, with a thud distinctly heard in the silence of the
woods. The leaves of the beech decay so gradually as
to lie in heaps beneath for months, filling up the hollows, so that an unwary passer-by may plunge knee-
deep in leaves. Rooks when feeding usually cross the
field facing the wind, perhaps to prevent the ruffling
of their feathers.

Wood-pigeons have apparently much increased in
numbers of recent years; they frequent sheltered spots
where the bushes diminish the severity of the frost.
Sometimes on the hills at a lonely farmhouse, where
the bailiff has a long-barrelled ancient fowling-piece,
he will lay a train of grain for them, and with a
double charge of shot, kill many at a time.

Men have boasted of shooting twenty at once. But
with an ordinary gun it is not credible; and the statement, without wilful exaggeration, may arise from
confusion in counting, for it is a fact that some of the
older uneducated country labourers cannot reckon

correctly. It is not unusual in parishes to hear of a
cottage woman who has had twenty children. Upon
investigation the real number is found to be sixteen or
seventeen, yet nothing on earth will convince the
mother that she has not given birth to a score. They
get hazy in figures when exceeding a dozen.

A pigeon is not easily brought down—the quills
are so stiff and strong that the shot, if it comes aslant,
will glance off. Many pigeons roost in the oaks of the
hedges, choosing by preference one well hung with
ivy, and when it is a moonlit night afford tolerable
sport. It requires a gun on each side of the hedge.
A stick flung up awakes the birds; they rise with a
rush and clatter, and in the wildness of their flight
and the dim light are difficult to hit. There is a belief
that pigeons are partially deaf. If stalked in the daytime they take little heed of footsteps or slight noises
which would alarm other creatures; but, on the other
hand, they are quick of eye, and are gone directly
anything suspicious appears in sight. You may get
quite under them and shoot them on the bough at
night. It is not their greater wakefulness but the noise
they make in rising which renders them good pro-
tectors of preserves; it alarms other birds and can be
heard at some distance.

When a great mound and hedgerow is grubbed up,
the men engaged in the work often anticipate making
a considerable bag of the rabbits, whose holes riddle
it in every direction, thinking to dig them out even
of those innermost chambers whence the ferret has
sometimes been unable to dislodge them. But this
hope is almost always disappointed; and when the
grub-axe and spade have laid bare the 'buries' only
recently teeming with life, not a rabbit is found. By

some instinct they have discovered the approach of destruction, and as soon as the first few yards of the hedge are levelled secretly depart. After a 'bury' has been ferreted it is some time before another colony takes possession: this is seemingly from the intense antipathy of the rabbit to the smell of the ferret. Even when shot at and pressed by dogs, a rabbit in his hasty rush will often pass a hole which would have afforded instant shelter because it has been recently ferreted.

At this season the labourers are busy with 'beetle' (pronounced 'bitel')—a huge mallet—and iron wedges, splitting the tough elm-butts and logs for firewood. In old times a cottager here and there with a taste for astrology used to construct an almanack by rule of thumb, predicting the weather for the ensuing twelve months from the first twelve days of January. As the wind blew on those days so the prevailing weather of the months might be foretold. The aged men, however, say that in this divination the old style must be adhered to, for the sequence of signs and omens still follows the ancient reckoning, which ought never to have been interfered with.

CHAPTER VI

THERE are other enemies of game life besides human
poachers whose numbers must be kept within bounds
to ensure successful sport. The thirst of the weasel
for blood is insatiable, and it is curious to watch the
persistency with which he will hunt down the particular rabbit he has singled out for destruction. Through
the winding subterranean galleries of the 'buries' with
their cross-passages, 'blind' holes and 'pop' holes
(*i.e.* those which end in undisturbed soil, and those
which are simply bored from one side of the bank to
the other, being only used for temporary concealment),
never once in the dark close caverns losing sight or
scent of his victim, he pursues it with a species of
eager patience. It is generally a long chase. The
rabbit makes a dash ahead and a double or two, and
then halts, usually at the mouth of a hole: perhaps
to breathe. By-and-by the weasel, baffled for a few
minutes, comes up behind. Instantly the rabbit slips
over the bank outside and down the ditch for a dozen
yards, and there enters the 'bury' again. The weasel
follows, gliding up the bank with a motion not unlike
that of the snake; for his body and neck are long and
slender and his legs short. Apparently he is not in
haste, but rather lingers over the scent. This is repeated five or six times, till the whole length of the
hedgerow has been traversed—sometimes up and
down again. The chase may be easily observed by
anyone who will keep a little in the background.

Although the bank be tenanted by fifty other rabbits, past whose hiding-place the weasel must go, yet they scarcely take any notice. One or two whom he has approached too closely bolt out and in again; but as a mass the furry population remain quiet, as if perfectly aware that they are not yet marked out for slaughter.

At last, having exhausted the resources of the bank the rabbit rushes across the field to a hedgerow, perhaps a hundred yards away. Here the wretched creature seems to find a difficulty in obtaining admittance. Hardly has he disappeared in a hole before he comes out again, as if the inhabitants of the place refused to give him shelter. For many animals have a strong tribal feeling, and their sympathy, like that of man in a savage state, is confined within their special settlement.

With birds it is the same: rooks, for instance, will not allow a strange pair to build in their trees, but drive them off with relentless beak, tearing down the half-formed nest, and taking the materials to their own use. The sentiment, 'If Jacob take a wife of the daughters of Heth, what good shall my life do me?' appears to animate the breasts of gregarious creatures of this kind. Rooks intermarry generation after generation; and if a black lover brings home a foreign bride they are forced to build in a tree at some distance. Near large rookeries several such outlying colonies may be seen.

The rabbit, failing to find a cover, hides in the grass and dry rushes; but across the meadow, stealing along the furrow, comes the weasel; and, shift his place how he may, in the end, worn out and weary, bunny succumbs, and the sharp teeth meet in the neck

behind the ear, severing the vein. Often in the end
the rabbit runs to earth in a hole which is a *cul-de-sac*,
with his back towards the pursuer. The weasel, unable to get at the poll, which is his desire, will mangle
the hinder parts in a terrible manner—as will the
civilised ferret under similar conditions. Now and
then the rabbit, scratching and struggling, fills the
hole in the rear with earth, and so at the last moment
chokes off his assailant and finds safety almost in the
death-agony. In the woods, once the rabbit is away
from the 'buries', the chase really does resemble a
hunt; from furze-bush to bracken, from fern to rough
grass, round and round, backwards, doubling, to and
fro, and all in vain.

At such times, eager for blood, the weasel will run
right across your path, almost close enough to be
kicked. Pursue him in turn, and if there be no hedge
or hole near, if you have him in the open, he will dart
hither and thither right between your legs, uttering a
sharp short note of anger and alarm, something composed of a tiny bark and a scream. He is easily killed
with a stick when you catch him in the open, for he
is by no means swift; but if a hedge be near it is impossible to secure him.

Weasels frequently hunt in couples, and sometimes
more than two will work together. I once saw five,
and have heard of eight. The five I saw were working
a sandy bank drilled with holes, from which the rabbits in wild alarm were darting in all directions. The
weasels raced from hole to hole and along the sides of
the bank exactly like a pack of hounds, and seemed
intensely excited. Their manner of hunting resembles
the motions of ants; these insects run a little way very
swiftly, then stop, turn to the right or left, make a

short detour, and afterwards on again in a straight line. So the pack of weasels darted forward, stopped, went from side to side, and then on a yard or two, and repeated the process. To see their reddish heads thrust for a moment from the holes, then withdrawn to reappear at another, would have been amusing had it not been for the reflection that their frisky tricks would assuredly end in death. They ran their quarry out of the bank and into a wood, where I lost sight of them. The pack of eight was seen by a labourer returning down a woodland lane from work one afternoon. He told me he got into the ditch, half from curiosity to watch them, and half from fear—laughable as that may seem—for he had heard the old people tell stories of men in the days when the corn was kept for years in barns, and so bred hundreds of rats, being attacked by those vicious brutes. He said they made a noise, crying to each other, short sharp snappy sounds; but the pack of five I myself saw hunted in silence.

Stoats, though not so numerous as weasels, probably do quite as much injury, being larger, swifter, stronger, and very bold, sometimes entering sheds close to dwelling-houses. The labouring people—at least, the elder folk—declare that they have been known to suck the blood of infants left asleep in the cradle upon the floor, biting the child behind the ear. They hunt in couples also—seldom in larger numbers. I have seen three at work together, and with a single shot killed two out of the trio. In elegance of shape they surpass the weasel, and the colour is brighter. Their range of destruction seems only limited by their strength: they attack anything they can manage.

The keeper looks upon weasel and stoat as bitter

foes, to be ruthlessly exterminated with shot and gin. He lays to their charge deadly crimes of murder, the death of rabbits, hares, birds, the theft and destruction of his young broods, even occasional abstraction of a chicken close to his very door, despite the dogs chained there. They are not easily shot, being quick to take shelter at the sight of a dog, and when hard hit with the pellets frequently escaping, though perhaps to die. Both weasel and stoat, and especially the latter, will snap viciously at the dog that overtakes them, even when sore wounded, always aiming to fix their teeth in his nose, and fighting savagely to the last gasp. The keeper slays a wonderful number in the course of a year, yet they seem as plentiful as ever. He traps perhaps more than he shoots.

It is not always safe to touch a stoat caught in a trap; he lies apparently dead, but lift him up, and instantly his teeth are in your hand, and it is said such wounds sometimes fester for months. Stoats are tough as leather: though severely nipped by the iron fangs of the gin, struck on the head with the butt of the gun, and seemingly quite lifeless, yet, if thrown on the grass and left, you will often find on returning to the place in a few hours' time that the animal is gone. Warned by experiences of this kind, the keeper never picks up a stoat till 'settled' with a stick or shot, and never leaves him till he is nailed to the shed. Stoats sometimes emit a disgusting odour when caught in a trap. The keeper has no mercy for such vermin, though he thinks some of his feathered enemies are even more destructive.

Twice a year the hawks and other birds of prey find a great feast spread before them; first, in the spring and early summer, when the hedges and fields are full of young creatures scarcely able to use their wings, and again in the severe weather of winter when cold and hunger have enfeebled them.

It is difficult to understand upon what principle the hawk selects his prey. He will pass by with apparent disdain birds that are within easy reach. Sometimes a whole cloud of birds will surround and chase him out of a field; and he pursues the even tenour of his way unmoved, though sparrow and finch almost brush against his talons. Perhaps he has the palate of an epicure, and likes to vary the dish of flesh torn alive from the breast of partridge, chicken, or mouse. He does not eat all he kills; he will sometimes carry a bird a considerable distance and then drop the poor thing. Only recently I saw a hawk, pursued by twenty or thirty finches and other birds across a ploughed field, suddenly drop a bird from his claws as he passed over a hedge. The bird fell almost perpendicularly, with a slight fluttering of the wings, just sufficient to preserve it from turning head-over-heels, and on reaching the hedge could not hold to the first branches, but brought up on one near the ground. It was a sparrow, and was not apparently hurt—simply breathless from fright.

All kinds of birds are sometimes seen with the tail feathers gone: have they barely escaped in this condition from the clutches of the hawk? Blackbirds, thrushes, and pigeons are frequently struck: the hawk seems to lay them on the back, for if he is disturbed that is the position his victim usually remains in. Though hawks do not devour every morsel, yet as a rule nothing is found but the feathers—usually scattered in a circle. Even the bones disappear: probably ground vermin make away with the fragments.

The hawk is not always successful in disabling his prey. I have seen a partridge dashed to the ground, get up again, and escape. The bird was flying close to the ground when struck; the hawk alighted on the grass a few yards further in a confused way as if over-balanced, and before he could reach the partridge the latter was up and found shelter in a thick hedge.

The power to hover or remain suspended in one place in the air does not, as some have supposed, depend upon the assistance of the wind, against which the hawk inclines the plane of his wings like an arti-ficial kite. He can accomplish the feat when the air is quite still and no wind stirring. Nor is he the only bird capable of doing this, although the others possess the power in a much less degree. The common lark sometimes hovers for a few moments low down over the young green corn, as if considering upon what spot to alight. The flycatcher contrives to suspend itself momentarily, but it is by a rapid motion of the wings, and is done when the first snap at the insect has failed. It is the rook that hovers by the assistance of the wind as he rises with his broad, flat wings over a hedge and meets its full force, which counterpoises his onward impetus and sustains him stationary, sometimes compelling him to return with the current.

Hawks have a habit of perching on the tops of bare poles or dead trees, and are there frequently caught in the gin the keeper sets for them. The cuckoo, which so curiously resembles the hawk, has the same habit, and will perch on a solitary post in the middle of a field, or on those upright stones sometimes placed for the cattle to rub themselves against. Though 'wild as a hawk' is a proverbial phrase, yet hawks are bold enough to enter gardens, and even take their prey from the ivy which grows over the gable of the house. The destruction they work among the young part-ridges in early summer is very great. The keeper is always shooting them, yet they come just the same, or nearly; for, if he exterminates them one season, others arrive from a distance. He is particularly careful to look out for their nests, so as to kill both the old birds and to prevent their breeding. There is little diffi-culty in finding the nest (which is built in a high tree) when the young get to any size; their cry is unmis-takable and audible at some distance.

Against sparrow-hawk and kestrel, and the rarer kinds that occasionally come down from the moun-tains of the north or the west—the magazines of these birds—the keeper wages ceaseless war.

So too with jay and magpie; he shoots them down whenever they cross his path, unless, as is sometimes the case, specially ordered to save the latter. For the magpie of recent years has become much less common. Though still often seen in some districts, there are other localities where this odd bird is nearly extinct. It does not seem to breed now, and you may ask to be shown a nest in vain. A magpie's nest in an orchard that I knew of was thought so great a curiosity that every now and then people came to see if from a dis-tance. In other places the bird may be frequently met with, almost always with his partner; and so jays usually go in couples, even in winter.

The jay is a handsome bird, whose chatter enlivens the plantations, and whose bright plumage contrasts pleasantly with the dull green of the firs. A pair will work a hedge in a sportsmanlike manner, one on one side, the second on the other; while the tiny wren, which creeps through the bushes as a mouse through the grass, cowers in terror, or slips into a knot-hole till the danger is past. When the husbandman has sown his field with the drill, hardly has he left the gateway before a legion of small birds pours out from the hedgerows and seeks for the stray seeds. Then you may see the jay hop out among them with an air of utter innocence, settling on the larger lumps of clay for convenience of view, swelling out his breast in pride of beauty, jerking his tail up and down, as if to say, Admire me. With a sidelong hop and two flaps of the wing, he half springs, half glides to another coign of vantage. The small birds, sparrows, chaffinches, greenfinches—instantly scatter swiftly right and left, not rising, but with a hasty run for a yard or so. They know well his murderous intent, and yet are so busy they only put themselves just out of reach, aware that, unlike the hawk, he cannot strike at a distance. This game will continue for a long time; the jay all the while affecting an utter indifference, yet ever on the alert till he spies his chance. It is the young or weakly partridges and pheasants that fall to the jay and magpie.

The keeper also destroys owls—on suspicion. Now and then someone argues with the keeper, assuring him that they do not touch game, but this he regards as pure sentimentalism. 'Look at his beak,' is his steady reply. 'Tell me that that there bill weren't made to tear a bird's breast to bits? Just see here—all crooked and pointed: why, an owl have got a hooked bill like an eagle. It stands to reason as he must be in mischief.' So the poor owls are shot and trapped, and nailed to the side of the shed.

But upon the crow the full vials of the keeper's wrath are poured, and not without reason. The crow among birds is like the local professional among human poachers: he haunts the place and clears everything—it would be hard to say what comes amiss to him. He is the impersonation of murder. His long, stout, pointed beak is a weapon of deadly power, wielded with surprising force by the sinewy neck. From a tiny callow fledgling, fallen out of the thrush's nest, to the partridge or a toothsome young rabbit, it is all one to him. Even the swift leveret is said sometimes to fall a prey, being so buffeted by the sooty wings of the assassin and so blinded by the sharp beak striking at his eyes as to be presently overcome. For the crow has a terrible penchant for the morsel afforded by another's eyes: I have seen the skull of a miserable thrush, from which a crow rose and slowly sailed away, literally split as if by a chisel —doubtless by the blow that destroyed its sight. Birds that are at all diseased or weakly, as whole broods sometimes are in wet unkindly seasons, rabbits touched by the dread parasite that causes the fatal 'rot', the young pheasant straying from the coop, even the chicken at the lone farmstead, where the bailiff only lives and is in the fields all day—these are the victims of the crow.

Crows work almost always in pairs—it is remarkable that hawks, jays, magpies, crows, nearly all birds of prey, seem to remain in pairs the entire year—and when they have once tasted a member of a brood, be it pheasant, partridge, or chicken, they stay till they have cleared off the lot. Slow of flight and somewhat lazy of habit, they will perch for hours on a low tree, croaking and pruning their feathers; they peer into every nook and corner of the woodlands, not like the swift hawk, who circles over and is gone and in a few minutes is a mile away. So that neither the mouse in the furrow nor the timid partridge cowering in the hedge can escape their leering eyes.

Therefore the keeper smites them hip and thigh whenever he finds them; and if he comes across the nest, placed on the broad top of a pollard-tree—not in the branches, but on the trunk—sends his shot through it to smash the eggs. For if the young birds come to maturity they will remain in that immediate locality for months, working every hedge and copse and ditch with cruel pertinacity. In consequence of this unceasing destruction the crow has become much rarer of late, and its nest is hardly to be found in many woods. They breed in the scattered trees of the meadows and fields, especially where no regular game preservation is attempted, and where no keeper goes his rounds. Even to this day a lingering superstition associates this bird with coming evil; and I have heard the women working in the fields remark that such and such a farmer then lying ill would not recover, for a crow had been seen to fly over his house but just above the roof-tree.

Trespassers give him a good deal of trouble, for a great wood seems to have an irresistible attraction for all sorts of semi-Bohemians, besides those who come for poaching purposes. The keeper thinks it much more difficult to watch a wood like this, which is continuous and all in one, than it is to guard a number of detached plantations, though in the aggregate they may cover an equal area. It is impossible to see into it any distance; to walk round it is a task of time. A poacher may slink from tree to tree and from thicket to thicket, and, unless the dogs chance to sniff him out, may lie hidden in tangled masses of fern and bramble, while the keeper passes not ten yards away. But plantations laid out in regular order with broad open spaces, sometimes with small fields between, do not afford anything like cover for human beings. If a man is concealed in one of these copses, and finds that the keeper or his assistants are about to go through it, he must move or be caught; and in moving he has to pass across an open space, and is nearly sure to be detected. In a continuous wood of large extent, if he hears the keepers coming he has but to slip as rapidly and silently as possible to one side, and often has the pleasure to see them pass right over the spot where only recently he was lying.

Therefore, although a wood is much more beautiful from an artistic point of view, with its lovely greens in spring and yellow and browns in autumn, its shades and recesses and fern-strewn glades, yet if a gentleman desires to imitate the monarch who laid out the New Forest and plant wood, and his object be simply game, the keeper is of opinion that the somewhat stiff and trim plantations are preferable. They are generally of fir; and fir is the most difficult of trees to slip past, being decidedly of an obstructive turn. The boughs grow so close to the ground that unless you crawl you cannot go under them. The trunks—unlike those of many other trees—will flourish so near together that the extremities of the branches touch and almost interweave, and they are rough and unpleasant to push through. To shoot or trap, or use a net or other poacher's implement, is very difficult in a young fir plantation, because of this thickness of growth; so that in a measure the tree itself protects the game. Then the cover afforded is warm and liked by the birds; and so for many reasons the fir has become a great favourite, notwithstanding that it is of very little value when finally cut down.

For fox preserving firs are hardly so suitable, because the needles, or small sharp leaves, quite destroy all undergrowth—not only by the turpentine they contain, but by forming a thick mat, as it were, upon the earth. This mass of needles takes years, to all appearance, to decay, and no young green blade or shoot can get through it; besides which the fir-boughs above make a roof almost impenetrable to air and light, the chief necessities of a plant's existence. Foxes like a close warm undergrowth, such as furze, sedges when the ground is dry, the underwood that springs up between the ash-stoles. Although constantly out of doors—if such a phrase be allowable—foxes seem to dislike cold and draught, as do weasels and all their kind, notably ferrets. But for pure game preserving, and for convenience of watching, the keeper thinks the detached plantations of fir preferable. Doubtless he is professionally right; and yet somehow a great wood seems infinitely more English and appeals to the heart far more powerfully, with its noble oaks and beeches and ash trees, its bramble-thickets and brake, and endless beauties which a life of study will not exhaust.

But the semi-Bohemians detested by the keeper do not prowl about the confines of a wood with artistic views; their objects are extremely prosaic, and though not always precisely injurious, yet they annoy him beyond endurance. He is like a spider in the centre of a vast spreading web, and the instant the most outlying threads—in this case represented by fences—are broken he is all agitation till he has expelled the intruder. Men and boys in the winter come stealing

into the wood where the blackthorn thickets are for
sloes, which are reputed to be improved by the first
frosts, and are used for making sloe gin, &c. Those
they gather they sell, of course; and although the pursuit may be perfectly harmless in itself, how is the
keeper to be certain that, if opportunity offered, these
gentry would not pounce upon a rabbit or anything
else? Others come for the dead wood; and it does on
the face of it seem hard to deny an old woman who
has worked all her days in the field a bundle of
fallen branches rotting under the trees. The accumu-
lations of such dead sticks in some places are astonishing: the soil under the ash-poles must slowly rise from
the mass of decaying wood and ultimately become
greatly enriched by this natural manure.

When a hard clay soil is revealed by the operations
for draining a meadow, and the crust of black or
reddish mould on which the sweet green grass flourishes
is seen to be but spade-deep, the idea naturally occurs
that that thin crust must have been originated by
some similar process to what is now going on in the
ash wood. Those six or nine inches of mould perhaps
represent several centuries of forest. But if the keeper
admits the old woman shivering over her embers in
the cottage to pick up these dead boughs, how can he
tell what further tricks others may be up to? The
privilege has often been offered and as often abused,
until at last it has been finally withdrawn—not only
because of the poaching carried on under the cloak
of picking up dead wood, but because the intruders
tore down fine living branches from the trees and
spoiled and disfigured them without mercy. Sometimes gentlemen go to the expense of having wood
periodically gathered and distributed among the poor,

which is a considerate system and worthy of imitation where possible.

Occasionally men come to search for walking-sticks, for which there is now a regular trade. Just at present 'natural' sticks—that is, those cut from the stem with the bark on—are rather popular, both for walking and for umbrella handles, which causes this kind of search to be actively prosecuted. The best 'natural' sticks are those which when growing were themselves young trees, sprung up direct from seed or shoots—saplings, which are stronger and more pliant than those cut from a stole or pollard. To cut such a stick as this is equivalent to destroying a future tree, and of course a good deal of mischief may be easily done in a short time.

Another kind of ash stick which is in demand is one round which there runs a spiral groove. This spiral is caused by the bine of honeysuckle or woodbine, and in some cases by wild hops. These climbing plants grow in great profusion when they once get fixed in the soil, and twist their tendrils or 'leaders' round and round the tall, straight, young ash poles with so tight a grasp as to partly strangle the stick and form a deep screw-like groove in it. When well polished, or sometimes in its rough state, such a stick attracts customers; and so popular is this 'style' of thing that the spiral groove is frequently cut by the lathe in more expensive woods than ash. Wild hops are common in many places, and will almost destroy a hedge or a little copse by the power with which they twine their coils about stem and branch. Young oak saplings, in the same way, are frequently cut; and the potential tree which might have grown large enough to form part of a ship's timbers is sold for a shilling.

Holly is another favourite wood for sticks, and fetches more money than oak or ash, on account of its ivory-like whiteness when peeled. To get a good stick with a knob to it frequently necessitates a considerable amount of cutting and chopping, and does far more damage than the loss of the stick itself represents. Neither blackthorn nor crabtree seem so popular as they once were for this purpose.

In the autumn scores of men, women, and children scour the hedges and woods for acorns, which bring a regular price per bushel or sack, affording a valuable food for pigs. Others seek elderberries to sell for making wine, and for a few weeks a trade is done in blackberries. Chair-menders and basket-makers frequent the shore of the little mere or lake looking for bulrushes or flags: the old rush-bottomed chairs are still to be found in country houses, and require mending; and flag-baskets are much used.

Hazel-nuts and filberts perhaps cause more trouble than all the rest; this fruit is now worth money, and in some counties the yield of nuts is looked forward to in the same way as any other crop—as in Kent, where cob-nuts are cultivated, and where the disorderly hop-pickers are great thieves. I have heard of owners of copses losing ten or fifteen pounds' worth of nuts by a single raid. Here, in this wood, no attempt is made to obtain profit from the fruit, yet it gives rise to much trouble. The nut-stealers take no care in pulling down the boughs, but break them shamefully, destroying entire bushes; and for this reason in many places, where nutting was once freely permitted, it is now rigidly repressed. Just before the nuts become ripe they are gathered by men employed on the place, and thrown down in sackfuls, making great heaps by the public footpaths—ocular evidence that it is useless to enter the wood a-nutting.

The keeper thinks that these trespassers grow more coarsely mischievous year by year. He can recollect when the wood in a measure was free and open, and, provided a man had not got a gun or was not suspected of poaching, he might roam pretty much at large; while the resident labouring people went to and fro by the nearest short cut they could find. But whether the railways bring rude strangers with no respect for the local authorities, or whether 'tramps' have become more numerous, it is certain that only by constant watchfulness can downright destruction be prevented. It is not only the game preserved within that closes these beautiful woodlands to the public, but the wanton damage to tree and shrub, the useless, objectless mischief so frequently practised. For instance, a column of smoke, curling like a huge snake round the limbs of a great tree and then floating away from the topmost branches, is a singular spectacle, so opposed to the ordinary current of ideas as to be certain of attracting the passer-by. It is the work, of course, of some mischievous lout who has set fire to the hollow interior of the tree.

Such a tree, as previously pointed out, is the favourite resort of bird and insect life. The heedless mischief of the bird-keeping boys, or the ploughlads rambling about on Sunday, destroys this Hôtel de Ville of the forest or hedgerow, the central house of assembly of the birds. To light a fire seems one of the special delights of these lads, and sometimes of men who should have learned better; and to light it in a hollow tree is the highest flight of genius. A few handfuls of withered grass and dead fern, half a dozen dry sticks, a lucifer match, and the thing is done. The hollow within the tree is shaped like an inverted funnel, large at the bottom and decreasing upwards, where at the pointed roof one thin streak of daylight penetrates. This formation is admirably adapted to 'draw' a fire at the bottom, and so, once lit, it is not easily put out. The 'touchwood' smoulders and smokes immensely, and a great black column rises in the air. So it will go on smouldering and smoking for days till nothing but a charred stump be left. Now and then there is sufficient sap yet remaining in the bark and outer ring of wood to check the fire when it reaches it; and finally it dies out, being unable to burn the green casing of the trunk. Even then, so strong is the vital force, the oak may stand for years and put forth leaves on its branches—leaves which, when dead, will linger, loth to fall, almost through the winter, rustling in the wind, till the buds of spring push them off.

Graver mischief is sometimes committed with the lucifer match, and with more of the set purpose of destruction. In the vast expanse of furze outside the wood on the high ground the huntsmen are almost certain of a find, and, if they can get between the fox and the wood, of a rattling burst along the edge of the downs; no wonder, therefore, that both they and the keeper set store by this breadth of 'bush'. To this great covert more than once some skulking scoundrel has set fire, taking good care to strike his match well to windward, so that the flames might drive across the whole, and to choose a wind which would also endanger the wood. Now nothing flares up with such a sudden fierceness as furze, and there is no possibility of stopping it. With a loud crackling,

and swaying of pointed tongues of flame visible miles
away even at noontide, and a cloud of smoke, the rift
rolls on, licking up grass and fern and heath; and its
hot breath goes before it, and the blast rises behind it.
As on the beach the wave seems to break at the foot,
and then in an instant the surf runs away along the
sand, so from its first start the flame widens out right
and left with a greedy eagerness, and what five
minutes ago was but a rolling bonfire is now a wall of
fire a quarter of a mile broad, and swelling as it goes.

Then happens on a lesser scale exactly the same
thing that travellers describe of the burning prairies of
the Far West—a stampede of the thousands of living
creatures, bird and beast: rabbits, hares, foxes, weasels,
stoats, badgers, wild cats, all rushing in a maddened
frenzy of fear they know not whither. Often, with a
strange reversal of instinct, so to say, they will crowd
together right in the way of the flames, huddling in
hundreds where the fire must pass, and no effort of
voice or presence of man will drive them away. The
hissing, crackling fire sweeps over, and in an instant
all have perished. No more miserable spectacle can
be witnessed than the terror of these wretched creatures. Birds seem to fly into the smoke and are
suffocated—they fall and are burned. Hares, utterly
beside themselves, will rush almost into the arms of
the crowd that assembles, and, of course, picks up
what it can seize. The flames blacken and scorch the
firs and trees on the edge of the wood, and the marks
of their passage are not obliterated for years.

Apart from the torture of animals, the damage to
sport—both hunting and shooting—is immense, and
takes long to remedy; for although furze and fern
soon shoot again, yet animal life is not so quickly

repaired. Sometimes a few sheep wandering from the downs are roasted alive in this manner; and one or more dogs from the crowd watching are sure to run into the flames, which seem to exercise a fascination over some canine minds. The keeper's wrath bubbles up years afterwards as he recalls the scene, and it would not be well for the incendiary if he fell into his hands. But the mischief can be so easily done that it is rarely these rascals are captured.

CHAPTER VII

THERE are three kinds of poachers, the local men, the raiders coming in gangs from a distance, and the 'mouchers'—fellows who do not make precisely a profession of it, but who occasionally loiter along the roads and hedges picking up whatever they can lay hands on. Philologists may trace a resemblance between the present provincial word 'mouching' and Shakspeare's 'mitcher', who ate blackberries. Of the three probably the largest amount of business is done by the local men, on the principle that the sitting gamester sweeps the board. They therefore deserve first consideration.

It is a popular belief that the village poacher is an idle, hang-dog ne'er-do-well, with a spice of sneaking romance in his disposition—the Bohemian of the hamlet, whose grain of genius has sprouted under difficulties, and produced weeds instead of wheat. This is a complete fallacy, in our day at least. Poaching is no longer an amusement, a thing to be indulged in because

It's my delight of a shiny night
In the season of the year;

but a hard, prosaic business, a matter of £ s. d., requiring a long-headed, shrewd fellow, with a power of silence, capable of a delicacy of touch which almost raises poaching into a fine art. The real man is often a sober and to all appearance industrious individual, working steadily during the day at some handicraft

in the village, as blacksmithing, hedge-carpentering—
i.e. making posts and rails, &c.—cobbling, tinkering,
or perhaps in the mill; a somewhat reserved, solitary
workman of superior intelligence and frequently advanced views as to the 'rights of labour'. He has no
appetite for thrilling adventure; his idea is simply
money, and he looks upon his night-work precisely as
he does upon his day-labour.

His great object is to avoid suspicion, knowing that
success will be proportionate to his skill in cloaking
his operations; for in a small community, when a man
is 'suspect', it is comparatively easy to watch him,
and a poacher knows that if he is watched he must
sooner or later be caught. Secrecy is not so very
difficult; for it is only with certain classes that he need
practise concealment: his own class will hold their
peace. If a man is seen at his work in the day, if he is
moderate in his public-house attendance, shows himself at church, and makes friends with the resident
policeman (not as a confederate, but to know his
beat and movements), he may go on for years without
detection.

Perhaps the most promising position for a man who
makes a science of it is a village at the edge of a range
of downs, generally fringed with large woods on the
lower slopes. He has then ground to work alternately,
according to the character of the weather and the
changes of the moon. If the weather be wet, windy, or
dark from the absence of the moon, then the wide
open hills are safe; while, on the other hand, the
woods are practically inaccessible, for a man must
have the eyes of a cat to see to do his work in the
impenetrable blackness of the plantations. So that
upon a bright night the judicious poacher prefers the

woods, because he can see his way, and avoids the hills, because, having no fences to speak of, a watcher may detect him a mile off.

Meadows with double mounds and thick hedges may be worked almost at any time, as one side of the hedge is sure to cast a shadow, and instant cover is afforded by the bushes and ditches. Such meadows are the happy hunting-grounds of the poacher for that reason, especially if not far distant from woods, and consequently overrun with rabbits. For, since the price of rabbits has risen so high, they are very profitable as game, considering that a dozen or two may be captured without noise and without having to traverse much space—perhaps in a single hedge.

The weather most unsuitable is that kind of frost which comes on in the early morning, and is accompanied with some rime on the grass—a duck's frost, just sufficient to check fox-hunting. Every footstep on grass in this condition when the sun comes out burns up as black as if the sole of the boot were of red-hot iron, and the poacher leaves an indelible trail behind him. But as three duck's frosts usually bring rain, a little patience is alone necessary. A real, downright six weeks' frost is, on the contrary, very useful—game lie close. But a deep snow is not welcome; for, although many starved animals may be picked up, yet it quite suspends the operations of the regular hand: he can neither use wire, net, nor ferret.

Windy nights are disliked, particularly by rabbit-catchers, who have to depend a great deal upon their sense of hearing to know when a rabbit is moving in the 'buries', and where he is likely to 'bolt', so as to lay hands on him the instant he is in the net. But with the 'oak's mysterious roar' overhead, the snapping of dead branches, and the moan of the gale as it rushes through the hawthorn, it is difficult to distinguish the low, peculiar thumping sound of a rabbit in his catacomb. The rabbit is not easily dislodged in rain; for this animal avoids getting wet as much as possible: he 'bolts' best when it is dry and still.

A judicious man rarely uses a gun, for the reason that noise is inconvenient, and a gun is an awkward tool to carry concealed about the person even when taken to pieces. There is a certain prejudice in rural places against a labouring man possessing a gun; it is sure to draw suspicion upon him. A professional poacher is pre-eminently a trapper, relying chiefly upon the dexterous employment of the snare. If he does shoot, by preference he chooses a misty day, knowing that the sound of the report travels scarcely half the usual distance through fog; and he beats the meadows rather than the preserves, where the discharge would instantly attract attention, while in the meadows or ploughed fields it may pass unnoticed as fired by a farmer with leave to kill rabbits.

When the acorns are ripe and the pheasants wander great distances from the plantations along the hedgerows is his best time for shooting; no keepers at that period can protect them. He also observes where the partridges which roost on the ground assemble nightly as it grows dark, easily ascertaining the spot by their repeated calls to each other, and sometimes knocks over three or four at a shot.

Occasionally, also, early in the season, before the legitimate sportsman perhaps has stepped into the stubble, and while the coveys are large, he sees a good chance, and with two or even three ounces of shot makes havoc among them. He invariably fires at his game sitting, first, because he cannot lose an opportunity, and, next, because he can kill several at once. He creeps up behind a hedge, much as the sportsman in Rubens's picture in the National Gallery is represented, stooping to get a view, himself unseen, at the brown birds on the ground. With the antique firelock such a practice was necessary; but nothing in our day so stamps a man a poacher as this total denial of 'law' to the game.

When the pheasant is shot his next difficulty is with the feathers. The fluffy, downy under-feathers fly in all directions, scattering over the grass, and if left behind would tell an unmistakable tale. They must therefore be collected as far as possible, and hidden in the ditch. The best pockets for carrying game are those made in the tails of the coat, underneath: many poachers' coats are one vast pocket behind the lining.

When there is special danger of being personally overhauled and searched, or when the 'bag' is large, the game is frequently hidden in a rabbit-hole, taking care to fence the hole some distance inside with a stout stick across it, the object of which is that if the keeper or a sportsman should pass that way his dogs, scenting the game, will endeavour to scratch out the earth and get in after it. This the cross stick will prevent, and the keeper will probably thrash his dog for refusing to obey when called off.

A great deal of poaching used to be accomplished by nets, into which both partridges and pheasants were driven. If skilfully alarmed—that is, not too much hurried—these birds will run a long way before rising, and, if their tracks are known, may be netted in considerable numbers. But of recent years, since pheasants especially have become so costly a luxury to keep, the preserves and roosting-places have been more effectually watched, and this plan has become more difficult to put in practice. In fact, the local man thinks twice before he puts his foot inside a preserve, and, if possible, prefers to pick up outside. If a preserve is broken into the birds are at once missed, and there is a hue and cry; but the loss of outsiders is not immediately noticed.

The wire is, perhaps, the regular poacher's best implement, and ground game his most profitable source of income. Hares exist in numbers upon the downs, especially near the localities where the great coursing meetings are held, where a dozen may be kicked out of the grass in five minutes. In these districts of course the downs are watched; but hares cannot be kept within bounds, and wander miles and miles at night, limping daintily with their odd gait (when undisturbed) along the lanes leading into the ploughed fields on the lower slopes and plains. The hills—wide and almost pathless, and practically destitute of fences—where the foot leaves no trail on the short grass and elastic turf, are peculiarly favourable to illicit sport.

Though apparently roaming aimlessly, hares have their regular highways or 'runs'; and it is the poacher's business to discover which of these narrow paths are most beaten by continuous use. He then sets his wire, as early in the evening as compatible with safety to himself, for hares are abroad with the twilight.

Long practice and delicate skill are essential to successful snaring. First, the loop itself into which the hare is to run his head must be of the exact size.

The Gamekeeper at Home

If it be too small he will simply thrust it aside; if too large his body will slip through, and his hind leg will be captured: being crooked, it draws the noose probably. Then if caught by the hind leg, the wretched creature, mad with terror, will shriek his loudest; and a hare shrieks precisely like a human being in distress. The sound, well understood by the watchers, will at once reveal what is going forward. But there may be no watchers about; and in that case the miserable animal will tug and tug during the night till the wire completely bares the lower bone of the leg, and in the morning, should anyone pass, his leaps and bounds and rolls will of course be seen. Sometimes he twists the wire till it snaps, and so escapes—but probably to die a lingering death, since the copper or brass is pretty sure to mortify the flesh. No greater cruelty can be imagined. The poacher, however, is very anxious to avoid it, as it may lead to detection; and if his wire is properly set the animal simply hangs himself, brought up with a sudden jerk which kills him in two seconds, and with less pain than is caused by the sting of the sportsman's cartridge.

Experience is required to set the loop at the right height above the ground. It is measured by placing the clenched fist on the earth, and then putting the extended thumb of the other open hand upon it, stretching it out as in the action of spanning, when the tip of the little finger gives the right height for the lower bend of the loop—that is, as a rule; but clever poachers vary it slightly to suit the conformation of the ground. A hare carries his head much higher than might be thought; and he is very strong, so that the plug which holds the wire must be driven in firmly to withstand his first convulsive struggle. The small

upright stick whose cleft suspends the wire across the
'run' must not be put too near the hare's path, or he
will see it, and it must be tolerably stiff, or his head
will push the wire aside. Just behind a 'tussocky'
bunch of grass is a favourite spot to set a noose; the
grass partially conceals it.

The poacher revisits his snares very early in the
morning, and if he is judicious invariably pulls them
up, whether successful or not, because they may be
seen in the day. Half the men who are fined by the
magistrates have been caught by keepers who, having
observed wires, let them remain, but keep a watch
and take the offenders red-handed. The professional
poacher never leaves his wires set up all day, unless
a sudden change of weather and the duck's frost
previously mentioned prevent him from approaching
them, and then he abandons those particular snares
for ever. For this reason he does not set up more than
he can easily manage. If he gets three hares a night
(wholesale price 2*s*. 6*d*. each) he is well repaid. Rabbits are also wired in great numbers. The loop is a
trifle smaller, and should be just a span from the
ground.

But the ferret is the poacher's chief assistant in
rabbiting: it takes two men, one on each side of the
'bury', and a ferret which will not 'lie in'—*i.e.* stay in
the hole and feast till overcome with sleep. Ferrets
differ remarkably in disposition, and the poacher
chooses his with care; otherwise, if the ferret will not
come out the keepers are certain to find him the next
day hunting on his own account. Part of the secret is
to feed him properly, so that he may have sufficient
appetite to hunt well and yet be quickly satisfied with
a taste of blood. Skill is essential in setting up the

nets at the mouth of the holes; but beyond the mere knack, easily acquired, there is little to learn in ferreting.

The greatest difficulty with any kind of game is to get home unobserved with the bag. Keepers are quite aware of this; and in the case of large estates, leaving one or two assistants near the preserves, they patrol the byways and footpaths, while the police watch the cross-roads and lanes which lead to the villages. If a man comes along at an exceptionally early hour with coat pockets violently bulging, there is a *prima facie* case for searching him. One advantage of wiring or netting over the gun is here very noticeable: anything shot bleeds and stains the pocket—a suspicious sign even when empty; strangulation leaves no traces.

Without a knowledge of the policeman's beat and the keeper's post the poacher can do nothing on a large scale. He has, however, no great trouble in ascertaining these things; the labourers who do not themselves poach sympathize warmly and whisper information. There is reason to think that men sometimes get drunk, or sufficiently so to simulate intoxication very successfully, with the express purpose of being out all night with a good excuse, and so discovering the policeman's ambuscade. Finding a man whom he knows to be usually sober overtaken with drink in a lonely road, where he injures none but himself, the policeman good-naturedly leads him home with a caution only.

The receivers of game are many and various. The low beer-shop keepers are known to purchase large quantities. Sometimes a local pork-butcher in a small way buys and transmits it, having facilities for sending hampers, &c., unsuspected. Sometimes the carriers are the channel of communication; and there is no doubt the lower class of game dealers in the provincial towns get a good deal in this way. The London dealer, who receives large consignments at once, has of course no means of distinguishing poached from other game. The men who purchase the rabbits ferreted by the keepers during the winter in the woods and preserves, and who often buy 100*l.* worth or more in the season, have peculiar opportunities for conveying poached animals, carefully stowed for them in a ditch on their route. This fact having crept out has induced gentlemen to remove these rabbit contracts from local men, and to prefer purchasers from a distance, who must take some time to get acquainted with the district poachers.

The raiders, who come in gangs armed with guns and shoot in the preserves, are usually the scum of manufacturing towns, led or guided by a man expelled through his own bad conduct from the village, and who has a knowledge of the ground. These gangs display no skill, relying on their numbers, arms, and known desperation of character to protect them from arrest, as it does in nine cases out of ten. Keepers and policemen cannot be expected to face such brutes as these fellows; they do sometimes, however, and get shattered with shot.

The 'mouchers' sneak about the hedgerows on Sundays with lurcher dogs, and snap up a rabbit or a hare; they do not do much damage except near great towns, where they are very numerous. Shepherds, also, occasionally mouch—their dogs being sometimes very expert; and ploughmen set wires in the gateways or gaps where they have noticed the track of a hare, but it is only for their own eating, and is not of much consequence in comparison with the work of the real local professional. These regular hands form a class which are probably more numerous now than ever; the reasons are—first, the high value of game and the immense demand for it since poultry has become so dear, and, secondly, the ease of transmission now that railways spread into the most out-lying districts and carry baskets or parcels swiftly out of reach. Poaching, in fact, well followed, is a lucrative business.

Some occasional poaching is done with no aid but the hand, especially in severe weather, which makes all wild animals 'dummel', in provincial phrase—*i.e.* stupid, slow to move. Even the hare is sometimes caught by hand as he crouches in his form. It requires a practised eye, that knows precisely where to look among the grass, to detect him hidden in the bunch under the dead, dry bennets. An inexperienced person chancing to see a hare sitting like this would naturally stop short in walking to get a better view; whereupon the animal, feeling that he was observed, would instantly make a rush. You must persuade the hare that he is unseen; and so long as he notices no start or sign of recognition—his eye is on you from first entering the field—he will remain still, believing that you will pass.

The poacher, having marked his game, looks steadily in front of him, never turning his head, but insensibly changes his course and quietly approaches sidelong. Then, in the moment of passing, he falls quick as lightning on his knee, and seizes the hare just behind the poll. It is the only place where the sudden grasp would hold him in his convulsive terror—he is surprisingly powerful—and almost ere he can shriek (as he will do) the left hand has tightened round the hind legs. Stretching him to his full length across the knee, the right thumb, with a peculiar twist, dislocates his neck, and he is dead in an instant. There is something of the hangman's knack in this, which is the invariable way of killing rabbits when ferreted or caught alive; and yet it is the most merciful, for death is instantaneous. It is very easy to sprain the thumb while learning the trick.

A poacher will sometimes place his hat gently on the ground, when first catching sight of a sitting hare, and then stealthily approach on the opposite side. The hare watches the hat, while the real enemy comes up unawares, or, if both are seen, he is in doubt which way to dash. On a dull, cold day hares will sit till the sportsman's dogs are nearly on them, almost till he has to kick them out. At other times in the same locality they are, on the contrary, too wild. Occasionally a labourer, perhaps a 'fogger', crossing the meadows with slow steps, finds a rabbit sitting in like manner among the grass or in a dry furrow. Instantly he throws himself all a-sprawl upon the ground, with the hope of pinning the animal to the earth. The manœuvre, however, frequently fails, and the rabbit slips away out of his very hands.

The poacher is never at rest; there is no season when his marauding expeditions cease for awhile; he acknowledges no 'close time' whatever. Almost every month has its appropriate game for him, and he can always turn his hand to something. In the very heat of the summer there are the young rabbits, for which there is always a sale in the towns, and the leverets, which are easily picked up by a lurcher dog.

I have known a couple of men take a pony and

trap for this special purpose, and make a pleasant excursion over hill and dale, through the deep country lanes, and across the open down land, carrying with them two or three such dogs to let loose as opportunity offers. Their appearance as they rattle along is certainly not prepossessing; the expression of their canine friends trotting under the trap, or peering over the side, stamps them at the first glance as 'snappers up of unconsidered trifles'; but you cannot arrest these gentlemen peacefully driving on the 'king's highway' simply because they have an ugly look about them. From the trap they get a better view than on foot; standing up they can see over a moderately high hedge, and they can beat a rapid retreat if necessary, with the aid of a wiry pony. Passing by some meadows, they note a goodly number oⳑ rabbits feeding in the short aftermath. They draw up by a gateway, and one of them dismounts. With the dogs he creeps along behind the hedge (the object being to get between the bunnies and their holes), and presently sends the dogs on their mission. The lurchers are tolerably sure of catching a couple—young rabbits are neither so swift nor so quick at doubling as the older ones. Before the farmer and his men, who are carting the summer-ricks in an adjacent field, can quite comprehend what the unusual stir is about yonder, the poachers are off, jogging comfortably along, with their game hidden under an old sack or some straw.

Their next essay is among the ploughed fields, where the corn is ripening and as yet no reapers are at work, so that the coast is almost clear. Here they pick up a leveret, and perhaps the dogs chop a weakly young partridge, unable to fly well, in the hedge. The keeper has just strolled through the copses bordering on the road, and has left them, as he thinks, safe. They watch his figure slowly disappearing in the distance from a bend of the lane, and then send the dogs among the underwood. In the winter men will carry ferrets with them in a trap like this.

The desperate gangs who occasionally sweep the preserves, defying the keepers in their strength of numbers and prestige of violence, sometimes bring with them a horse and cart, not so much for speed of escape as to transport a heavy bag of game. Such a vehicle, driven by one man, will, moreover, often excite no suspicion though it may be filled with pheasants under sacks and hay. A good deal of what may be called casual poaching is also done on wheels.

Some of the landlords of the low beer-houses in the country often combine with the liquor trade the business of dealing in pigs, calves, potatoes, &c., and keep a light cart, or similar conveyance. Now, if anyone will notice the more disreputable of these beerhouses, they will observe that there are generally a lot of unkempt, rough-looking dogs about them. These, of course, follow their master when he goes on his short journeys from place to place; and they are quite capable of mischief. Such men may not make a business of poaching, yet if in passing a preserve the dogs stray and bring back something eatable, why, it is very easy to stow it under the seat with the potatoes. Sometimes a man is bold enough to carry a gun in this way —to jump out when he sees a chance and have a shot, and back and off before anyone knows exactly what is going on.

Somehow there always seems to be a market for game out of season: it is 'passed' somewhere, just as thieves pass stolen jewellery. So also fish, even when manifestly unfit for table, in the midst of spawning time, commands a ready sale if overlooked by the authorities. It is curious that people can be found to purchase fish in such a condition; but it is certain that they do. In the spring, when one would think bird and beast might be permitted a breathing space, the poacher is as busy as ever after eggs. Pheasant and partridge eggs are largely bought and sold in the most nefarious manner. It is suspected that some of the less respectable breeders who rear game birds like poultry for sale, are not too particular of whom they purchase eggs; and, as we have before observed, certain keepers are to blame in this matter also.

Plovers' eggs, again, are an article of commerce in the spring; they are protected now by law, but it is to be feared that the enactment is to a great extent a dead letter. The eggs of the peewit, or lapwing, as the bird is variously called, are sought for with great perseverance, and accounted delicacies. These birds frequent commons where the grass is very rough, and interspersed with bunches of rushes, marshy places, and meadows liable to be flooded in the winter. The nest on the ground is often made in the depression left by a horse's hoof in the soft earth —any slight hole, in fact; and it is so concealed, or rather differs so little from the appearance of the general sward around, as to be easily passed unnoticed. You may actually step on it, and so smash the eggs, before you see it.

Aware that the most careful observation may fail to find what he wants, the egg-stealer adopts a simple but effective plan by which he ensures against omitting to examine a single foot of the field. Drop a pocket-knife or some such object in the midst of a great meadow, and you will find the utmost difficulty in discovering it again, when the grass is growing tall as in spring. You may think that you have traversed every inch, yet it is certain that you have not; the inequalities of the ground insensibly divert your footsteps, and it is very difficult to keep a straight line. What is required is something to fix the eye—what a sailor would call a 'bearing.' This the egg-stealer finds in a walking-stick. He thrusts the point into the earth, and then slowly walks round and round it, enlarging the circle every time, and thus sweeps every inch of the surface with his eye. When he has got so far from the stick as to feel that his steps are becoming uncertain, he removes it, and begins again in another spot. A person not aware of this simple trick will search a field till weary and declare there is nothing to be found; another, who knows the dodge, will go out and return in an hour with a pocketful of eggs.

On those clear, bright winter nights when the full moon is almost at the zenith, and the 'definition' of tree and bough in the flood of light seems to equal if not to exceed that of the noonday, some poaching used to be accomplished with the aid of a horsehair noose on the end of a long slender wand. There are still some districts in the country more or less covered with forest, and which on account of ancient rights cannot be enclosed. Here the art of noosing lingers; the loop being insidiously slipped over the bird's head while at roost. By constant practice a wonderful dexterity may be acquired in this trick; men will snare almost any bird in broad daylight. With many birds a favourite place for a nest is in a hollow tree, access being had by a decayed knothole, and they are sometimes noosed as they emerge. A thin flexible copper wire is said to be substituted for large game. This method of capture peculiarly suits the views of the ornithologist, with whom it is an object to avoid the spoiling of feathers by shot.

Every now and then a bird-catcher comes along decoying the finches from the hedges, for sale as cage-birds in London. Some of these men, without any mechanical assistance, can imitate the 'call' note of the bird they desire to capture so as to deceive the most practised ear. These fellows are a great nuisance, and will completely sweep a lane of all the birds whose song makes them valuable. In this way some localities have been quite cleared of goldfinches, which used to be common. The keepers, of course, will not permit them on private property; but in all rural districts there are wide waste spaces—as where two or more roads meet—broad bands of green sward running beside the highway, and the remnants of what in former days were commons; and here the bird-catcher plies his trade. It so happens that these very waste places are often the most favourite resorts of goldfinches, for instance, who are particularly fond of thistledown, and thistles naturally chiefly flourish on uncultivated land. These men, and the general class of loafers, have a wholesome dread of gamekeepers, who look on them with extreme suspicion.

The farmers and rural community at large hardly give the gamekeeper his due as a protection against thieves and mischievous rascals. The knowledge that he may at any time come round the corner, even in the middle of the night, has a decidedly salutary effect upon the minds of those who are prowling about. Intoxicated louts think it fine fun to unhinge gates, and let cattle and horses stray abroad, to tear down rails, and especially to push the coping-stones off the parapets of the bridges which span small streams. They consider it clever to heave these over with a splash into the water, or to throw down half a dozen yards of 'dry wall'. In many places fields are commonly enclosed by the roadside with such walls, which are built of a flat stone dug just beneath the surface, and used without mortar. There are men who make a business of building these walls; it requires some skill and patience to select the stones and fit them properly. They serve the purpose very well, but the worst is that if once started the process of destruction is easy and quick. Much more serious offences than these are sometimes committed, as cutting horses with knives, and other mutilations. The fact that the fields are regularly perambulated by keepers and their assistants night and day cannot but act as a check upon acts of this kind.

CHAPTER VIII

THE FIELD DETECTIVE—FISH POACHING

THE footpaths through the plantations and across the fields have no milestones by which the pedestrian can calculate the distance traversed; nor is the time occupied a safe criterion, because of the varying nature of the soil—now firm and now slippery—so that the pace is not regular. But these crooked paths —no footpath is ever straight—really represent a much greater distance than would be supposed if the space from point to point were measured on a map. So that the keeper as he goes his rounds, though he does not rival the professional walker, in the course of a year covers some thousands of miles. He rarely does less than ten, and probably often twelve miles a day, visiting certain points twice—*i.e.* in the morning and evening—and often in addition, if he has any suspicions, making *détours*. It is easy to walk a mile in a single field of no great dimensions when it is necessary to go up and down each side of four long hedgerows, and backwards and forwards, following the course of the furrows.

The keeper's eye is ever on the alert for the poacher's wires; and where the grass is tall to discover these is often a tedious task, since he may go within a few yards and yet pass them. The ditches and the great bramble-bushes are carefully scanned, because in these the poacher often conceals his gun, nets, or game, even when not under immediate apprehension of capture. The reason is that his cottage may perhaps be suddenly searched: if not by authority, the policeman on some pretext or other may unexpectedly lift the latch or peer into the outhouses, and feathers and fur are apt to betray their presence in the most unexpected manner. One single feather, one single fluffy little piece of fur overlooked, is enough to ruin him, for these are things of which it is impossible to give an acceptable explanation.

In dry weather the poacher often hides his implements: especially is this the case after a more than usually venturesome foray, when he knows that his house is tolerably certain to be overhauled and all his motions watched. A hollow tree is a common resource—the pollard willow generally becomes hollow in its old age—and with a piece of the decaying 'touchwood' or a strip of dead bark his tools are ingeniously covered up. Under the eaves of sheds and outhouses the sparrows make holes by pulling out the thatch and roost in these sheltered places in severe weather, warmly protected from the frost; other small birds, as wrens and tomtits, do the same; and the poacher avails himself of these holes to hide his wires.

A gun has been found before now concealed in a heap of manure, such as are frequently seen in the corners of the fields. These heaps sometimes remain for a year or more in order that the materials may become thoroughly decomposed, and the surface is quickly covered with a rank growth of weeds. The poacher, choosing the side close to the hedge, where no one would be likely to go, excavated a place beneath these weeds, partly filled it in with dry straw, and laid his gun on this. A rough board placed over it shielded it from damp; and the aperture was closed with 'bull-polls'—that is, the rough grass of the furrows chopped up (not unlike the gardener's 'turves')

—and thrown on the manure-heap to decay. If the keeper detects anything of this kind he allows it to stay undisturbed, but sets a watch, and so surprises the owner of the treasure.

The keeper is particularly careful to observe the motions of the labourers engaged in the fields; especially at luncheon-time, when men with a hunch of bread and a slice of bacon—kept on the bread with a small thumb-piece of crust, and carved with a pocket-knife—are apt to ramble round the hedges, of course with the most innocent of motives, admiring the beauties of nature. Slowly wandering like this, they cast a sidelong glance at their wire, set up in a 'drock'—*i.e.* a bridge over a ditch formed of a broad flat stone—which chances to be a favourite highway of the rabbits. Nowadays, in this age of draining, short barrel drains of brick or large glazed pipes are often let through thick banks; these are dry for weeks together, and hares slip through them. A wire or trap set here is quite out of ordinary observation; and the keeper, who knows that he cannot examine every inch of ground, simplifies the process by quietly noting the movements of the men. As he passes and repasses a field where they are at work day after day, and understands agricultural labour, he is aware that they have no necessity to visit hedgerows and mounds a hundred yards distant, and should he see anything of that kind the circle of his suspicions gradually narrows till he hits the exact spot and person.

The gateways and gaps receive careful attention —unusual footmarks in the mud are looked for. Sometimes he detects a trace of fur or feathers, or a blood-stain on the spars or rails, where a load of rabbits or game has been hung for a few minutes while the bearer rested. The rabbit-holes in the banks are noted: this becomes so much a matter of habit as to be done almost unconsciously and without effort as he walks; and anything unusual—as the sand much disturbed, the imprint of a boot, the bushes broken or cut away for convenience of setting a net—is seen in an instant. If there be any high ground—woods are often on a slope—the keeper has here a post whence to obtain a comprehensive survey, and he makes frequent use of this natural observatory, concealing himself behind a tree trunk.

The lanes and roads and public footpaths that cross the estate near the preserves are a constant source of uneasiness. Many fields are traversed by a perfect network of footpaths, half of which are of very little use but cannot be closed. Nothing causes so much ill-will in rural districts as the attempt to divert or shut up a track like this. Cottagers are most tenacious of these 'rights', and will rarely exchange them for any advantage. 'There always wur a path athwert thuck mead in the ould volk's time' is their one reply endlessly reiterated; and the owner of the property, rather than make himself unpopular, desists from persuasion. The danger to game from these paths arises from the impossibility of stopping a suspicious character at once. If he breaks through a hedge it is different; but the law is justly jealous of the subject's liberty on a public footpath, and you cannot turn him back.

Neither is it of any use to search a man whose tools, to a moral certainty, are concealed in some hedge. With his hands in his pockets, and a short pipe in his mouth, he can saunter along the side of a preserve if only a path, as is often the case, follows the edge; and by-and-by it grows dusk, and the keeper

or keepers cannot be everywhere at once. There is
nothing to prevent such fellows as these from sneaking
over an estate with a lurcher dog at their heels—a
kind of dog gifted with great sagacity, nearly as swift
as a greyhound, and much better adapted for picking up the game when overtaken, which is the greyhound's difficulty. They can be taught to obey the
faintest sign or sound from their owners. If the latter
imagine watchers to be about, the lurcher slinks along
close behind, keeping strictly to the path. Presently,
if the poacher but lifts his finger, away dashes the dog,
and will miss nothing he comes across. The lurcher
has always borne an evil repute, which of course is
the due not of the dog but of his master. If a man
had to get his living by the chase in Red Indian
fashion, probably this would be the best breed for his
purpose. Many shepherds' dogs now have a cross of
the lurcher in their strain, and are good at poaching.

Sunday is the gamekeeper's worst day; the idle,
rough characters from the adjacent town pour out
into the country, and necessitate extra watchfulness.
On Sunday the keeper, out of respect to the day, does
not indeed carry his gun, but he works yet harder
than on week-days. While the chimes are ringing to
church he is on foot by the edge of the preserves. He
has to maintain a sort of surveillance over the beer-
houses in the village, which is done with the aid of the
district policeman, for they are not only the places
where much of the game is sold, but the rendezvous
of those who are planning a raid.

If the policeman notices an unusual stir, or the
arrival of strange men without any apparent business,
he acquaints the keeper, who then takes care to double
his sentinels, and personally visit them during the

night. This nightwork is very trying after his long walks by day. A great object is to be about early in the morning—just before the dawn: that is the time when the poachers return to examine their wires. By day he often varies his rounds so as to appear upon the scene when least expected; and has regular trysting places, where his assistants meet him with their reports.

The gipsies, who travel the road in caravans, give him endless trouble; they are adepts at poaching, and each van is usually accompanied by a couple of dogs. The movements of these people are so irregular that it is impossible to be always ready for them. They are suspected of being recipients of poached game, purchasing it from the local professionals. Under pretence of cutting skewer-wood, often called dog-wood, which they split and sharpen for the butchers, they wander across the open downs where it grows, camping in wild, unfrequented places, and finding plenty of opportunities for poaching. Down land is most difficult to watch.

Then the men who come out from the towns, ostensibly to gather primroses in the early spring, or ferns, which they hawk from door to door; and the watercress men, who are about the meadows and brooks twice a year, in spring and autumn, require constant supervision. An innocent-looking basket or small sack-bag of mushrooms has before now, when turned upside down, been discovered to contain a couple of rabbits or a fine young leveret. This detective work is, in fact, never finished. There is no end to the tricks and subterfuges practised, and with all his experience and care the gamekeeper is frequently outwitted.

The relations between the agricultural labourers and the keeper are not of the most cordial character; in fact, there is a ceaseless distrust upon the one hand and incessant attempts at over-reaching upon the other. The ploughmen, the carters, shepherds, and foggers have so many opportunities as they go about the fields, and they never miss the chance of a good dinner or half-a-crown when presented to them. Higher wages have not in the slightest degree diminished poaching, regular or occasional; on the contrary, from whatever cause, there is good reason to believe it on the increase. If a labourer crossing a field sees a hare or rabbit crouching in his form, what is to prevent him from thrusting his prong like a spear suddenly through the animal and pinning him to the turf? There are plenty of ways of hiding dead game, under straw or hay, in the thick beds of nettles which usually spring up outside or at the back of a cowshed.

Why does the keeper take such a benevolent interest in the progress of spade-husbandry, as exemplified in allotment gardens near the village, which allotments are generally in a field set apart by the principal landowner for the purpose? In person or by proxy the keeper is very frequently seen looking over the close-cropped hedge which surrounds the spot, and now and then he takes a walk up and down the narrow paths between the plots. His dog sniffs about among the heaps of rubbish or under the potato-vines. The men at work are remarkably civil and courteous to the gentleman in the velveteen jacket, who, on his side, is equally chatty with them; but both in their hearts know very well the why and wherefore of this interest in agriculture. Almost all kinds of game are attracted by gardens, presupposing, of course, that they are situated at a distance from houses, as these allotments are. There is a supply of fresh, succulent, food of various kinds: often too, after a large plot has been worked for garden produce, the tenant will sow it for barley or beans or oats, on the principle of rotation; and these small areas of grain have a singular fascination for pheasants, and hares linger in them.

Rabbits, if undisturbed, are particularly fond of garden vegetables. In spring and early summer they will make those short holes in which they bring forth their young under the potato-vines, finding the soil easy to work, dry, and the spot sheltered by the thick green stems and leaves. Both rabbits and hares do considerable damage if they are permitted the run of the place unchecked. The tenants of the allotments, however, instead of driving them off, are anxious that they should come sniffing and limping over the plots in the gloaming, and are strongly suspected of allowing crops specially pleasing to game to remain in the ground till the very latest period in order that they may snare it.

Much kindly talk has been uttered over allotments, and undoubtedly they are a great encouragement to the labourer; yet even this advantage is commonly abused. The tenants have no ground of complaint as to damage to their crops, because the keeper, at a word from them, would lose not a moment of time in killing or driving away the intruder; and as an acknowledgment of honesty and in reparation of the mischief, if any, a couple of rabbits would be presented to the man who carried the complaint. But the labourer, if he spies the tracks of a hare running into his plot of corn, or suspects that a pheasant is hiding there, carefully keeps that knowledge to himself. He knows that a pheasant, if you can get close enough to it before it rises, is a clumsy bird, and large enough to offer a fair mark, and may be brought down with a stout stick dexterously thrown. As very probably the pheasant is a young one and (not yet having undergone its baptism of fire) only recently regularly fed, it is almost tame and may be approached without difficulty. This is why the keeper just looks round the allotment gardens now and then, and lets his dogs run about; for their noses are much more clever at discovering hidden fur or feathers than his eyes.

In winter if the weather be severe, hares and rabbits are very bold, and will enter gardens though attached to dwelling-houses. Sometimes when a vast double-mound hedge is grubbed, the ditches each side are left, and the interior space is ultimately converted into an osier-bed, osiers being rather profitable at present. But before these are introduced it is necessary that the ground be well dug up, for it is full of roots and the seeds of weeds, which perhaps have lain dormant for years, but now spring up in wonderful profusion. In consideration of cleansing the soil, and working it by digging, burning the weeds and rubbish, &c., the farmer allows one or two of his labourers to use it as a garden for the growth of potatoes, free of rent, for say a couple of years. Potatoes are a crop which flourish in fresh-turned soil, and so they do very well over the arrangement. But unfortunately as they dig and weed, &c., in the evenings after regular work, they have an excuse for their presence in the fields, and perhaps near preserves at a tempting period of the twenty-four hours. The keeper, in short, is quite aware that some sly poaching goes on in this way.

Another cause of unpleasantness between him and the cottagers arises from the dogs they maintain, generally curs, it is true, and not to all appearance capable of harm. But in the early summer a mongrel cur can do as much mischief as a thoroughbred dog. Young rabbits are easily overtaken when not much larger than rats, and at other seasons, when the game has grown better able to take care of itself, any kind of dog rambling loose in the woods and copses frightens it and unsettles it to an annoying degree. Consequently, when a dog once begins to trespass, it is pretty sure to disappear for good—it is not necessary to indicate how—and though no actual evidence can be got against the keeper, he is accused of the destruction of the ugly, ill-bred 'pet'. If a dog commences to hunt on his own account, he can only be broken of the habit by the utmost severity; and so it sometimes happens that other dogs besides those of the cottagers come to an untimely end by shot and gin.

The keeper being a man with some true sense of sport, dislikes shooting dogs, though compelled to do so occasionally; he never fires at his own, and candidly admits that he hates to see a sportsman give way to anger in that manner. The custom of 'peppering' with shot a dog for disobedience or wildness, which was once very common in the field, has however gone a great deal into disuse.

Shepherds, who often have to visit their flocks in the night—as at this season of the year, while lambing is in progress—who, in fact, sometimes sleep in the fields in a little wooden house on wheels built for the purpose, are strongly suspected of tampering with the hares scampering over the turnips by moonlight. At harvest-time many strange men come into the district for the extra wages of reaping. They rarely take lodgings—which, indeed, they might find some difficulty in obtaining—but in the warm summer weather sleep in the outhouses and sheds, with the permission of the owner. Others camp in the open in the corner of a meadow, where the angle made by meeting hedges protects them from the wind, crouching round the embers of the fire which boils the pot and kettle. This influx of strangers is not without its attendant anxiety to the keeper, who looks round now and then to see what is going on.

Despite the ill-will in their hearts, the labourers are particularly civil to the keeper; he is, in fact, a considerable employer of labour—not on his own account—but in the woods and preserves. He can often give men a job in the dead of winter, when farm work is scarce and the wages paid for it are less; such as hedge-cutting, mending the gaps in the fences, cleaning out ditches or the watercourses through the wood.

Then there is an immense amount of ferreting to be done, and there is such an instinctive love of sport in every man's breast, that to assist in this work is almost an ambition; besides which, no doubt the chances afforded of an occasional private 'bag' form a secret attraction. One would imagine that there could be but little pleasure in crouching all day in a ditch, perhaps ankle-deep in ice-cold water, with flakes of snow driving in the face, and fingers numbed by the biting wind as it rushes through the bare hawthorn bushes, just to watch a rabbit jump out of a hole into a net, and to break his neck afterwards.

Yet so it is; and some men become so enamoured of this slow sport as to do nothing else the winter through; and as of course their employment depends entirely upon the will of the keeper, they are anxious to conciliate him.

Despite therefore of missing cur dogs and straying cats which never return, the keeper is treated with marked deference by the cottagers. He is, nevertheless, fully aware of the concealed ill-will towards him; and perhaps this knowledge has contributed to render him more morose, and sharper of temper, and more suspicious of human nature than he would otherwise have been; for it never improves a man's character to have to be constantly watching his fellows.

The streams are no more sacred from marauders than the woods and preserves. The brooks and upper waters are not so full of fish as formerly, the canal into which they fall being netted so much; and another cause of the diminution is the prevalence of fish-poaching, especially for jack, during the spawning season and afterwards. Though the keepers can check this within their own boundaries, it is not of much use.

Fish-poaching is simple and yet clever in its way. In the spawning time jack fish, which at other periods are apparently of a solitary disposition, go in pairs, and sometimes in trios, and are more tame than usual. A long slender ash stick is selected, slender enough to lie light in the hand and strong enough to bear a sudden weight. A loop and running noose are formed of a piece of thin copper wire, the other end of which is twisted round and firmly attached to the smaller end of the stick. The loop is adjusted to the size of the fish—it should not be very much larger, else it will not

draw up quick enough, nor too small, else it may
touch and disturb the jack. It does not take much
practice to hit the happy medium. Approaching the
bank of the brook quietly, so as not to shake the
ground, to the vibrations of which fish are peculiarly
sensitive, the poacher tries if possible to avoid letting
his shadow fall across the water.

Some persons' eyes seem to have an extraordinary
power of seeing through water, and of distinguishing
at a glance a fish from a long swaying strip of dead
brown flag, or the rotting pieces of wood which lie at
the bottom. The ripple of the breeze, the eddy at the
curve, or the sparkle of the sunshine cannot deceive
them; while others, and by far the greater number,
are dazzled and see nothing. It is astonishing how few
persons seem to have the gift of sight when in the field.

The poacher, having marked his prey in the shallow yonder, gently extends his rod slowly across the
water three or four yards higher up the stream, and
lets the wire noose sink without noise till it almost or
quite touches the bottom. It is easier to guide the
noose to its destination when it occasionally touches
the mud, for refraction distorts the true position of
objects in water, and accuracy is important. Gradually the wire swims down with the current, just as
if it were any ordinary twig or root carried along, such
as the jack is accustomed to see, and he therefore feels
no alarm. By degrees the loop comes closer to the
fish, till with steady hand the poacher slips it over the
head, past the long vicious jaws and gills, past the first
fins, and pauses when it has reached a place corre-
sponding to about one-third of the length of the fish,
reckoning from the head. That end of the jack is
heavier than the other, and the 'lines' of the body are

there nearly straight. Thus the poacher gets a firm hold—for a fish, of course, is slippery—and a good balance. If the operation is performed gently the jack will remain quite still, though the wire rubs against his side: silence and stillness have such a power over all living creatures. The poacher now clears his arm and, with a sudden jerk, lifts the fish right out of the stream and lands him on the sward.

So sharp is the grasp of the wire that it frequently cuts its way through the scales, leaving a mark plainly visible when the jack is offered for sale. The suddenness and violence of the compression seem to disperse the muscular forces, and the fish appears dead for the moment. Very often, indeed, it really is killed by the jerk. This happens when the loop either has not passed far enough along the body or has slipped and seized the creature just at the gills. It then garottes the fish. If, on the other hand, the wire has been passed too far towards the tail, it slips off that way, the jack falling back into the water with a broad white band where the wire has scraped the scales. Fish thus marked may not unfrequently be seen in the stream. The jack, from its shape, is specially liable to capture in this manner; long and well balanced, the wire has every chance of holding it. This poaching is always going on; the implement is so easily obtained and concealed. The wire can be carried in the pocket, and the stick may be cut from an adjacent copse.

The poachers observe that after a fish has once escaped from an attempt of the kind it is ever after far more difficult of capture. The first time the jack was still and took no notice of the insidious approach of the wire gliding along towards it; but the next—unless a long interval elapses before a second trial—the moment it comes near he is away. At each succeeding attempt, whether hurt or not, he grows more and more suspicious, till at last to merely stand still or stop while walking on the bank is sufficient for him; he is off with a swish of the tail to the deeper water, leaving behind him a cloud, so to say, of mud swept up from the bottom to conceal the direction of his flight. For it would almost seem as if the jack throws up this mud on purpose; if much disturbed he will quite discolour the brook. The wire does a good deal to depopulate the stream, and is altogether a deadly implement.

But a clever fish-poacher can land a jack even without a wire, and with no better instrument than a willow stick cut from the nearest osier-bed. The willow, or withy as it is usually called, is remarkably pliant, and can be twisted into any shape. Selecting a long slender wand, the poacher strips it of leaves, gives the smaller end a couple of twists, making a noose and running knot of the stick itself. The mode of using it is precisely similar to that followed with a wire, but it requires a little more dexterity, because, of course, the wood, flexible as it is, does not draw up so quickly or so closely as the metal, neither does it take so firm a grip. A fish once caught by a wire can be slung about almost anyhow, it holds so tightly. The withy noose must be jerked up the instant it passes under that part of the jack where the weight of the fish is balanced—the centre of gravity; if there is an error in this respect it should be towards the head, rather than towards the tail. Directly the jack is thrown out upon the sward he must be seized, or he will slip from the noose, and possibly find his way back again into the water. With a wire there is little risk of that; but then the withy does not cut its way into the fish.

This trick is often accomplished with the common withy—not that which grows on pollard trees, but in osier-beds; that on the trees is brittle. But a special kind is sought for the purpose, and for any other requiring extreme flexibility. It is, I think, locally called the stone osier, and it does not grow so tall as the common sorts. It will tie like string. Being so short, for poaching fish it has to be fastened to a thicker and longer stick, which is easily done; and some prefer it to wire because it looks more natural in the water and does not alarm the fish, while, should the keeper be about, it is easily cut up in several pieces and thrown away. I have heard of rabbits, and even hares, being caught with a noose of this kind of withy, which is as 'tough as wire'; and yet it seems hardly possible, as it is so much thicker and would be seen. Still, both hares and rabbits, when playing and scampering about at night, are sometimes curiously heedless, and foolish enough to run their necks into anything.

With such a rude implement as this some fish-poachers will speedily land a good basket of pike. During the spawning season, as was observed previously, jack go in pairs, and now and then in trios, and of this the poacher avails himself to take more than one at a haul. The fish lie so close together— side by side just at that time—that it is quite practicable, with care and judgment, to slip a wire over two at once. When near the bank two may even be captured with a good withy noose: with a wire a clever hand will make a certainty of it. The keeper says that on one occasion he watched a man operating just without his jurisdiction, who actually succeeded in wiring three jacks at once and safely landed them on the grass. They were small fish, about a pound to a pound and a half each, and the man was but a few minutes in accomplishing the feat. It sometimes happens that after a heavy flood, when the brook has been thick with suspended mud for several days, so soon as it has gone down fish are more than usually plentiful, as if the flood had brought them up-stream: poachers are then particularly busy.

Fresh fish—that is, those who are new to that particular part of the brook—are, the poachers say, much more easily captured than those who have made it their home for some time. They are, in fact, more easily discovered; they have not yet found out all the nooks and corners, the projecting roots and the hollows under the banks, the dark places where a black shadow falls from overhanging trees and is with difficulty pierced even by a practised eye. They expose themselves in open places, and meet an untimely fate.

Besides pike, tench are occasionally wired, and now and then even a large roach; the tench, though a bottom fish, in the shallow brooks may be sometimes detected by the eye, and is not a difficult fish to capture. Every one has heard of tickling trout: the tench is almost equally amenable to titillation. Lying at full length on the sward, with his hat off lest it should fall into the water, the poacher peers down into the hole where he has reason to think tench may be found. This fish is so dark in colour when viewed from above that for a minute or two, till the sight adapts itself to the dull light of the water, the poacher cannot distinguish what he is searching for. Presently, having made out the position of the tench, he slips his bared

arm in slowly, and without splash, and finds little or
no trouble as a rule in getting his hand close to the
fish without alarming it: tench, indeed, seem rather
sluggish. He then passes his fingers under the belly
and gently rubs it. Now it would appear that he has
the fish in his power, and has only to grasp it. But
grasping is not so easy; or rather it is not so easy to
pull a fish up through two feet of superincumbent
water which opposes the quick passage of the arm.
The gentle rubbing in the first place seems to soothe
the fish, so that it becomes perfectly quiescent, except
that it slowly rises up in the water, and thus enables
the hand to get into proper position for the final
seizure. When it has risen up towards the surface
sufficiently far—the tench must not be driven too near
the surface, for it does not like light and will glide away
—the poacher suddenly snaps as it were; his thumb
and fingers, if he possibly can manage it, closing on
the gills. The body is so slimy and slippery that there
alone a firm hold can be got, though the poacher will
often flick the fish out of water in an instant so soon as
it is near the surface. Poachers evidently feel as much
pleasure in practising these tricks as the most enthu-
siastic angler using the implements of legitimate sport.

No advantage is thought too unfair to be taken of
fish; nothing too brutally unsportsmanlike. I have
seen a pike killed with a prong as he lay basking in
the sun at the top of the water. A labourer stealthily
approached, and suddenly speared him with one of
the sharp points of the prong or hayfork he carried:
the pike was a good sized one too.

The stream, where not strictly preserved, is frequently netted without the slightest regard to season.
The net is stretched from bank to bank, and watched

by one man, while the other walks up the brook thirty or forty yards, and drives the fish down the current into the bag. With a long pole he thrashes the water, making a good deal of splash, and rousing up the mud, which fish dislike and avoid. The pole is thrust into every hiding-place, and pokes everything out. The watcher by the net knows by the bobbing under of the corks when a shoal of roach and perch, or a heavy pike, has darted into it, and instantly draws the string and makes his haul. In this way, by sections at a time, the brook, perhaps for half a mile, is quite cleared out. Jack, however, sometimes escape; they seem remarkably shrewd and quick to learn. If the string is not immediately drawn when they touch the net, they are out of it without a moment's delay: they will double back up stream through all the splashing and mud, and some will even slide as it were between the net and the bank if it does not quite touch in any place, and so get away.

In its downward course the brook irrigates many water meadows, and to drive the stream out upon them there are great wooden hatches. Sometimes a gang of men, discovering that there is a quantity of fish thereabouts, will force down a hatch which at once shuts off or greatly diminishes the volume of water flowing down the brook, and then rapidly construct a dam across the current below it with the mud of the shore. Above this dam they thrash the water with poles and drive all the fish towards it, and then make a second dam above the first so as to enclose them in a short space. In the making of these dams speed is an object, or the water will accumulate and flow over the hatch; so hurdles are used, as they afford a support to the mud hastily thrown up. Then with buckets, bowls, and 'scoops', they bale out the water between the two dams, and quickly reduce their prey to wriggling helplessness. In this way whole baskets full of fish have been taken, together with eels; and nothing so enclosed can escape.

The mere or lake by the wood is protected by sharp stakes set at the bottom, which would tear poachers' nets; and the keeper does not think any attempt to sweep it has been made of late years, it is too well watched. But he believes that night lines are frequently laid: a footpath runs along one shore for some distance, and gives easy access, and such lines may be overlooked. He is certain that eels are taken in that way despite his vigilance.

Trespassing for crayfish, too, causes much annoyance. I have known men to get bodily up to the waist into the great ponds, a few of which yet remain, after carp. These fish have a curious habit of huddling up in hollows under the banks; and those who know where these hollows and holes are situate can take them by hand if they can come suddenly upon them. It is said that now and then fish are raked out of the ponds with a common rake (such as is used in haymaking) when lying on the mud in winter.

CHAPTER IX

GUERILLA WARFARE—GUN ACCIDENTS—BLACK SHEEP

SCARCELY a keeper can be found who has not got one or more tales to tell of encounters with poachers, sometimes of a desperate character. There is a general similarity in most of the accounts, which exhibit a mixture of ferocity and cowardice on the side of the intruders. The following case, which occurred some years since, brings these contradictory features into relief. The narrator was not the owner of the man-trap described previously.

There had been a great deal of poaching before the affray took place, and finally it grew to horse-stealing: one night two valuable horses were taken from the home park. This naturally roused the indignation of the owner of the estate, who resolved to put a stop to it. Orders were given that if shots were heard in the woods the news should be at once transmitted to headquarters, no matter at what hour of the night.

One brilliant moonlight night, frosty and clear, the gang came again. A messenger went to the house, and, as previously arranged, two separate parties set out to intercept the rascals. The head keeper had one detachment, whose object it was to secure the main outlet from the wood towards the adjacent town —to cut off retreat. The young squire had charge of the other, which, with the under keeper as guide, was to work its way through the wood and drive the gang into the ambuscade. In the last party were six men and a mastiff dog; four of the men had guns, the gentleman only a stout cudgel.

They came upon the gang—or rather a part of it, for the poachers were somewhat scattered—in a 'drive' which ran between tall firs, and was deep in shadow. With a shout the four or five men in the 'drive', or green lane, slipped back behind the trees, and two fired, killing the mastiff dog on the spot and 'stinging' one man in the legs. Quick as they were the under keeper, to use his own words, 'got a squint of one fellow as I knowed; and I lets drive both barrels in among the firs. But, bless you! it were all over in such a minute that I can't hardly tell 'ee how it were. Our squire ran straight at 'em; but our men hung back, though they had their guns and he had nothing but a stick. I just seen him, as the smoke rose, hitting at a fellow; and then, before I could step, I hears a crack, and the squire he was down on the sward. One of them beggars had come up behind, and swung his gun round, and fetched him a purler on the back of his head. I picked him up, but he was as good as dead, to look at;' and in the confusion the poachers escaped. They had probably been put up to the ambuscade by one of the underlings, as they did not pass that way, but seemed to separate and get off by various paths. The 'young squire' had to be carried home, and was ill for months, but ultimately recovered.

Not one of the gang was ever captured, notwithstanding that a member of it was recognized. Next day an examination of the spot resulted in the discovery of a trail of blood upon the grass and dead leaves, which proved that one of them had been wounded at the first discharge. It was traced for a short distance and then lost. Not till the excitement had subsided did the under keeper find that he had been hit; one pellet had scored his cheek under the eye, and left a groove still visible.

Some time afterwards a gun was picked up in the ferns, all rusty from exposure, which had doubtless been dropped in the flight. The barrel was very short—not more than eighteen inches in length—having been filed off for convenience of taking to pieces, so as to be carried in a pocket made on purpose in the lining of the coat. Now, with a barrel so short as that, sport, in the proper sense of the term, would be impossible; the shot would scatter so quickly after leaving the muzzle that the sportsman would never be able to approach near enough. The use of this gun was clearly to shoot pheasants at roost.

The particular keeper in whose shed the man-trap still lies among the lumber thinks that the class of poachers who come in gangs are as desperate now as ever, and as ready with their weapons. Breech-loading guns have rendered such affrays extremely dangerous on account of the rapidity of fire. Increased severity of punishment may deter a man from entering a wood; but once he is there and compromised, the dread of a heavy sentence is likely to make him fight savagely.

The keeper himself is not altogether averse to a little fisticuffing, in a straightforward kind of way, putting powder and shot on one side. He rather relishes what he calls 'leathering' a poacher with a good tough ground-ash stick. He gets the opportunity now and then, coming unexpectedly on a couple of fellows rabbiting in a ditch, and he recounts the 'leathering' he has frequently administered with great gusto. He will even honestly admit that on one occasion—just one, not more—he got himself most thoroughly thrashed by a pair of hulking fellows.

'Some keepers', he says, 'are always summoning people, but it don't do no good. What's the use of summoning a chap for sneaking about with a cur dog and a wire in his pocket? His mates in the village clubs together and pays his fine, and he laughs at you. Why, down in the town there them mechanic chaps have got a regular society to pay these here fines for trespass, and the bench they claps it on strong on purpose. But it ain't no good; they forks out the tin, and then goes and haves a spree at a public. Besides which, if I can help it I don't much care to send a man to gaol—this, of course, is between you and me—unless he uses his gun. If he uses his gun there ain't nothing too bad for him. But these here prisons—every man as ever I knowed go to gaol always went twice, and kept on going. There ain't nothing in the world like a good ground-ash stick. When you gives a chap a sound dressing with that there article, he never shows his face in your wood no more. There's fields about here where them mechanics goes as regular as Saturday comes to try their dogs, as they calls it—and a precious lot of dogs they keeps among 'em. But they never does it on this estate: they knows my habits, you see. There's less summonses goes up from this property than any other for miles, and it's all owing to this here stick. A bit of ash is the best physic for poaching as I knows on.'

I suspect that he is a little mistaken in his belief that it is the dread of his personal prowess which keeps trespassers away—it is rather due to his known vigilance and watchfulness. His rather hasty notions of taking the law into his own hands are hardly in accord

with the spirit of the times; but some allowance must
be made for the circumstances of his life, and it is my
object to picture the man as he is.

There are other dangers from guns beside these.
A brown gaiter indistinctly seen moving some distance off in the tall dry grass or fern—the wearer
hidden by the bushes—has not unfrequently been
mistaken for game in the haste and excitement of
shooting, and received a salute of leaden hail. This
is a danger to which sportsman and keeper are both
liable, especially when large parties are engaged in
rapid firing; sometimes a particular corner gets very
'hot', being enfiladed for the moment by several guns.
Yet, when the great number of men who shoot is considered, the percentage of serious accidents is small
indeed; more fatal accidents probably happen through
unskilled persons thoughtlessly playing with guns supposed not to be loaded, or pointing them in joke, than
ever occur in the field. The ease with which the
breechloader can be unloaded or reloaded again prevents most persons from carrying it indoors charged;
and this in itself is a gain on the side of safety, for perhaps half the fatal accidents take place within doors.

In farmsteads where the owner had the right of
shooting the muzzle-loader was—and still is, when
not converted—kept loaded on the rack. The starlings, perhaps, are making havoc of the thatch, tearing
out straw by straw, and working the holes in which
they form their nests right through, till in the upper
story daylight is visible. When the whistling and
calling of the birds tell him they are busy above, the
owner slips quickly out with his gun, and brings down
three or four at once as they perch in a row on the
roof-tree. Or a labourer leaves a message that there

is a hare up in the meadow or some wild ducks have settled in the brook. But men who have a gun always in their hands rarely meet with a mishap. The starlings, by-the-by, soon learn the trick, and are cunning enough to notice which door their enemy generally comes out at, where he can get the best shot; and the moment the handle of that particular door is turned, off they go.

The village blacksmith will tell you of more than one narrow escape he has had with guns, and especially muzzle-loaders, brought to him to repair. Perhaps a charge could not be ignited through the foulness of the nipple, and the breech had to be unscrewed in the vice; now and then the breech-piece was so tightly jammed that it could not be turned. Once, being positively assured that there was nothing but some dirt in the barrel and no powder, he was induced to place it in the forge fire; when—bang! a charge of shot smashed the window, and the burning coals flew about in a fiery shower. In one instance a blacksmith essayed to clear out a barrel which had become choked with a long iron rod made red-hot: the explosion which followed drove the rod through his hand and into the wooden wall of the shed. Smiths seem to have a particular fondness for meddling with guns, and generally have one stowed away somewhere.

It was not wonderful that accidents happened with the muzzle-loaders, considering the manner in which they were handled by ignorant persons. The keeper declares that many of the cottagers, who have an old single-barrel, ostensibly to frighten the birds from their gardens, do not think it properly loaded until the ramrod jumps out of the barrel. They ram the charge and especially the powder, with such force that the rebound sends the rod right out, and he has seen those who were not cottagers follow the same practice. A close-fitting wad, too tight for the barrel, will sometimes cause the rod to spring high above the muzzle: as it is pushed quickly down it compresses the air in the tube, which expands with a sharp report and drives the rod out.

Loading with paper, again, has often resulted in mischief: sometimes a smouldering fragment remains in the barrel after the discharge, and on pouring in powder from the flask it catches and runs like a train up to the flask, which may burst in the hand. For this reason to this day some of the old farmers, clinging to ancient custom, always load with a clay tobacco pipe-bowl, snapped off from the stem for the purpose. It is supposed to hold just the proper charge, and as it is detached from the horn or flask there is no danger of fire being communicated to the magazine; so that an explosion, if it happened, would do no serious injury, being confined to the loose powder of the charge itself. Paper used as wads will sometimes continue burning for a short time after being blown out of the gun, and may set fire to straw, or even dry grass.

The old folk, therefore, when it was necessary to shoot the starlings on the thatch, or the sparrows and chaffinches which congregate in the rickyards in such extraordinary numbers—in short, to fire off a gun anywhere near inflammable materials—made it a rule to load with green leaves, which would not burn and could do no harm. The ivy leaf was a special favourite for the purpose—the broad-leaved ivy which grows against houses and in gardens—because it is stout, about the right size to double up and fold into a wad, and is available in winter, being an evergreen, when most other leaves are gone. I have seen guns loaded with ivy leaves many times. When a gun gets foul the ramrod is apt to stick tight if paper is used after pushing it home, and unless a vice be handy no power will draw it out. In this dilemma the old plan used to be to fire it into a hayrick, standing at a short distance; the hay, yielding slightly, prevented the rod from breaking to pieces when it struck.

Most men who have had much to do with guns have burst one or more. The keeper in the course of years has had several accidents of the kind; but none since the breechloader has come into general use, the reason of course being that two charges cannot be inadvertently inserted one above the other, as frequently occurred in the old guns.

I had a muzzle-loading gun burst in my hands some time since: the breech-piece split, and the nipple, hammer, and part of the barrel there blew out. Fortunately no injury was done; and I should not note it except for the curious effect upon the tympanum of the ear. The first sense was that of a stunning blow on the head; on recovering from which the distinction between one sound and another seemed quite lost. The ear could not separate or define them, and whether it was a person speaking, a whistle, the slamming of a door, or the neigh of a horse, it was all the same. Tone, pitch, variation there was none. Though perfectly, and in fact painfully, audible, all sounds were converted into a miserable jangling noise, exactly like that made when a wire in a piano has come loose and jingles. This annoying state of things lasted three days, after which it gradually went off, and in a week had entirely disappeared. Probably the sound of the explosion had been much increased by the cheek slightly touching the stock in the moment of firing, the jar of the wood adding to the vibration. This gun belonged to another person, and was caught up, already loaded, to take advantage of a favourable chance; it is noticeable that half the accidents happen with a strange gun.

Shot plays curious freaks sometimes: I know a case in which a gun was accidentally discharged in a dairy paved as most dairies are with stone flags. The muzzle was pointed downwards at the time—the shot struck the smooth stone floor, glanced off and up and hit another person standing almost at right angles, causing a painful wound. It is a marvel that more bird-keepers do not get injured by the bursting of the worn-out firelocks used to frighten birds from the seed. Some of these are not only rusty, but so thin at the muzzle as almost to cut the hand if it accidentally comes into contact with any force.

A collection of curious old guns might be made in the villages; the flint-locks are nearly all gone, but there are plenty of single-barrels in existence and use which were converted from that ancient system. In the farmhouses here and there may be found such a weapon, half a century old or more, with a barrel not quite equal in length to the punt-gun, but so long that, when carried under the arm of a tall man, the muzzle touches the ground where it is irregular in level. It is slung up to the beam across the ceiling with leathern thongs—one loop for the barrel and the other for the stock. It is still serviceable, having been kept dry; and the owner will tell you that he has brought down pigeons with it at seventy yards.

Every man believes that his particular gun is the

best in the locality to kill. The owner of this cumbrous weapon, if you exhibit an interest in its history, will take you into the fields and point out a spot where forty years ago he or his immediate ancestor shot four or five wild geese at once, resting the barrel on the branch of a tree in the hedge and sending a quarter of a pound of lead whistling among the flock. The spot the wild geese used to visit in the winter is still remembered, though they come there no more; drains and cultivation having driven them away from that southern district. In the course of the winter, perhaps, a small flock may be seen at a great height passing over, but they do not alight, and in some years are not observed at all.

There is a trick sometimes practised by poachers which enables them to make rabbits bolt from their holes without the assistance of a ferret. It is a chemical substance emitting a peculiar odour, and, if placed in the burrows, drives the rabbits out. Chemical science, indeed, has been called to the aid of poaching in more ways than one: fish, for instance, are sometimes poisoned, or killed by an explosion of dynamite. These later practices have, however, not yet come into general use, being principally employed by those only who have had some experience of mining or quarrying.

There is a saying that an old poacher makes the best gamekeeper, on the principle of setting a thief to catch a thief: a maxim, however, of doubtful value, since no other person could so thoroughly appreciate the tempting opportunities which must arise day after day. That keepers themselves are sometimes the worst of depredators must be admitted. Hitherto I have chiefly described the course of action followed by honest and conscientious men, truly anxious for their employers' interests, and taking a personal pride in a successful shooting season. But there exists a class of keepers of a very different order, who have done much to bring sport itself into unmerited odium.

The blackleg keeper is often a man of some natural ability—a plausible, obsequious rascal, quick in detecting the weak points of his employer's character, and in practising upon and distorting what were originally generous impulses. His game mainly depends upon gaining the entire confidence of his master; and, not being embarrassed by considerations of self-esteem, he is not choice in the use of means to that end. He knows that if he can thoroughly worm himself into his employer's good opinion the unfavourable reports which may be set afloat against him will be regarded as the mere tittle-tattle of envy; for it is often an amiable weakness on the part of masters who are really attached to their servants to maintain a kind of partisanship on behalf of those whom they have once trusted.

Such a servant finds plentiful occasions for dexterously gratifying the love of admiration innate in us all. The manliest athlete and frankest amateur—who would blush at the praise of social equals—finds it hard to resist the apparently bluff outspoken applause of his inferiors bestowed on his prowess in field sports, whether rowing or riding, with rod or gun. Of course it frequently happens that the sportsman really does excel as a shot; but that in no degree lessens the insidious effect of the praise which seems extorted in the excitement of the moment, and to come forth with unpremeditated energy.

The next step is to establish a common ground of indignation; for it is to be observed that those who unite in abuse of a third person have a stronger bond of sympathy than those who mutually admire another. If by accident some unfortunate *contretemps* should cause a passing irritation between his master and the owner of a neighbouring estate, the keeper loses no opportunity of heaping coals upon the fire. He brings daily reports of trespass. Now the other party's keepers have been beating a field beyond their boundaries; now they have ferreted a bank to which they have no right. Another time they have prevented straying pheasants from returning to the covers by intercepting their retreat; and a score of similar tricks. Or perhaps it is the master of a pack of hounds against whom insinuations are directed: cubs are not destroyed sufficiently, and the pheasants are eaten daily.

Sometimes it is a tenant-farmer with a long lease, who cannot be quickly ejected, who has to bear the brunt of these attacks. He is accused of trapping hares and rabbits: he sets the traps so close to the preserves that the pheasants are frequently caught and mortally injured; he is suspected of laying poisoned grain about. Not content with this he carries his malice so far as to cause the grass or other crops in which outlying nests or young broods are sheltered to be cut before it is ripe, with the object of destroying or driving them away; and he presents the mowers whose scythes mutilate game with a quart of beer as reward, or furnishes his shepherds with lurchers for poaching. He encourages the gipsies to encamp in the neighbourhood and carry on nightly expeditions by allowing them the use of a field in which to put their vans and horses. With such accounts as these, supported by what looks like evidence, the blackleg keeper gradually works his employer into a state of intense irritation, meantime reaping the reward of the incorruptible guardian and shrewd upright servitor.

At the same time, in the haze of suspicion he has created, the rascal finds a cloak for his own misdeeds. These poachers, trespassers, gipsies, foxes, and refractory tenants afford a useful excuse to account for the comparative scarcity of game. What on earth has become of the birds, and where the dickens are the hares? asks the angry proprietor. In the spring he recollects being shown by the keeper, with modest pride, some hundreds of young pheasants, flourishing exceedingly. Now he finds the broods have strangely dwindled, and he is informed that these enemies against whom all along he has been warned have made short work of them. If this explanation seems scarcely sufficient, there is always some inexplicable disease to bear the blame: the birds had been going on famously when suddenly they were seized by a mysterious epidemic which decimated their numbers.

All this is doubly annoying, because, in addition to the loss of anticipated sport, there has been an exorbitant expenditure. The larger the number of young broods of pheasants early in the year the better for the dishonest keeper, who has more chances of increasing his own profit, both directly and indirectly. In the first place, there is the little business of buying eggs, not without commissions. More profit is found in the supply of food for the birds: extras and petty disbursements afford further room for pickings.

Then, when the game has been spirited away, the keeper's object is to induce his employer to purchase full-grown pheasants—another chance of secret gratuities—and to turn them out for the battue. That institution is much approved of by keepers of this character, for, the pheasants being confined to a small area, there is less personal exertion than is involved in walking over several thousand acres to look after hares and partridges.

By poisoning his master's mind against some one he not only covers these proceedings but secures himself from the explanation which if listened to might set matters right. The accused, attempting to explain, finds a strong prejudice against him, and turns away in dudgeon. Such underhand tricks sometimes cause mischief in a whole district. An unscrupulous keeper may set people of all ranks at discord with each other.

In these malpractices, and in the disposal of game which is bulky, he is occasionally assisted by other keepers of congenial character engaged upon adjacent estates. Gentlemen on intimate terms naturally imagine that their keepers mutually assist each other in the detection of poaching—meeting by appointment, for instance, at night, as the police do, to confer upon their beats. When two or three are thus in league it is not difficult for them to dispose of booty: they quickly get into communication with professional receivers; and instances have been known in which petticoats have formed a cover for a steady if small illegal transport of dead game over the frontier.

For his own profit a keeper of this kind may indeed be trusted to prevent poaching on the part of other persons, whose gains would be his loss, since there would remain less for him to smuggle. Very probably it may come to be acknowledged on all sides that he is watchful and always about: an admission that naturally tends to raise him in the esteem of his employer.

Those who could tell tales—his subordinate assistants—are all more or less implicated, as in return for their silence they are permitted to get pickings: a dozen rabbits now and then, good pay for little work, and plenty of beer. If one of them lets out strange facts in his cups, it signifies nothing: no one takes any heed of a labourer's beerhouse talk. The steward or bailiff has strong suspicions, perhaps, but his motions are known, and his prying eyes defeated. As for the tenants, they groan and bear it.

It is to be regretted that now and then the rural policeman becomes an accomplice in these nefarious practices. His position of necessity brings him much into contact with the keepers of the district within his charge. If they are a 'shady' lot, what with plenty of drink, good fellowship, presents of game, and insidious suggestions of profit, it is not surprising that a man whose pay is not the most liberal should gradually fall away from the path of duty. The keeper can place a great temptation in his way—*i.e.* occasional participation in shooting when certain persons are absent: there are few indeed who can resist the opportunity of enjoying sport. The rural constable often has a beat of very wide area, thinly populated: it is difficult to tell where he may be; he has a reasonable pretext for being about at all hours, and it is impossible that he should be under much supervision. Perhaps he may have a taste for dogs, and breed them for sale, if not openly, on the sly. Now the keeper can try these animals, or even break them in in a friendly way; and when once he has committed himself, and winked at what is going on, the constable feels that he may as well join and share altogether. At outlying wayside 'publics' the keeper and the constable may carouse to the top of their bent: the landlord is only too glad to be on good terms with them; his own little deviations pass unnoticed, and if by accident they are discovered he has a friend at court to give him a good character.

The worthy pair have an engine of oppression in their hands which effectually overawes the cottagers: they can accuse them of poaching; and if not proceeding to the ultimatum of a summons, which might not suit their convenience, can lay them under suspicion, which may result in notice to quit their cottages, or to give up their allotment gardens; and a garden is almost as important to a cottager as his weekly wages. In this way a landlord whose real disposition may be most generous may be made to appear a perfect tyrant, and be disliked by the whole locality. It is to the interest of the keeper and the constable to obtain a conviction now and then; it gives them the character of vigilance.

Sometimes a blackleg keeper, not satisfied with the plunder of the estate under his guardianship must needs encroach on the lands of neighbouring farmers occupying under small owners; and so further ill-will is caused. In the end an exposure takes place, and the employer finds to his extreme mortification how deeply he has been deceived; but the discovery may not be made for years. Of course all keepers of this character are not systematically vicious: many are only guilty occasionally, when a peculiarly favourable opportunity offers.

Another class of keeper is rather passively than actively bad. This is the idle man, whose pipe is ever in his mouth and whose hands are always in his pockets. He is often what is called a good-natured fellow—soft-spoken, respectful, and willing; liked by everybody; a capital comrade in his own class, and, in fact, with too many friends of a certain set.

Gamekeeping is an occupation peculiarly favourable to loafing if a man is inclined that way. He can sit on the rails and gates, lounge about the preserves, go to sleep on the sward in the shade; call at the roadside inn, and, leaning his gun against the tree from which the sign hangs, quaff his quart in indolent dignity. By degrees he easily falls into bad habits, takes too much liquor, finds his hands unsteady, becomes too lazy to repress poaching (which is a weed that must be constantly pulled up, or it will grow with amazing rapidity), and finally is corrupted, and shares the proceeds of bolder rascals. His assistants do as they please. He has no control over them: they know too much about him.

It is a curious fact that there are poaching villages and non-poaching villages. Out of a dozen or more parishes forming a petty sessional district one or two will become notorious for this propensity. The bench never meet without a case from them, either for actual poaching or some cognate offence. The drinking, fighting, dishonesty, low gambling, seem ceaseless —like breeding like—till the place becomes a nest of rascality. Men hang about at the public-houses all day, betting on horses, loitering; a blight seems to fall upon them, and a bad repute clings to the spot for years after the evil itself has been eradicated.

If a weak keeper gets among such a set as this he succumbs; and the same cause hastens the moral decay of the constable. The latter has a most difficult part to maintain. If he is disposed to carry out the strict letter of his instructions, that does not do—

there is a prejudice against too much severity. English feeling is anti-Draconian; and even the respectable inhabitants would rather endure some little rowdyism than witness an over interference with liberty. If the constable is good-natured, and loth to take strong measures, he either becomes a semi-accomplice or sinks to a nonentity. It is difficult to find a man capable of controlling such a class; it requires tact, and something of the gift of governing men.

By contact with bad characters a weak keeper may be contaminated without volition of his own at first: for we know the truthful saying about touching pitch. The misfortune is that the guilty when at last exposed become notorious; and their infamy spreads abroad, smirching the whole class to which they belong. The honest conscientious men remain in obscurity and get no public credit, though they may far outnumber the evil-disposed.

To make a good keeper it requires not only honesty and skill, but a considerable amount of 'backbone' in the character to resist temptation and to control subordinates. The keeper who has gone to the bad becomes one of the most mischievous members of the community: the faithful and upright keeper is not only a valuable servant, but a protection to all kinds of property.

The Amateur
Poacher

===

BY THE AUTHOR OF
'THE GAMEKEEPER AT HOME' AND
'WILD LIFE IN A SOUTHERN COUNTY'

PREFACE

THE following pages are arranged somewhat in the order of time, beginning with the first gun, and attempts at shooting. Then come the fields, the first hills, and woods explored, often without a gun, or any thought of destruction: and next the poachers, and other odd characters observed at their work. Perhaps the idea of shooting with a matchlock, or wheel-lock, might, if put in practice, at least afford some little novelty.

R. J.

CHAPTER I

THE FIRST GUN

THEY burned the old gun that used to stand in the dark corner up in the garret, close to the stuffed fox that always grinned so fiercely. Perhaps the reason why he seemed in such a ghastly rage was that he did not come by his death fairly. Otherwise his pelt would not have been so perfect. And why else was he put away up there out of sight?—and so magnificent a brush as he had too. But there he stood, and mounted guard over the old flintlock that was so powerful a magnet to us in those days. Though to go up there alone was no slight trial of moral courage after listening to the horrible tales of the carters in the stable, or the old women who used to sit under the hedge in the shade, on an armful of hay, munching their crusts at luncheon time.

The great cavernous place was full of shadows in the brightest summer day; for the light came only through the chinks in the shutters. These were flush with the floor and bolted firmly. The silence was intense, it being so near the roof and so far away from the inhabited parts of the house. Yet there were sometimes strange acoustical effects—as when there came a low tapping at the shutters, enough to make your heart stand still. There was then nothing for it but to dash through the doorway into the empty cheese-room adjoining, which was better lighted. No doubt it was nothing but the labourers knocking the stakes in for the railing round the rickyard, but why did it sound just exactly outside the shutters?

When that ceased the staircase creaked, or the pear-tree boughs rustled against the window. The staircase always waited till you had forgotten all about it before the loose worm-eaten planks sprang back to their place.

Had it not been for the merry whistling of the starlings on the thatch above, it would not have been possible to face the gloom and the teeth of Reynard, ever in the act to snap, and the mystic noises, and the sense of guilt—for the gun was forbidden. Besides which there was the black mouth of the open trap-door overhead yawning fearfully—a standing terror and temptation; for there was a legend of a pair of pistols thrown up there out of the way—a treasure-trove tempting enough to make us face anything. But Orion must have the credit of the courage; I call him Orion because he was a hunter and had a famous dog. The last I heard of him he had just ridden through a prairie fire, and says the people out there think nothing of it.

We dragged an ancient linen-press under the trap-door, and put some boxes on that, and finally a straight-backed oaken chair. One or two of those chairs were split up and helped to do the roasting on the kitchen hearth. So, climbing the pile, we emerged under the rafters, and could see daylight faintly in several places coming through the starlings' holes. One or two bats fluttered to and fro as we groped among the lumber, but no pistols could be discovered: nothing but a cannon-ball, rusty enough and about as big as an orange, which they say was found in the wood, where there was a brush in Oliver's time.

In the middle of our expedition there came the well-known whistle, echoing about the chimneys, with which it was the custom to recall us to dinner. How else could you make people hear who might be cutting a knobbed stick in the copse half a mile away or bathing in the lake? We had to jump down with a run; and then came the difficulty; for black dusty cobwebs, the growth of fifty years, clothed us from head to foot. There was no brushing or picking them off, with that loud whistle repeated every two minutes.

The fact where we had been was patent to all; and so the chairs got burned—but one, which was rickety. After which a story crept out, of a disjointed skeleton lying in a corner under the thatch. Though just a little suspicious that this might be a *ruse* to frighten us from a second attempt, we yet could not deny the possibility of its being true. Sometimes in the dusk, when I sat poring over 'Kœnigsmark, the Robber', by the little window in the cheese-room, a skull seemed to peer down the trapdoor. But then I had the flintlock by me for protection.

There were giants in the days when that gun was made; for surely no modern mortal could have held that mass of metal steady to his shoulder. The linen-press and a chest on the top of it formed, however, a very good gun-carriage; and, thus mounted, aim could be taken out of the window at the old mare feeding in the meadow below by the brook, and a 'bead' could be drawn upon Molly, the dairy-maid, kissing the fogger behind the hedge, little dreaming that the deadly tube was levelled at them. At least this practice and drill had one useful effect—the eye got accustomed to the flash from the pan, instead of blinking the discharge, which ruins the shooting. Almost everybody and everything on the place got shot dead in this way without knowing it.

It was not so easy as might be supposed to find proper flints. The best time to look for them was after a heavy storm of rain had washed a shallow channel beside the road, when you might select some handy splinters which had lain hidden under the dust. How we were found out is not quite clear: perhaps the powder left a smell of sulphur for any one who chanced to go up in the garret.

But, however that may be, one day, as we came in unexpectedly from a voyage in the punt, something was discovered burning among the logs on the kitchen hearth; and, though a desperate rescue was attempted, nothing was left but the barrel of our precious gun and some crooked iron representing the remains of the lock. There are things that are never entirely for-given, though the impression may become fainter as years go by. The sense of the cruel injustice of that act will never quite depart.

But they could not burn the barrel, and we almost succeeded in fitting it to a stock of elder. Elder has a thick pith running down the centre: by removing that the gouge and chisel had not much work to do to make a groove for the old bell-mouthed barrel to lie in. The matchlock, for as such it was intended, was nearly finished when our hopes were dashed to the ground by a piece of unnatural cunning. One morning the breechpiece that screwed in was missing. This was fatal. A barrel without a breechpiece is like a cup without a bottom. It was all over.

There are days in spring when the white clouds go swiftly past, with occasional breaks of bright sun-shine lighting up a spot in the landscape. That is like the memory of one's youth. There is a long dull blank, and then a brilliant streak of recollection.

Doubtless it was a year or two afterwards when, seeing that the natural instinct could not be suppressed but had better be recognized, they produced a real gun (single-barrel) for me from the clock-case.

It stood on the landing just at the bottom of the dark flight that led to the garret. An oaken case six feet high or more, and a vast dial, with a mysterious picture of a full moon and a ship in full sail that somehow indicated the quarters of the year, if you had been imitating Rip Van Winkle and after a sleep of six months wanted to know whether it was spring or autumn. But only to think that all the while we were puzzling over the moon and the ship and the queer signs on the dial a gun was hidden inside! The case was locked, it is true; but there are ways of opening locks, and we were always handy with tools.

This gun was almost but not quite so long as the other. That dated from the time between Stuart and Hanover; this might not have been more than seventy years old. And a beautiful piece of workmanship it was: my new double breechloader is a coarse common thing to compare with it. Long and slender and light as a feather, it came to the shoulder with wonderful ease. Then there was a groove on the barrel at the breech and for some inches up which caught the eye and guided the glance like a trough to the sight at the muzzle and thence to the bird. The stock was shod with brass, and the trigger-guard was of brass, with a kind of flange stretching half-way down to the butt and inserted in the wood. After a few minutes' polishing it shone like gold, and to see the sunlight flash on it was a joy.

You might note the grain of the barrel, for it had not been browned; and it took a good deal of sand to get the rust off. By aid of a little oil and careful wiping after a shower it was easy to keep it bright. Those browned barrels only encourage idleness. The lock was a trifle dull at first, simply from lack of use. A small screwdriver soon had it to pieces, and it speedily clicked again sweet as a flute. If the hammer came back rather far when at full-cock, that was because the lock had been converted from a flint, and you could not expect it to be absolutely perfect. Besides which, as the fall was longer the blow was heavier, and the cap was sure to explode.

By old farmhouses, mostly in exposed places (for which there is a reason), one or more huge walnut trees may be found. The provident folk of those days planted them with the purpose of having their own gunstocks cut out of the wood when the tree was thrown. They could then be sure it was really walnut, and a choice piece of timber thoroughly well seasoned. I like to think of those times, when men settled themselves down, and planted and planned and laid out their gardens and orchards and woods, as if they and their sons and sons' sons, to the twentieth generation, were sure to enjoy the fruit of their labour.

The reason why the walnuts are put in exposed places, on the slope of a rise, with open aspect to the east and north, is because the walnut is a foolish tree that will not learn by experience. If it feels the warmth of a few genial days in early spring, it immediately protrudes its buds; and the next morning a bitter frost cuts down every hope of fruit for that year, leaving the leaf as black as may be. Wherefore the east wind is desirable to keep it as backward as possible.

There was a story that the stock of this gun had been cut out of a walnut tree that was thrown on the place by my great-grandfather, who saw it well seasoned, being a connoisseur of timber, which is, indeed, a sort of instinct in all his descendants. And a vast store of philosophy there is in timber if you study it aright.

After cleaning the gun and trying it at a mark, the next thing was to get a good shot with it. Now there was an elm that stood out from the hedge a little, almost at the top of the meadow, not above five-and-twenty yards from the other hedge that bounded the field. Two mounds could therefore be commanded by any one in ambush behind the elm, and all the angular corner of the mead was within range.

It was not far from the house; but the ground sank into a depression there, and the ridge of it behind shut out everything except just the roof of the tallest hayrick. As one sat on the sward behind the elm, with the back turned on the rick and nothing in front but the tall elms and the oaks in the other hedge, it was quite easy to fancy it the verge of the prairie with the backwoods close by.

The rabbits had scratched the yellow sand right out into the grass—it is always very much brighter in colour where they have just been at work—and the fern, already almost yellow too, shaded the mouths of their buries. Thick bramble bushes grew out from the mound and filled the space between it and the elm: there were a few late flowers on them still, but the rest were hardening into red sour berries. Westwards, the afternoon sun, with all his autumn heat, shone full against the hedge and into the recess, and there was not the shadow of a leaf for shelter on that side.

The gun was on the turf, and the little hoppers kept jumping out of the grass on to the stock: once their king, a grasshopper, alighted on it and rested, his green limbs tipped with red rising above his back. About the distant wood and the hills there was a soft faint haze, which is what Nature finishes her pictures with. Something in the atmosphere which made it almost visible: all the trees seemed to stand in a liquid light—the sunbeams were suspended in the air instead of passing through. The butterflies even were very idle in the slumberous warmth; and the great green dragon-fly rested on a leaf, his tail arched a little downwards, just as he puts it when he wishes to stop suddenly in his flight.

The broad glittering trigger-guard got quite hot in the sun, and the stock was warm when I felt it every now and then. The grain of the walnut-wood showed plainly through the light polish: it was not varnished like the stock of the double-barrel they kept padlocked to the rack over the high mantelpiece indoors. Still you could see the varnish. It was of a rich dark horse-chestnut colour, and yet so bright and clear that if held close you could see your face in it. Behind it the grain of the wood was just perceptible; especially at the grip, where hard hands had worn it away somewhat. The secret of that varnish is lost—like that of the varnish on the priceless old violins.

But you could feel the wood more in my gun: so that it was difficult to keep the hand off it, though the rabbits would not come out; and the shadowless recess grew like a furnace, for it focussed the rays of the sun. The heat on the sunny side of a thick hedge between three and four in the afternoon is almost tropical if you remain still, because the air is motionless: the only relief is to hold your hat loose; or tilt it against your head, the other edge of the brim on the ground. Then the grass-blades rise up level with the forehead. There is a delicious smell in growing grass, and a sweetness comes up from the earth.

Still it got hotter and hotter; and it was not possible to move in the least degree, lest a brown creature sitting on the sand at the mouth of his hole, and hidden himself by the fern, should immediately note it. And Orion was waiting in the rickyard for the sound of the report, and very likely the shepherd too. We knew that men in Africa, watched by lions, had kept still in the sunshine till, reflected from the rock, it literally scorched them, not daring to move; and we knew all about the stoicism of the Red Indians. But Ulysses was ever my pattern and model: that man of infinite patience and resource.

So, though the sun might burn and the air become suffocating in that close corner, and the quivering line of heat across the meadow make the eyes dizzy to watch, yet not a limb must be moved. The black flies came in crowds; but they are not so tormenting if you plunge your face in the grass, though they titillate the back of the hand as they run over it. Under the bramble bush was a bury that did not look much used; and once or twice a great blue fly came out of it, the buzz at first sounding hollow and afar off and becoming clearer as it approached the mouth of the hole. There was the carcass of a dead rabbit inside no doubt.

A humble-bee wandering along—they are restless things—buzzed right under my hat, and became entangled in the grass by my ear. Now we knew by experience in taking their honey that they could sting

sharply if irritated, though good-tempered by nature.
How he 'burred' and buzzed and droned!—till by-
and-by, crawling up the back of my head, he found
an open space and sailed away. Then, looking out
again, there was a pair of ears in the grass not ten
yards distant: a rabbit had come out at last. But the
first delight was quickly over: the ears were short and
sharply pointed, and almost pinkly transparent.

What would the shepherd say if I brought home
one of his hated enemies no bigger than a rat? The
young rabbit made waiting still more painful, being
far enough from the hedge to get a clear view into
the recess if anything attracted his notice. Why the
shepherd hated rabbits was because the sheep would
not feed where they had worn their runs in the grass.
Not the least movement was possible now—not even
that little shifting which makes a position just endur-
able: the heat seemed to increase; the thought of
Ulysses could hardly restrain the almost irresistible
desire to stir.

When, suddenly, there was a slight rustling among
the boughs of an oak in the other hedge, as of wings
against twigs: it was a woodpigeon, better game than
a rabbit. He would, I knew, first look round before
he settled himself to preen his feathers on the branch,
and, if everything was still while that keen inspection
lasted, would never notice me. This is their habit—
and the closer you are underneath them the less
chance of their perceiving you: for a pigeon perched
rarely looks straight downwards. If flying, it is just
the reverse; for then they seem to see under them
quicker than in any other direction.

Slowly lifting the long barrel of the gun—it was
fortunate the sunlight glancing on the bright barrel

was not reflected towards the oak—I got it to bear upon the bird; but then came a doubt. It was all eight-
and-twenty yards across the angle of the meadow to
the oak—a tremendous long shot under the circumstances. For they would not trust us with the large
copper powder-flask, but only with a little pistol-flask
(it had belonged to the pair of pistols we tried to find),
and we were ordered not to use more than a charge
and a half at a time. That was quite enough to kill
blackbirds. (The noise of the report was always a
check in this way; such a trifle of powder only made a
slight puff.)

Shot there was in plenty—a whole tobacco-pipe
bowl full, carefully measured out of the old yellow
canvas money-bag that did for a shot belt. A starling
could be knocked off the chimney with this charge
easily, and so could a blackbird roosting in a bush at
night. But a woodpigeon nearly thirty yards distant
was another matter; for the old folk (and the bird-
keepers too) said that their quills were so hard the
shot would glance aside unless it came with great force.
Very likely the pigeon would escape, and all the rabbits in the buries would be too frightened to come out
at all.

A beautiful bird he was on the bough, perched
well in view and clearly defined against the sky
behind; and my eye travelled along the groove on
the breech and up the barrel, and so to the sight and
across to him; and the finger, which always would
keep time with the eye, pulled at the trigger.

A mere puff of a report, and then a desperate
fluttering in the tree and a cloud of white feathers
floating above the hedge, and a heavy fall among the
bushes. He was down, and Orion's spaniel (that came

racing like mad from the rickyard the instant he heard the discharge) had him in a moment. Orion followed quickly. Then the shepherd came up, rather stiff on his legs from rheumatism, and stepped the distance, declaring it was thirty yards good; after which we all walked home in triumph.

Molly the dairy-maid came a little way from the rickyard, and said she would pluck the pigeon that very night after work. She was always ready to do anything for us boys; and we could never quite make out why they scolded her so for an idle hussy indoors. It seemed so unjust. Looking back, I recollect she had very beautiful brown eyes.

'You mind you chaws the shot well, measter,' said the shepherd, 'afore you loads th' gun. The more you chaws it the better it sticks thegither, an' the furder it kills um': a theory of gunnery which was devoutly believed in in his time and long anticipated the wire cartridges. And the old soldiers that used to come round to haymaking, glad of a job to supplement their pensions, were very positive that if you bit the bullet and indented it with your teeth, it was perfectly fatal, no matter to what part of the body its billet took it.

In the midst of this talk as we moved on, I carrying the gun at the trail with the muzzle downwards, the old ramrod, long disused and shrunken, slipped half out; the end caught the ground, and it snapped short off in a second. A terrible disaster this, turning everything to bitterness: Orion was especially wroth, for it was his right next to shoot. However, we went down to the smithy at the inn, to take counsel of the blacksmith, a man of knowledge and a trusty friend. 'Aha!' said he, 'it's not the first time I've made a ramrod. There's a piece of lancewood in the store overhead which I keep on purpose; it's as tough as a bow—they make carriage-shafts of it; you shall have a better rod than was ever fitted to a Joe Manton.' So we took him down some pippins, and he set to work on it that evening.

CHAPTER II

THE OLD PUNT: A CURIOUS 'TURNPIKE'

THE sculls of our punt, being short and stout, answered very well as levers to heave the clumsy old craft off the sand into which it sank so deeply. That sheltered corner of the mere, with a shelving sandy shore, and a steep bank behind covered with trees, was one of the best places to fish for roach: you could see them playing under the punt in shoals any sunny day.

There was a projecting bar almost enclosing the creek, which was quite still, even when the surf whitened the stony strand without, driven before a wet and stormy south-wester. It was the merest routine to carry the painter ashore and twist the rotten rope round an exposed root of the great willow tree; for there was not the slightest chance of that ancient craft breaking adrift.

All our strength and the leverage of the sculls could scarcely move her, so much had she settled. But we had determined to sail that lovely day to visit the island of Calypso, and had got all our arms and munitions of war aboard, besides being provisioned and carrying some fruit for fear of scurvy. There was of course the gun, placed so as not to get wet; for the boat leaked, and had to be frequently baled out with a tin mug—one that the haymakers used.

Indeed, if we had not caulked her with some dried moss and some stiff clay, it is doubtful if she would have floated far. The well was full of dead leaves that had been killed by the caterpillars and the blight,

and had fallen from the trees before their time; and
there were one or two bunches of grass growing at the
stern part from between the decaying planks.

Besides the gun there was the Indian bow, scooped
out inside in a curious way, and covered with strange
designs or coloured hieroglyphics: it had been brought
home by one of our people years before. There was
but one man in the place who could bend that bow
effectually; so that though we valued it highly we
could not use it. By it lay another of briar, which was
pliable enough and had brought down more than one
bird.

Orion hit a rabbit once; but though sore wounded
it got to the bury, and, struggling in, the arrow caught
the side of the hole and was drawn out. Indeed, a
nail filed sharp is not of much avail as an arrowhead:
you must have it barbed, and that was a little beyond
our skill. Ikey the blacksmith had forged us a spear-
head after a sketch from a picture of a Greek warrior;
and a rake-handle served as a shaft. It was really a
dangerous weapon. He had also made us a small
anchor according to plan; nor did he dip too deeply
into our pocket-money.

Then the mast and square-sail, fitted out of a win-
dow-blind, took up a considerable space; for although
it was perfectly calm, a breeze might arise. And what
with these and the pole for punting occasionally, the
deck of the vessel was in that approved state of confusion which always characterizes a ship on the point
of departure. Nor must Orion's fishing-rod and gear
be forgotten, nor the cigar-box at the stern (a present
from the landlady at the inn) which contained a chart
of the mere and a compass.

With a 'yeo—heave-ho!' we levered her an inch

at a time, and then loosened her by working her from side to side, and so, panting and struggling, shoved the punt towards the deep. Slowly a course was shaped out of the creek—past the bar and then along the edge of the thick weeds, stretching so far out into the water that the moorhen feeding near the land was beyond reach of shot. From the green matted mass through which a boat could scarcely have been forced came a slight uncertain sound, now here now yonder, a faint 'suck-sock'; and the dragon-flies were darting to and fro.

The only ripple of the surface, till broken by the sculls, was where the swallows dipped as they glided, leaving a circle of tiny wavelets that barely rolled a yard. Past the low but steep bluff of sand rising sheer out of the water, drilled with martins' holes and topped by a sapling oak in the midst of a great furze bush: yellow bloom of the furze, tall brake fern nestling under the young branches, woodbine climbing up and bearing sweet coronals of flower.

Past the barley that came down to the willows by the shore—ripe and white under the bright sunshine, but yonder beneath the shadow of the elms with a pale tint of amber. Past broad rising meadows, where under the oaks on the upper ground the cattle were idly lying out of the sultry heat.

Then the barren islands, strewn with stone and mussel-shells glistening in the sunshine, over which in a gale the waves made a clean sweep, rendered the navigation intricate; and the vessel had to be worked in and out, now scraping against rocky walls of sandstone, now grounding and churning up the bottom, till presently she floated in the bay beneath the firs. There a dark shadow hung over the black water—

still and silent, so still that even the aspens rested from their rustling.

Out again into the sunshine by the wide mouth of the Green River, as the chart named the brook whose level stream scarce moved into the lake. A streak of blue shot up it between the banks, and a shrill pipe came back as the kingfisher hastened away. By the huge boulder of sarsen, whose shoulder projected but a few inches—in stormy times a dangerous rock to mariners—and then into the unknown narrow seas between the endless osier-beds and withy-covered isles.

There the chart failed; and the known-landmarks across the open waters—the firs and elms, the green knoll with the cattle—were shut out by thick branches on either hand. In and out and round the islets, sounding the depth before advancing, winding now this way, now that, till all idea of the course was lost, and it became a mere struggle to get forward. Drooping boughs swept along the gunwales, thick-matted weeds cumbered the way; 'snags', jagged stumps of trees, threatened to thrust their tops through the bottom; and, finally, panting and weary of poling through the maze, we emerged in a narrow creek all walled in and enclosed with vegetation.

Running her ashore on the soft oozy ground, we rested under a great hawthorn bush that grew at the very edge, and, looking upwards, could see in the canopy above the black interlaced twigs of a dove's nest. Tall willow poles rose up all around, and above them was the deep blue of the sky. On the willow stems that were sometimes under water the bark had peeled in scales; beneath the surface bunches of red fibrous roots stretched out their slender filaments tipped with white, as if feeling like a living thing for prey.

A dreamy, slumberous place, where the sedges slept, and the green flags bowed their pointed heads. Under the bushes in the distant nook the moorhen, reassured by the silence, came out from the grey-green grass and the rushes. Surely Calypso's cave could not be far distant, where she with

> work and song the time divides,
> And through the loom the golden shuttle guides.

For the Immortals are hiding somewhere still in the woods; even now I do not weary searching for them.

But as we rested a shadow fell from a cloud that covered the sun, and immediately a faint sigh arose from among the sedges and the reeds, and two pale yellow leaves fell from the willows on the water. A gentle breeze followed the cloud, chasing its shadow. Orion touched his rod meaningly.

So I stepped ashore with the gun to see if a channel could be found into the open water, and pushed through the bush. Briar and bramble choked the path, and hollow willow stoles; but, holding the gun upright, it was possible to force through, till, pushing between a belt of reeds and round an elder thicket, I came suddenly on a deep, clear pool—all but walking into it. Up rose a large bird out of the water with a bustling of wings and splashing, compelled to 'rocket' by the thick bushes and willow poles. There was no time to aim; but the old gun touched the shoulder and went off without conscious volition on my part.

The bird flew over the willows, but the next moment there was a heavy splash somewhere beyond out of sight. Then came an echo of the report sent back from the woods adjoining, and another, and a third and fourth, as the sound rolled along the side of the hill, caught in the coombes and thrown to and fro like a ball in a tennis-court. Wild with anxiety, we forced the punt at the bulrushes, in the corner where it looked most open, and with all our might heaved it over the weeds and the mud, and so round the islet into the next pool, and thence into the open water. It was a wild duck, and was speedily on board.

Stepping the mast and hoisting the sail, we drifted before the faint breath of air that now just curled the surface, steering straight across the open for the stony barren islands at the mouth of the bay. The chart drawn in pencil—what labour it cost us!—said that there, a few yards from the steep shore, was a shoal with deep water round it. For some reason there always seemed a slight movement or current—a set of the water there, as if it flowed into the little bay.

In swimming we often came suddenly out of a cold into a stratum of warm water (at the surface); and perhaps the difference in the temperature may have caused the drift, for the bay was in shadow half the day. Now, wherever there is motion there will fish assemble; so as the punt approached the shoal the sail was doused, and at twenty yards' distance I *put* the anchor into the water—not dropping it, to avoid the splash—and let it slip gently to the bottom.

Then, paying out the cable, we drifted to the edge of the shoal without the least disturbance, and there brought up. Orion had his bait ready—he threw his line right to windward, so that the float might drag the worm naturally with the wind and slight current towards the shoal.

The tiny blue buoy dances up and down on the

miniature waves; beyond it a dazzling path of gold stretches away to the distant osier-islands—a path down which we came without seeing it, till we looked back. The wavelets strike with a faint 'sock-sock' against the bluff overhanging bow, and then roll on to the lee-shore close at hand.

It rises steep; then a broad green ledge; and after that, still steeper, the face of a long-deserted sandpit, where high up a rabbit sits at the mouth of his hole, within range, but certain to escape even if hit, and therefore safe. On the turf below is a round black spot, still showing, though a twelvemonth has gone by since we landed with half a dozen perch, lit a fire, and cooked the fishes. For Molly never could 'a-bear' perch, because of the hardness of the scales, saying she would as soon 'scrape a vlint'; and they laughed to scorn our idea of skinning them as you do moorhens, whose 'dowl' no fingers can pick.

So we lit a fire and blew it up, lying on the soft short grass in a state of nature after a swim, there being none to see us but the glorious sun. The skinned perch were sweeter than any I have tasted since.

'Look!' whispers Orion, suddenly. The quill above the blue buoy nods as it lifts over the wavelets—nods again, sinks a little, jerks up, and then goes down out of sight. Orion feels the weight. 'Two pounds, if he's an ounce!' he shouts: soon after a splendid perch is in the boat, nearer three pounds perhaps than two. Flop! whop! how he leaps up and down on the planks, soiled by the mud, dulling his broad back and barred sides on the grit and sand!

Roaming about like this with the gun, now on the water in the punt, and now on land, we gradually came to notice very closely the game we wished to shoot. We saw, for instance, that the rabbit when feeding or moving freely, unless quickened by alarm, has a peculiar way of dwelling upon his path. It almost resembles creeping; for both fore feet stop while the hinder come up—one hinder foot slightly behind the other, and rather wide apart.

When a fall of snow presents a perfect impression of his passage, it appears as if the animal had walked slowly backwards. This deceives many who at such times go out to pick up anything that comes in their way; for they trace the trail in the wrong direction. The truth is, that when the rabbit pauses for the hinder feet to come up he again rests momentarily upon these before the two foremost are put forth, and so presses not only the paw proper but the whole first joint of the hind leg upon the snow. A glance at the hind feet of a rabbit will show what I mean: they will be found to display plain signs of friction against the ground.

The habit has given the creature considerable power of standing up on the hinder feet; he can not only sit on his haunches, but raise himself almost upright, and remain in that position to listen for some little time. For the same reason he can bark the ash saplings higher up than would be imagined: where he cannot reach, the mice climb up and nibble straight lines across the young pole, as if done with a single stroke from a saw that scraped away the rind but did not reach the wood.

In front of a large rabbit bury the grass will be found discoloured with sand at some distance from the mouth of the hole. This is explained by particles adhering to the rabbits' hind feet, and rubbing off against the grass blades. Country people call this

peculiar gait 'sloppetting;' and one result of it is that
the rabbits wear away the grass where they are
numerous almost as much as they eat it away.

There was such a space worn by the attrition of
feet sprinkled with sand before the extensive burrow
at the top of the meadow where I shot the woodpigeon. These marks suggested to us that we should
attempt some more wholesale system of capture than
shooting. It was not for the mere desire of destruction,
but for a special purpose that we turned our attention
to wiring. The punt, though much beloved, was, like
all punts, a very bad sailer. A boat with a keel that
could tack, and so work into the wind's eye, was our
ambition.

The blacksmith Ikey readily purchased every rabbit we obtained at sixpence each. Rabbits were not
so dear then as now; but of course he made a large
profit even then. The same rabbits at present would
be worth fifteen or eighteen pence. Every sixpence
was carefully saved, but it was clear that a long time
must elapse before the goal was attained. The blacksmith started the idea of putting up a 'turnpike'—*i.e.*
a wire—but professed ignorance as to the method of
setting it. That was a piece of his cunning—that he
might escape responsibility.

The shepherd, too, when obliquely questioned,
shook his head, pursed his lips, threw his pitching-bar
over his shoulder, and marched off with a mysterious
hint that our friend Ikey would some day put his 'vut
in it'. It did not surprise us that the shepherd should
turn his back on anything of the kind; for he was a
leading man among the 'Ranters', and frequently ex-
horted them in his cottage.

The carter's lad was about at the time, and for the

moment we thought of applying to him. He was
standing on the threshold of the stable, under the
horseshoes and weasels' feet nailed up to keep the
witches away, teasing a bat that he had found under
the tiles. But suddenly the dusky thing bit him
sharply, and he uttered an oath; while the creature,
released, flew aimlessly into the elms. It was better
to avoid him.

Indoors, they would have put a very heavy hand
upon the notion had they known of it: so we had to
rely solely upon the teaching of experiment. In the
first attempt, a stick that had been put by for the
thatcher, but which he had not yet split, was cut short
and sharpened for the plug that prevents the animal
carrying away the wire when snared. This is driven
into the earth; at the projecting end a notch was cut
to hold the string attached to the end of the wire away
from the run.

A smaller stick supported the wire above the ground;
this latter only just sufficiently thrust into the sward
to stand firmly upright. Willow was used for this at
first; but it is a feeble wood: it split too much, or bent
and gave way instead of holding the wire in its place.
The best for the purpose we found were the nut-tree
rods that shoot up among the hazel thickets, no
larger than the shaft of an arrow, and almost as
straight. A slit about half an inch deep was made
in the upper end, and in this slit the shank of the wire
was sunk. Once or twice the upright was peeled; but
this was a mistake, for the white wand was then too
conspicuous. The bark should be left on.

Three copper wires twisted tight formed the snare
itself; we twisted them like the strands of a rope, thinking it would give more strength. The wire projected

horizontally, the loop curling downwards. It was first set up at a spot where a very broad and much-worn run—more like a footpath than a rabbit track—forked into several lesser runs, and at about five yards from the hedge. But though adjusted, as we thought, with the utmost nicety, no rabbit would put his neck into it—not even in the darkness of the night. By day they all played round it in perfect safety.

After waiting some time it was removed and reset just over a hole—the loop close to the opening. It looked scarcely possible for a rabbit to creep out without being caught, the loop being enlarged to correspond with the mouth of the hole. For a while it seemed as if the rabbits declined to use the hole at all; presently, however, the loop was pushed back, showing that one must have got his nose between it and the bank and so made a safe passage sideways. A run that crossed the field was then selected, and the wire erected at about the middle of it, equidistant from either hedge. Near the entrance of the buries the rabbits moved slowly, sniffing their way along and pausing every yard or so. But they often increased their speed farther away, and sometimes raced from one mound to the other. When going at that rate it appeared natural to conclude that they would be less careful to pick and choose their road.

The theory proved so far correct that next day the upright was down, but the wire had snapped and the rabbit was gone. The character of the fracture clearly indicated how it had happened: the rabbit, so soon as he found his head in the noose, had rolled and tumbled till the wire, already twisted tight, parted. Too much twisting, therefore, weakened instead of strengthening. Next a single wire, somewhat thicker, was used, and set up nearly in the same place; but it broke again.

Finally, two strands of medium size, placed side by side, but only twisted once—that is, just enough to keep them together—were employed. The lesser loop—the slip-knot, as it might be called—was at the same time eased in order to run quicker and take a closer grip. Experiments with the hand proved that this style of wire would bear a great strain, and immediately answered to a sudden jerk. The running noose slipped the more easily because the wires were smooth; when twisted the strands checked the noose, the friction causing a slight sound. The wire itself seemed nearly perfect; but still no rabbit was caught.

Various runs were tried in succession; the size of the loop, too, was now enlarged and now decreased; for once it seemed as if a rabbit's ears had struck it aside, and on another as if, the loop being too large or too low down, one of the fore feet had entered and drawn it. Had it been the hind leg the noose would have held, because of the crook of the leg; but the forefoot came through, leaving the noose drawn up to a size not much larger than a finger-ring. To decide the point accurately, a full-grown rabbit was shot, and Orion held it in a position as near as possible to that taken in running, while I adjusted the wire to fit exactly. Still no success.

At last the secret was revealed by a hare. One day, walking up the lane with the gun, and peeping over into the ploughed field, I saw a hare about sixty yards away. The distance was too great to risk a shot, or rather it was preferable to wait for the chance of his coming nearer. Stepping back gently behind the bushes, I watched him run to and fro, gradually approaching in a zig-zag line that must carry him right across in front. I was positive that he had not seen me, and felt sure of bagging him; when suddenly —without any apparent cause—up went his head, he glanced round, and was off like the wind.

Yet there had not been the faintest noise, and I could not understand it, till all at once it occurred to me that it must be the scent. The slight, scarcely perceptible, breeze blew in that direction: instantly he crossed the current from me he detected it and fled. Afterwards I noticed that in the dusky twilight, if the wind is behind him, a hare will run straight at you as if about to deliberately charge your legs. This incident by the ploughed field explained the failure of the wire. Every other care had been taken, but we had forgotten to allow for the extreme delicacy of a wild animal's sense of smell.

In walking to the spot selected for the snare it is best to avoid even stepping on the run, and while setting it up to stand back as far as convenient and lean forward. The grass that grows near must not be touched by the hand, which seems to impart a very strong scent. The stick that has been carried in the hand must not be allowed to fall across the run: and be careful that your handkerchief does not drop out of your pocket on or near it. If a bunch of grass grows very tall and requires parting, part it with the end (not the handle) of your stick.

The same holds good with gins, especially if placed for a rat. Some persons strew a little freshly plucked grass over the pan and teeth of the trap, thinking to hide it; but it not only smells of the hand, but withers up and turns brown, and acts as a warning to that wary creature. It is a better plan if any dead leaves are lying near to turn them over and over with the end of a twig till they fall on the trap, that is if they are dry: if wet (unless actually raining at the time), should one chance to be left with the drier under surface uppermost, the rat may pause on the brink.

Now that the remotest chance of leaving a scent was avoided the wire became a deadly instrument. Almost every morning two or three rabbits were taken: we set up a dozen snares when we had mastered the trick. They were found lying at full length in the crisp white grass, for we often rose to visit the wires while yet the stars were visible. Thus extended a person might have passed within a few yards and never noticed them, unless he had an out-of-doors eye; for the whiter fur of the belly as they lay aside was barely distinguishable from the hoar frost. The blacksmith Ikey sauntered down the lane every evening, and glanced casually behind the ash tree—the northern side of whose trunk was clothed with dark green velvet-like moss—to see if a bag was lying for him there among the nettles in the ditch. The rabbits were put in the bag, which was pushed through the hedge.

CHAPTER III

TREE-SHOOTING: A FISHING EXPEDITION

JUST on the verge and borderland of the territory that could be ranged in safety there grew a stunted oak in a mound beside the brook. Perhaps the roots had been checked by the water; for the tree, instead of increasing in bulk, had expended its vigour in branches so crooked that they appeared entangled in each other. This oak was a favourite perching-place, because of its position: it could also be more easily climbed than straight-grown timber, having many boughs low down the trunk. With a gun it is difficult to ascend a smooth tree; these boughs therefore were a great advantage.

One warm afternoon late in the summer I got up into this oak, and took a seat astride a large limb, with the main trunk behind like the back of a chair and about twenty feet above the mound. Some lesser branches afforded a fork on which the gun could be securely lodged, and a limb of considerable size came across in front. Leaning both arms on this, a view could be obtained below and on three sides easily and without effort.

The mound immediately beneath was grown over with thick blackthorn, a species of cover that gives great confidence to game. A kick or blow upon the bushes with a stick will not move anything in an old blackthorn thicket. A man can scarcely push through it: nothing but a dog can manage to get about. On the meadow side there was no ditch, only a narrow fringe of tall pointed grass and rushes, with one or two small furze bushes projecting out upon the sward. Behind such bushes, on the slope of the mound, is rather a favourite place for a rabbit to sit out, or a hare to have a form.

The brook was shallow towards the hedge, and bordered with flags, among which rose up one tall bunch of beautiful reeds. Some little way up the brook a pond opened from it. At the entrance the bar of mud had hardly an inch of water; within there was a clear small space, and the rest all weeds, with moorhens' tracks. The farther side of the pond was covered with bramble bushes. It is a good plan to send the dogs into bushes growing on the banks of ponds; for though rabbits dislike water itself they are fond of sitting out in such cover near it. A low railing enclosed the side towards me: the posts had slipped by the giving way of the soil, and hung over the still pool.

One of the rails—of willow—was eaten out into hollow cavities by the wasps, which came to it generation after generation for the materials of their nests. The particles they detach are formed into a kind of paste or paper: in time they will quite honeycomb a pole. The third side of the pond shelved to the 'leaze', that the cattle might drink. From it a narrow track went across the broad field up the rising ground to the distant gateway leading to the meadows, where they grazed on the aftermath. Marching day by day, one after the other in single file, to the drinking-place, the hoofs of the herd had cut a clean path in the turf, two or three inches deep and trodden hard. The reddish soil thus exposed marked the winding line athwart the field, through the tussocky bunches.

By the pond stood a low three-sided merestone or

landmark, the initials on which were hidden under
moss. Up in the tree, near the gun, there was a dead
branch that had decayed in the curious manner that
seems peculiar to oak. Where it joined the trunk the
bark still remained, though covered with lichen, and
for a foot or so cut; then there was a long space where
the bark and much of the wood had mouldered away;
finally, near the end the bough retained its original
size and the bark adhered. At the junction with the
trunk and at the extremity its diameter was perhaps
three inches: in the middle rather less than half as
much. The grey central piece, larger and darker at
either end, suggested the thought of the bare neck of
a vulture.

Far away, just rising above the slope of the leaze,
the distant tops of elms, crowded with rooks' nests
(not then occupied), showed the site of the residence
of an old gentleman of whom at that time we stood
in much fear. The 'Squire' of Southlands alarmed
even the hardened carters' lads as much by the prestige
of a singular character as by the chastisement he
personally gave those who ventured into his domain.
Not a bird's nest, not a nut, must be touched: still less
anything that could be called game. The watch kept
was so much the stricter because he took a personal
part in it, and was often round the fields himself
armed with a great oak staff. It seemed, indeed, as if
the preservation of the game was of far greater im-
portance to him than the shooting of it afterwards.
All the fowls of the air flocked to Southlands, as if it
had been a refuge; yet it was not a large estate. Into
the forest we had been, but Southlands was a mystery,
a forbidden garden of delight, with the terror of an
oaken staff (and unknown penalties) turning this way

and that. Therefore the stunted old oak on the verge
—the moss-grown merestone by the pond marked the
limit—was so favourite a perching-place.

That beautiful afternoon I leaned both arms idly
on the great bough that crossed in front of the seat,
and listened to the 'Caw—caw!' of the rooks as they
looked to see if the acorns were yet ripening. A dead
branch that had dropped partly into the brook was
swayed continually up and down by the current,
the water as it chafed against it causing a delicious
murmur. This lulled me to sleep.

I woke with a start, and had it not been for the
bough crossing in front must have fallen twenty feet.
Looking down into the meadow as soon as my eyes
were thoroughly open, I instantly noticed a covey of
young partridges a little way up beside the hedge
among the molehills. The neighbourhood of those
hillocks has an attraction for many birds; especially
in winter. Then fieldfares, redwings, starlings, and
others prefer the meadows that are dotted with them.
In a frost if you see a thrush on a molehill it is very
likely to thaw shortly. Moles seem to feel the least
change in the temperature of the earth; if it slackens
they begin to labour, and cast up, unwittingly, food
for the thrushes.

It would have been easy to kill three or four of the
covey, which was a small one, at a single shot; but it
had been a late summer, and they were not full-
grown. Besides which they roosted, I knew, about the
middle of the meadow, and to shoot them near the
roost would be certain to break them up, and perhaps drive them into Southlands. 'Good poachers
preserve their own game': so the birds fed safely,
though a pot shot would not have seemed the crime

then that it would now. While I watched them suddenly the old bird 'quat', and ran swiftly into the hedge, followed by the rest. A kestrel was hovering in the next meadow: when the beat of his wings ceased he slid forward and downwards, then rose and came over me in a bold curve. Well those little brown birds in the blackthorn knew that, fierce as he was, he dared not swoop even on a comparatively open bush, much less such thick covert, for fear of ruffling his proud feathers and beating them out. Nor could he follow them through the intricate hidden passages.

In the open water of the pond a large jack was basking in the sunshine, just beneath the surface; and though the shot would scatter somewhat before reaching him, he was within range. If a fish lies a few inches under water he is quite safe from shot unless the muzzle of the gun is so close that the pellets travel together like a bullet. At a distance the shot is supposed to glance as it strikes the water at an angle; for that reason the elevation of the tree was an advantage, since from it the charge would plunge into the pool. A jack may be killed in some depth of water when the gun is nearly perpendicularly above the mark; but in any case the aim must be taken two inches or more, according to circumstances, beneath the apparent position of the fish, to allow for refraction.

Sometimes the jack when hit comes to the surface belly upwards, but sometimes keeps down or sinks, and floats a considerable distance away from the spot; so that in the muddy water disturbed by the shot it is difficult to find him. If a snake be shot at while swimming he will sometimes sink like a stone, and can be seen lying motionless at the bottom. After we got hold of a small deer rifle we used to practise at the snakes in

the mere—aiming at the head, which is about the size
of a nut, and shows above the surface wobbling as they
move. I recollect cutting a snake's head clean off with
a ball from a pistol as he hastened away through the
grass.

In winter, when the jacks came up and lay immediately under the ice, they could be easily shot. The
pellets cut a round hole through an inch and a half of
ice. The jack now basking in the pond was the more
tempting because we had often tried to wire him in
vain. The difficulty was to get him if hit. While I was
deliberating a crow came flying low down the leaze,
and alighted by the pond. His object, no doubt, was
a mussel. He could not have seen me, and yet no
sooner did he touch the ground than he looked uneasily about, sprang up, and flew straight away, as if
he had smelt danger. Had he stayed he would have
been shot, though it would have spoiled my ambush:
the idea of the crows picking out the eyes of dying
creatures was always peculiarly revolting to me.

If the pond was a haunt of his, it was too near the
young partridges, which were weakly that season. A
kestrel is harmless compared to a crow. Surely the
translators have wrongly rendered Don Quixote's remark that the English did not kill crows, believing that
King Arthur, instead of dying, was by enchantment
turned into one, and so fearing to injure the hero.
Must he not have meant a rook?[1]

Soon afterwards something moved out of the
mound into the meadow a long distance up: it was a
hare. He came slowly along beside the hedge towards
me—now stopping and looking into it as if seeking a

[1] It has since been pointed out to me that the Don
may have meant a raven.

convenient place for a form, having doubtless been disturbed from that he had first chosen. It was some minutes before he came within range: had I been on the ground most likely he would have scented me, the light air going that way; but being in the tree the wind that passed went high over him. For this reason a tree ambush is deadly. It was necessary to get the line of sight clear of twigs which check and divert shot, and to take a steady aim; for I had no second barrel, no dog, and had to descend the tree before running. Some leaves were blackened by the flame: the hare simply fell back, stretched his hind legs, quivered, and lay still. Part of the leaf of a plant was fixed in his teeth; he had just had a nibble.

With this success I was satisfied that day; but the old oak was always a favourite resort, even when nothing particular was in hand. From thence, too, as a base of operations, we made expeditions varying in their object with the season of the year.

Some distance beyond the stunted oak the thick blackthorn hedge was succeeded by a continuous strip of withy-bed bordering the brook. It often occurred to us that by entering these withies it would be possible to reconnoitre one side of Southlands; for the stream skirted the lower grounds: the tall willows would conceal anyone passing through them. So one spring morning the attempt was made.

It was necessary to go on hands and knees through the mowing grass for some yards while passing an open space where the blackthorn cover ended, and then to leap a broad ditch that divided the withy-beds from the meadow. The lissom willow wands parted easily and sprang back to their places behind, leaving scarce a trace. Their slender tops rose overhead; be-

neath, long dead grasses, not yet quite supplanted by
the spring growth, filled the space between. These
rustled a little under foot, but so faint a sound could
scarcely have been audible outside; and had anyone
noticed it it would have been attributed to a hare or
a fox moving: both are fond of lying in withy-beds
when the ground is dry.

The way to walk noiselessly is to feel with the foot
before letting your weight press on it; then the dead
stick or fallen hemlock is discovered and avoided.
A dead stick cracks; the dry hollow hemlock gives a
splintering sound when crushed. These old hemlock
stems were numerous in places, together with 'gicksies',
as the haymakers call a plant that resembles it, but
has a ribbed or fluted instead of a smooth stalk. The
lads use a long 'gicks' cut between the joints as a
tube to blow haws or peggles at the girls. When
thirsty, and no ale is handy, the men search for one
to suck up water with from the brook. It is difficult
to find one free from insects, which seem to be remarkably fond of anything hollow. The haymakers
do not use the hemlock, thinking it would poison the
water; they think, too, that drinking through a tube
is safer when they are in a great heat from the sun than
any other way.

Nor is it so easy to drink from a stream without
this simple aid. If the bank be flat it is wet, and what
looks like the grass of the meadow really grows out
of the water; so that there it is not possible to lie at
full length. If the bank be dry the level of the water
is several inches lower, and in endeavouring to drink
the forehead is immersed; often the water is so much
lower than its banks that it is quite impossible to drink
from it lying. By the edge grasses, water-plantains,

forget-me-nots, frequently fill the space within reach. If you brush these aside it disturbs the bottom, and the mud rises, or a patch of brown 'scum' comes up and floats away. A cup, though gently used, generally draws some insects in with the water, though the liquid itself be pure. Lapping with the hollowed palm requires practice, and, unless the spot be free from weeds and of some little depth, soon disturbs the bottom. But the tube can be inserted in the smallest clear place, and interferes with nothing.

Each of us carried a long hazel rod, and the handle of a 'squailer' projected from Orion's coat-pocket. For making a 'squailer' a teacup was the best mould: the cups then in use in the country were rather larger than those at present in fashion. A ground ash sapling with the bark on, about as thick as the little finger, pliant and tough, formed the shaft, which was about fifteen inches long. This was held upright in the middle of a teacup, while the mould was filled with molten lead. It soon cooled, and left a heavy conical knob on the end of the stick. If rightly thrown it was a deadly missile, and would fly almost as true as a rifle ball. A rabbit or leveret could thus be knocked over; and it was peculiarly adapted for fetching a squirrel out of a tree, because, being so heavy at one end, it rarely lodged on the boughs, as an ordinary stick would, but overbalanced and came down.

From the outlook of the oak some aspen trees could be seen far up in the withy-beds; and it had been agreed that there the first essay of the stream should be made. On arriving at these trees we paused, and began to fix the wires on the hazel rods. The wire for fish must slip very easily, and the thinner it is, if strong enough, the better, because it takes a firmer grip. A single wire will do; but two thin ones are preferable. Thin copper wire is as flexible as thread. Brass wire is not so good; it is stiffer, and too conspicuous in the water.

At the shank end a stout string is attached in the middle of its length. Then the wire is placed against the rod, lying flat upon it for about six inches. The strings are now wound round tightly in opposite directions, binding it to the stick, so that at the top the ends cross and are in position to tie in the slight notch cut for the purpose. A loop that will allow four fingers to enter together is about large enough, though of course it must be varied according to the size of the jack in view. Heavy jacks are not often wired, and scarcely ever in brooks.

For jack the shape of the loop should be circular; for trout it should be oval, and considerably larger in proportion to the apparent bulk of the fish. Jack are straight-grown and do not thicken much in the middle; with trout it is different. The noose should be about six inches from the top of the rod. Orion said he would go twenty yards farther up; I went direct from the centre of the withy-bed to the stream.

The bank rose a little above the level of the withy-bed; it was a broad mound full of ash stoles and willow —the sort that is grown for poles. At that spot the vines of wild hops had killed all the underwood, leaving open spaces between the stoles; the vines were matted so thickly that they hid the ground. This was too exposed a place, so I went back and farther up till I could just hear Orion rustling through the hemlocks. Here the dead grass and some elder bushes afforded shelter, and the water could be approached unseen.

It was about six or eight inches deep; the opposite

shore was bordered for several yards out with flags and rushes. The cattle nibbled their tender tops off, as far as they could reach; farther out they were pushing up straight and pointed. The rib and groove of the flag so closely resemble those of the ancient bayonet that it might be supposed the weapon was modelled from the plant. Indoors among the lumber there was a rusty old bayonet that immediately called forth the comparison: the modern make seem more triangular.

The rushes grew nearer the shore of the meadow—the old ones yellow, the young green: in places this fringe of rush and sedge and flag must have been five or six yards wide, and it extended as far as could be seen up the brook. No doubt the cattle trod in the edge of the firm ground by degrees every year to get at the water, and thus widened the marsh. It was easy to understand now why all the water-fowl, teal and duck, moorhen and snipe, seemed in winter to make in this direction.

The ducks especially exercised all our ingenuity and quite exhausted our patience in the effort to get near them in winter. In the large water-meadows a small flock sometimes remained all day: it was possible to approach near enough by stalking behind the hedges to see the colour of the mallards; but they were always out of gunshot. This place must be full of teal then; as for moorhens, there were signs of them everywhere, and several feeding in the grass. The thought of the sport to be got here when the frosty days came was enough to make one wild.

After a long look across, I began to examine the stream near at hand: the rushes and flags had forced the clear sweet current away from the meadow, so that it ran just under the bank. I was making out the brown sticks at the bottom, when there was a slight splash—caused by Orion about ten yards farther up—and almost at the same instant something shot down the brook towards me. He had doubtless landed a jack, and its fellow rushed away. Under a large dead bough that had fallen across its top in the stream I saw the long slender fish lying a few feet from the bank, motionless save for the gentle curving wave of the tail edges. So faint was that waving curl that it seemed caused rather by the flow of the current than the volition of the fish. The wings of the swallow work the whole of the longest summer day, but the fins of the fish in running water are never still: day and night they move continuously.

By slow degrees I advanced the hazel rod, keeping it at first near to and parallel with the bank, because jack do not like anything that stretches across them; and I imagine other fish have the same dislike to right angles. The straight shadow even seems to arouse suspicion—no boughs are ever straight. Perhaps, if it were possible to angle without a rod, there would be more success, particularly in small streams. But after getting the stick almost out far enough, it became evident that the dead branch would not let me slip the wire into the water in front of the jack in the usual way. So I had to draw it back again as gradually as it had been put forth.

With fish everything must be done gradually and without a jerk. A sudden, jerking movement immediately alarms them. If you walk gently by they remain still, but start or lift the arm quickly and they dart for deep water. The object of withdrawing the rod was to get at and enlarge the loop in order that it might be slipped over his tail, since the head was protected by the bough. It is a more delicate operation to pass the wire up from behind; it has to go farther before the spot that allows a firm grip is reached, and fish are well aware that natural objects such as twigs float down with the current. Anything, therefore, approaching from behind or rubbing upwards is suspicious. As this fish had just been startled, it would not do to let the wire touch him at all.

After enlarging the loop I put the rod slowly forth again, worked the wire up stream, slipped the noose over his tail, and gently got it up to the balance of the fish. Waiting a moment to get the elbow over the end of the rod so as to have a good leverage, I gave a sudden jerk upwards, and felt the weight instantly. But the top of the rod struck the overhanging bough, and there was my fish, hung indeed, but still in the water near the surface. Nor could I throw it on the bank, because of the elder bushes. So I shortened the rod, pulling it in towards me quickly and dragging the jack through the water. The pliant wire had cut into the scales and skin—he might have been safely left suspended over the stream all day; but in the eagerness of the moment I was not satisfied till I had him up on the mound.

We did not see much of Southlands, because the withy-beds were on the lowest ground; but there were six jacks strung on a twisted withy when we got back to the stunted oak and rested there tasting acid sorrel leaves.

CHAPTER IV

THERE is no sweeter time in the woods than just before the nesting begins in earnest. Is it the rising sap that causes a pleasant odour to emanate from every green thing? Idling along the hedgerows towards the woodlands there may perchance be seen small tufts of white rabbit's fur in the grass, torn from herself by the doe to form a warm lining to the hole in which her litter will appear: a 'sign' this that often guides a robber to her nest.

Yonder on the rising ground, towering even in their fall over the low (lately cut) ash plantation, lie the giant limbs of the mighty oaks, thrown just as they felt the quickening heat. The bark has been stripped from the trunk and branches; the sun has turned the exposed surface to a deep buff colour, which contrasts with the fresh green of the underwood around and renders them visible afar.

When the oak first puts forth its buds the woods take a ruddy tint. Gradually the background of green comes to the front, and the oak-apples swell, streaked with rosy stains, whence their semblance to the edible fruit of the orchard. All unconscious of the white or red cross daubed on the rough bark, the tree prepares its glory of leaf, though doomed the while by that sad mark to the axe.

Cutting away the bushes with his billhook, the woodman next swings the cumbrous grub-axe, whose wide edge clears the earth from the larger roots. Then he puts his pipe in his pocket, and settles to the serious

work of the 'great axe', as he calls it. I never could
use this ungainly tool aright: a top-heavy, clumsy,
awkward thing, it rules you instead of you ruling it.
The handle, too, is flat—almost with an edge itself
sometimes—and is quite beyond the grasp of any but
hands of iron. Now, the American axe feels balanced
like a sword; this is because of the peculiar curve of
the handle. To strike you stand with the left foot
slightly forward, and the left hand uppermost; the
'S' curve (it is of course not nearly so crooked as
the letter) of the American axe adjusts itself to the
anatomy of the attitude, so to speak.

The straight English handle does not; it is stiff,
and strains the muscles; but the common 'great axe'
has the advantage that it is also used for splitting logs
and gnarled 'butts'. An American axe is too beautiful
a tool for that rude work. The American was designed
to strike at the trunk of the tree several feet from the
ground, the English axe is always directed to the great
roots at the base.

A dexterous woodman can swing his tool alternately
left hand or right hand uppermost. The difference
looks trifling; but try it, and you will be astonished
at the difficulty. The blows echo and the chips fly,
till the base of the tree, that naturally is much larger,
is reduced to the size of the trunk or less. Now a pause,
while one swarms up to 'line' it—*i.e.* to attach a rope
as high as possible to guide the 'stick' in its fall.

It is commonly said that in climbing it is best to
look up—a maxim that has been used for moral
illustrations; but it is a mistake. In ascending a tree
you should never look higher than the brim of your
hat, unless when quite still and resting on a branch;
temporary blindness would be the penalty in this case,

Particles of decayed bark, the borings of insects in dead wood, dust and fragments of twigs, rush down in little streams and fill the eyes. The quantity of woody powder that adheres to a tree is surprising; every motion dislodges it from a thousand minute crevices. As for firs, in climbing a fir one cannot look up at all— dead sticks, needles, and dust pour down, and the branches are so thick together that the head has to be forced through them. The line fixed, the saw is applied, and by slow degrees the butt cut nearly through. Unless much overbalanced on one side by the limbs, an oak will stand on a still day when almost off.

Some now seize the rope, and alternately pull and slacken, which gives the great tree a tottering movement. One more daring than the rest drives a wedge into the saw-cut as it opens when the tree sways. It sways—it staggers; a loud crack as the fibres part, then with a slow heave over it goes, and, descending, twists upon the base. The vast limbs plough into the sward; the twigs are crushed; the boughs, after striking the earth, rebound and swish upwards. See that you stand clear, for the least branch will thresh you down. The flat surface of the exposed butt is blue with stains from the steel of the saw.

Light taps with a small sharp axe, that cut the rind but no deeper, ring the trunk at intervals. Then the barking irons are inserted; they are rods of iron, forged at the top something like a narrow shallow spoon. The bark from the trunk comes off in huge semi-cylinders almost large enough for a canoe. But that from the branches is best. You may mark how at the base the bark is two inches thick, lessening to a few lines on the topmost boughs. If it sticks a little, hammer it with the iron: it peels with a peculiar sound, and the juicy sap glistens white between. It is this that, drying in the sun, gives the barked tree its colour: in time the wood bleaches paler, and after a winter becomes grey. Inside, the bark is white streaked with brown; presently it will be all brown. While some strip it, others collect the pieces, and with them build toy-like sheds of bark, which is the manner of stacking it.

From the peeled tree there rises a sweet odour of sap: the green mead, the green underwood and hawthorn around, are all lit up with the genial sunbeams. The beautiful wind-anemones are gone, too tender and lovely for so rude an earth; but the wild hyacinths droop their blue bells under the wood, and the cowslips rise in the grass. The nightingale sings without ceasing; the soft 'coo-coo' of the dove sounds hard by; the merry cuckoo calls as he flies from elm to elm; the wood-pigeons rise and smite their wings together over the firs. In the mere below the coots are at play; they chase each other along the surface of the water and indulge in wild evolutions. Everything is happy. As the plough-boys stroll along they pluck the young succulent hawthorn leaves and nibble them.

It is the sweetest time of all for wandering in the wood. The brambles have not yet grown so bushy as to check the passage; the thistles that in autumn will be as tall as the shoulder and thick as a walking-stick are as yet no bar; burrs do not attach themselves at every step, though the broad burdock leaves are spreading wide. In its full development the burdock is almost a shrub rather than a plant, with a woody stem an inch or more in diameter.

Up in the fir trees the nests of the pigeons are sometimes so big that it appears as if they must use the same year after year, adding fresh twigs, else they could hardly attain such bulk. Those in the ash-poles are not nearly so large. In the open drives blue cartridge-cases lie among the grass, the brass part tarnished by the rain, thrown hurriedly aside from the smoking breech last autumn. But the guns are silent in the racks, though the keeper still carries his gun to shoot the vermin, which are extremely busy at this season. Vermin, however, do not quite agree among themselves: weasels and stoats are deadly enemies of mice and rats. Where rats are plentiful there they are sure to come; they will follow a rat into a dwelling-house.

Here the green drive shows traces of the poaching it received from the thick-planted hoofs of the hunt when the leaves were off and the blast of the horn sounded fitfully as the gale carried the sound away. The vixen is now at peace, though perhaps it would scarcely be safe to wander too near the close-shaven mead where the keeper is occupied more and more every day with his pheasant-hatching. And far down on the lonely outlying farms, where even in fox-hunting England the music of the hounds is hardly heard in three years (because no great coverts cause the run to take that way), foul murder is sometimes done on Reynard or his family. A hedge-cutter marks the sleeping-place in the withies where the fox curls up by day; and with his rusty gun, that sometimes slaughters a roaming pheasant, sends the shot through the red side of the slumbering animal. Then, thrust ignobly into a sack, he shoulders the fox and marches round from door to door, tumbling the limp body rudely down on the pitching stones to prove that fowls will now be safe, and to be rewarded with beer and small coin. A dead fox is profit to him for a fortnight. These evil deeds of course are cloaked as far as possible.

Leaving now the wood for the lane that wanders through the meadows, a mower comes sidling up, and, looking mysteriously around with his hand behind under his coat, 'You med have un for sixpence', he says, and produces a partridge into whose body the point of the scythe ran as she sat on her nest in the grass, and whose struggles were ended by a blow from the rubber or whetstone flung at her head. He has got the eggs somewhere hidden under a swathe.

The men that are so expert at finding partridges' eggs to sell to the keepers know well beforehand whereabouts the birds are likely to lay. If a stranger who had made no previous observations went into the fields to find these eggs, with full permission to do so, he would probably wander in vain. The grass is long, and the nest has little to distinguish it from the ground; the old bird will sit so close that one may pass almost over her. Without a right of search in open daylight the difficulty is of course much greater. A man cannot quarter the fields when the crop is high and leave no trail.

Farmers object to the trampling and damage of their property; and a keeper does not like to see a labourer loafing about, because he is not certain that the eggs when found will be conscientiously delivered to him. They may be taken elsewhere, or they may even be broken out of spite if the finder thinks he has a grudge to repay. Now that every field is enclosed, and for the most part well cultivated and looked after, the business of the egg-stealer is considerably diminished.

He cannot roam over the country at his fancy; his egg-finding is nearly restricted to the locality of which he possesses minute knowledge. .

Thus workmen engaged in the towns, but sleeping several miles out in the villages, can keep a register of the slight indications they observe morning after morning as they cross the fields by the footpath to their labour. Early in the spring they notice that the partridges have paired; as time advances they see the pair day after day in the same meadow, and mark the spot. Those who work in the fields, again, have still better opportunities: the bird-keeping lads too have little else to do at that season than watch for nests. In the meadows the labourer as he walks to and fro with the 'bush' passes over every inch of the ground. The 'bush' is a mass of thorn bushes fixed in a frame and drawn by a horse; it acts like a light harrow, and leaves the meadow in strips like the pile of green velvet, stroked in narrow bands, one this way, one that, laying the grass blades in the directions it travels. Solitary work of this kind—for it requires but one man—is very favourable to observation. When the proper time arrives the searcher knows within a little where the nest must be, and has but a small space to beat.

The pheasant being so large a bird, its motions are easy to watch; and the nest is speedily found, because, being in the hedge or under bushes, there is a definite place in which to look, instead of the broad surface of the field. Pheasants will get out of the preserves in the breeding season and wander into the mounds, so that the space the keeper has to range is then enlarged threefold. Both pheasants and partridges are frequently killed on their nests; when the eggs are hard the birds remain to the last moment, and are often knocked over.

Besides poachers, the eggs have to run the chance of being destroyed by carrion crows, and occasionally by rooks. Rooks, though generally cleanly feeders, will at times eat almost anything, from a mussel to a fledgeling bird. Magpies and jays are accused of being equally dangerous enemies of eggs and young birds, and so too are snakes. Weasels, stoats, and rats spare neither egg, parents, nor offspring. Some of the dogs that run wild will devour eggs; and hawks pounce on the brood if they see an opportunity. Owls are said to do the same. The fitchew, the badger, and the hedgehog have a similarly evil reputation; but the first is rare, the second almost exterminated in many districts; the third—the poor hedgehog—is common, and some keepers have a bitter dislike to them. Swine are credited with the same mischief as the worst of vermin at this particular season; but nowadays swine are not allowed to run wild in cultivated districts, except in the autumn when the acorns are falling.

As the nests are on the ground they are peculiarly accessible, and the eggs, being large, are tempting. Perhaps the mowing machine is as destructive as anything; and after all these there is the risk of a wet season and of disease. Let the care exercised be never so great, a certain amount of mortality must occur.

While the young partridges gradually become strong and swift, the nuts are increasing in size, and ripening upon the bough. The very word hazel has a pleasant sound—not a nut-tree hedge existed in the neighbourhood that we did not know and visit. We noted the progress of the bushes from the earliest spring, and the catkins to the perfect nut.

There are threads of brilliant scarlet upon the hazel
in February, though the gloom of winter lingers and
the 'Shuck—a—sheck!' of the fieldfare fleeing before
the snow sounds overhead. On the slender branches
grow green ovals, from whose tips tiny scarlet plumes
rise and curl over.

It often happens that while the tall rods with
speckled bark grow vigorously the stole is hollow and
decaying when the hardy fern flourishes around it.
Before the summer ricks are all carted the nuts are
full of sweet milky matter, and the shell begins to
harden. A hazel bough with a good crook is then
sought by the men that are thinking of the wheat harvest: they trim it for a 'vagging' stick, with which to
pull the straw towards them. True reaping is now
never seen: 'vagging' makes the short stubble that
forces the partridges into the turnips. Maple boughs,
whose bark is so strongly ribbed, are also good for
'vagging' sticks.

Nut tree is used for bonds to tie up faggots, and
split for the shepherds' hurdles. In winter sometimes
a store of nuts and acorns may be seen fallen in a
stream down the side of a bank, scratched out from a
mouse's hole, as they say, by Reynard, who devours
the little provident creature without regard for its wisdom. So that man and wild animals derive pleasure
or use from the hazel in many ways. When the nuts
are ripe the carters' lads do not care to ride sideways
on the broad backs of the horses as they jog homewards along the lane, but are ever in the hedges.

There were plenty in the double-mounds to which
we had access; but the shepherd, who had learned
his craft on the Downs, said that the nuts grew there
in such immense quantities as determined us to see

them. Sitting on the felled ash under the shade of the hawthorn hedge, where the butcher-birds every year used to stick the humble-bees on the thorns, he described the route—a mere waggon track—and the situation of the largest copses.

The waggon track we found crossed the elevated plains close under and between the Downs, following at the foot, as it seemed, for an endless distance the curve of a range. The slope bounded the track on one side: on the other it was enclosed by a low bank covered with dead thorn thickly entangled, which enclosed the cornfields. The space between the hedge and the hill was as far as we could throw one of the bleached flints lying on the sward. It was dotted with hawthorn trees and furze, and full of dry brown grass. A few scattered firs, the remnants of extinct plantations, grew on the slope, and green 'fairy rings' marked it here and there.

These fairy rings have a somewhat different appearance from the dark green semicircles found in the meadows and called by the same name: the latter are often only segments of circles, are found near hedges, and almost always either under a tree or where a tree has been. There were more mushrooms on the side of the hill than we cared to carry. Some eat mushrooms raw—fresh as taken from the ground, with a little salt: to me the taste is then too strong. Of the many ways of cooking them the simplest is the best; that is, on a gridiron over wood embers on the hearth.

Every few minutes a hare started out of the dry grass: he always scampered up the Down and stopped to look at us from the ridge. The hare runs faster up hill than down. By the cornfields there were wire nettings to stop them; but nothing is easier than for

any passer-by who feels an interest in hares and rabbits, and does not like to see them jealously excluded,
to open a gap. Hares were very numerous—tempt-
ingly so. Not far from where the track crossed a lonely
road was a gipsy encampment; that swarthy people
are ever about when anything is going on, and the
reapers were busy in the corn. The dead dry thorns
of the hedge answered very well to boil their pot with.
Their tents, formed by thrusting the ends of long bent
rods like half-hoops into the turf, looked dark like the
canvas of a barge.

These 'gips'—country folk do not say gipsy—were
unknown to us; but we were on terms with some members of a tribe who called at our house several times in
the course of the year to buy willow. The men wore
golden earrings, and bought 'Black Sally', a withy
that has a dark bark, for pegs, and 'bolts' of osier for
basket-making. A bolt is a bundle forty inches in cir-
cumference. Though the women tell fortunes, and
mix the 'dark man' and the 'light man', the 'journey'
and the 'letter' to perfection, till the ladies half believe,
I doubt if they know much of true palmistry. The
magic of the past always had a charm for me. I had
learned to know the lines, from that which winds along
at the base of the thumb-ball and if clear means health
and long life, to that which crosses close to the fingers
and indicates the course of love, and had traced them
on many a delicate palm. So that the 'gips' could tell
me nothing new.

The women are the hardiest in the country; they
simply ignore the weather. Even the hedgers and
ditchers and the sturdiest labourers choose the lee
side of the hedge when they pause to eat their lun-
cheons; but the 'gips' do not trouble to seek such

shelter. Passing over the hills one winter's day, when
the Downs looked all alike, being covered with snow,
I came across a 'gip' family sitting on the ground
in a lane, old and young exposed to the blast. In that
there was nothing remarkable, but I recollect it because the young mother, handsome in the style of her
race, had her neck and brown bust quite bare, and
the white snowflakes drove thickly aslant upon her.
Their complexion looks more dusky in winter, so that
the contrast of the colours made me wish for an artist
to paint it. And he might have put the grey embers of
a fire gone out, and the twisted stem of a hawthorn
bush with red haws above.

A mile beyond the gipsy tents we entered among the
copses: scattered ash plantations, and hazel thickets
with narrow green tracks between. Further in the nut-
tree bushes were more numerous, and we became
separated though within call. Presently a low whistle
like the peewit's (our signal) called me to Orion. On
the border of a thicket, near an open field of swedes,
he had found a hare in a wire. It was a beauty—the
soft fur smooth to stroke, not so much as a shot-hole in
the black-marked ears. Wired or netted hares and
rabbits are much preferred by the dealers to those that
have been shot—and so, too, netted partridges—because they look so clean and tempt the purchaser. The
blacksmith Ikey, who bought our rabbits, used to sew
up the shot wounds when they were much knocked
about, and trimmed up the shattered ones in the
cleverest way.

To pull up the plug and take wire and hare too
was the first impulse; yet we hesitated. Why did the
man who set the snare let his game lie till that hour of
the day? He should have visited it long before: it had

a suspicious look altogether. It would also have been nearly impossible to carry the hare so many miles by daylight and past villages: even with the largest pockets it would have been doubtful, for the hare had stiffened as he lay stretched out. So, carefully replacing him just as we found him, we left the spot and re-entered the copse.

The shepherd certainly was right; the quantity of nuts was immense: the best and largest bunches grew at the edge of the thickets, perhaps because they received more air and light than the bushes within that were surrounded by boughs. It thus happened that we were in the green pathway when someone suddenly spoke from behind, and, turning, there was a man in a velveteen jacket who had just stepped out of the bushes. The keeper was pleasant enough and readily allowed us to handle his gun—a very good weapon, though a little thin at the muzzle—for a man likes to see his gun admired. He said there were finer nuts in a valley he pointed out, and then carefully instructed us how to get back into the waggon track without returning by the same path. An old barn was the landmark; and, with a request from him not to break the bushes, he left us.

Down in the wooded vale we paused. The whole thing was now clear: the hare in the wire was a trap laid for the 'gips', whose camp was below. The keeper had been waiting about doubtless where he could command the various tracks up the hill, had seen us come that way, and did not wish us to return in the same direction; because if the 'gip' saw anyone at all he would not approach his snare. Whether the hare had actually been caught by the wire, or had been put in by the keeper, it was not easy to tell.

We wandered on in the valley wood, going from bush to bush, little heeding whither we went. There are no woods so silent as the nut-tree; there is scarce a sound in them at that time except the occasional rustle of a rabbit, and the 'thump, thump' they sometimes make underground in their buries after a sudden fright. So that the keen plaintive whistle of a kingfisher was almost startling. But we soon found the stream in the hollow. Broader than a brook and yet not quite a river, it flowed swift and clear, so that every flint at the bottom was visible. The nut-tree bushes came down to the edge: the ground was too firm for much rush or sedge; the streams that come out of the chalk are not so thickly fringed with vegetation as others.

Some little way along there was a rounded sarsen boulder not far from shore, whose brown top was so nearly on a level with the surface that at one moment the water just covered it, and the next left it exposed. By it we spied a trout; but the hill above gave 'Velvet' the command of the hollow; and it was too risky even to think of. After that the nuts were tame; there was nothing left but to turn homewards. As for trout-fishing, there is nothing so easy. Take the top joint off the rod, and put the wire on the second, which is stronger, fill the basket, and replace the fly. There were fellows who used to paddle in canoes up a certain river (not this little stream), pick out the largest trout, and shoot them with pistols, under pretence of practising at water-rats.

CHAPTER V

In a hedge that joined a wood, and about a hundred yards from it, there was a pleasant hiding-place beside a pollard ash. The bank was hollow with rabbit-buries: the summer heat had hardened the clay of the mound and caused it to crack and crumble wherever their excavations left a precipitous edge. Some way up the trunk of the tree an immense flat fungus projected, roughly resembling the protruding lip of a savage enlarged by the insertion of a piece of wood. It formed a black ledge standing out seven or eight inches, two or three inches thick, and extending for a foot or more round the bark. The pollard, indeed, was dead inside, and near the ground the black touchwood showed. Ash timber must become rarer year by year; for, being so useful, it is constantly cut down, while few new saplings are planted or encouraged to become trees.

In front a tangled mass of bramble arched over the dry ditch; it was possible to see some distance down the bank, for nothing grew on the top itself, the bushes all rising from either side—a peculiarity of clay mounds. This narrow space was a favourite promenade of the rabbits; they usually came out there for a few minutes first, looking about before venturing forth into the meadows. Except a little moss, scarcely any vegetation other than underwood clothed the bare hard soil of the mound; and for this reason every tiny aperture that suited their purpose was occupied by wasps.

They much prefer a clear space about the entrance to their nests, affording an unencumbered passage: there were two nests within a few yards of the ash. Though so generally dreaded, wasps are really inoffensive insects, never attacking unless previously buffeted. You may sit close to a wasps' nest for hours, and, if you keep still, receive no injury. Humble-bees, too, congregate in special localities: along one hedge half a dozen nests may be found, while other fields are searched for them in vain.

The best time to enter such a hiding-place is a little before the sun sinks; for as his beams turn red all the creatures that rest during the day begin to stir. Then the hares start down from the uplands and appear on the short stubble, where the level rays throw exaggerated shadows behind them. When six or eight hares are thus seen near the centre of a single field they and their shadows seem to take possession of and occupy it.

Pheasants, though they retire to roost on the trees, often before rising come forth into the meadows adjacent to the coverts. The sward in front of the pollard ash sloped upwards gradually to the foot of a low hill planted with firs, and just outside these about half a dozen pheasants regularly appeared in the early evening. As the sun sank below the hill, and the shadow of the great beeches some distance away began to extend into the mead, they went back one by one into the firs. There they were nearly safe, for no trees give so much difficulty to the poacher. It is not easy even to shoot anything inside a fir plantation at night: as for the noose, it is almost impossible to use it. The lowest pheasant is taken first, and then the next above, like fowls perched on the rungs of a ladder; and, indeed, it is not unlikely that those who excel in this kind of work base their operations upon previous experiences in the hen roost.

The wood pigeons begin to come home, and the wood is filled with their hollow notes: now here, now yonder, for as one ceases another takes it up. They cannot settle for some time: each as he arrives perches awhile, and then rises and tries a fresh place, so that there is a constant clattering. The green woodpecker approaches at a rapid pace—now opening, now closing his wings, and seeming to throw himself forward rather than to fly. He rushes at the trees in the hedge as though he could pierce the thick branches like a bullet. Other birds rise over or pass at the side: he goes through, arrow-like, avoiding the boughs. Instead of at once entering the wood, he stays awhile on the sward of the mead in the open.

As the pheasants generally feed in a straight line along the ground, so the lesser pied woodpecker travels across the fields from tree to tree, rarely staying on more than one branch in each, but, after examining it, leaves all that may be on other boughs and seeks another ahead. He rises round and round the dead branch in the elm, tapping it with blows that succeed each other with marvellous rapidity. He taps for the purpose of sounding the wood to see if it be hollow or bored by grubs, and to startle the insects and make them run out for his convenience. He will ascend dead branches barely half an inch thick that vibrate as he springs from them, and proceeds down the hedge towards the wood. The 'snop-top' sounds in every elm, and grows fainter as he recedes. The sound is often heard, but in the thick foliage of summer the bird escapes unseen, unless you are sitting almost under the tree when he arrives in it.

Then the rooks come drifting slowly to the beeches: they are uncertain in their hour at this season—some, indeed, scarce care to return at all; and even when quite dusk and the faint stars of summer rather show themselves than shine, twos and threes come occasionally through the gloom. A pair of doves pass swiftly, flying for the lower wood, where the ashpoles grow. The grasshoppers sing in the grass, and will continue till the dew descends. As the little bats flutter swiftly to and fro just without the hedge, the faint sound of their wings is audible as they turn: their membranes are not so silent as feathers, and they agitate them with extreme velocity. Beetles go by with a loud hum, rising from those isolated bunches of grass that may be seen in every field; for the cows will not eat the rank green blades that grow over and hide dried dung.

A large white spot, ill-defined and shapeless in the distance and the dimness, glides along the edge of the wood, then across in front before the fir plantation, next down the hedge to the left, and presently passes within two yards, going towards the wood again along this mound. It is a white owl: he flies about five feet from the ground and absolutely without a sound. So when you are walking at night it is quite startling to have one come overhead, approaching from behind and suddenly appearing. This owl is almost fearless; unless purposely alarmed he will scarcely notice you, and not at all if you are still.

As he reaches the wood he leaves the hedge, having gone all round the field, and crosses to a small detached circular fir plantation in the centre. There he goes out of sight a minute or two; but presently appears skirting the low shed and rickyard yonder, and is finally lost behind the hedges. This round he will go every evening, and almost exactly at the same time—that is, in reference to the sun, which is the clock of nature.

Step never so quietly out from the mound, the small birds that unnoticed have come to roost in the bushes will hear it and fly off in alarm. The rabbits that are near the hedge rush in; those that are far from home crouch in the furrows and the bunches. Crossing the open field, they suddenly start as it seems from under your feet—one white tail goes dapping up and down this way, another jerks over the 'lands' that way. The moonbeams now glisten on the double-barrel; and a bright sparkle glitters here and there as a dewdrop catches a ray.

Upon the grass a faint halo appears; it is a narrow band of light encircling the path, an oval ring—perhaps rather horseshoe shape than oval. It glides in front, keeping ever at the same distance as you walk, as if there the eye was focussed. This is only seen when the grass is wet with dew, and better in short grass than long. Where it shines the grass looks a paler green. Passing gently along a hedge thickly timbered with oak and elm, a hawk may perhaps start forth: hawks sometimes linger by the hedges till late, but it is not often that you can shoot one at roost except in spring. Then they invariably return to roost in the nest tree, and are watched there and so shot, a gunner approaching on each side of the hedge. In the lane dark objects—rabbits—hasten away, and presently the footpath crosses the still motionless brook near where it flows into the mere.

The low brick parapet of the bridge is overgrown with mosses; great hedges grow each side, and the willows, long uncut, almost meet in the centre. In one hedge an opening leads to a drinking-place for cattle: peering noiselessly over the parapet between the boughs, the coots and moorhens may be seen there feeding by the shore. They have come up from the mere as the ducks and teal do in the winter. The broader waters can scarcely be netted without a boat, but the brook here is the very place for a moonlight haul. The net is stretched first across the widest spot nearest to the pool, that no fish may escape. They swim up here in the daytime in shoals, perch especially; but the night poachers are often disappointed, for the fish seem to retire to deeper waters as the darkness comes on. A black mass of mud-coated sticks, rotten twigs, and thorn bushes, entangled in the meshes, is often the only result of much toil.

Once now and then, as when a preserved pond is netted, a tremendous take occurs; but nets are rather gone by, being so unwieldy and requiring several men to manage effectually. If they are not hung out to dry properly after being used, they soon rot. Now, a large net stretched along railings or a hedge is rather a conspicuous object, and brings suspicion on the owner. It is also so heavy after use that until wrung, which takes time, a strong man can barely carry it; and if a sudden alarm comes it must be abandoned.

It is pleasant to rest awhile on the parapet in the shadow of the bushes. The low thud-thud of sculls in the rowlocks of a distant punt travels up the water. By-and-by a hare comes along, enters on the bridge, and almost reaches the gate in the middle before he spies anything suspicious. Such a spot, and, indeed, any gateway, used to be a favourite place to set a net, and then drive the hares towards it with a cur dog that ran silent. Bold must be the man that would set a net in a footpath now, with almost every field preserved by owner or tenant. With a bound the hare hies back and across the meadow: the gun comes to the shoulder as swiftly.

On the grass lit by the moon the hare looked quite distinct, but the moment the gaze is concentrated up the barrel he becomes a dim object with no defined outline. In shooting on the ground by twilight or in the moonbeams, waste no time in endeavouring to aim, but think of the hare's ears—say a couple of feet in front of his tail—and the moment the gun feels steady pull the trigger. The flash and report come together; there is a dull indescribable sound ahead, as some of the shot strikes home in fur and some drills into the turf, and then a rustling in the grass. The moorhens dive, and the coots scuttle down the brook towards the mere at the flash. While yet the sulphurous smoke lingers, slow to disperse, over the cool dewy sward, there comes back an echo from the wood behind, then another from the mere, then another and another beyond.

The distant sculls have ceased to work in the rowlocks—those in the punt are listening to the echoes: most likely they have been fishing for tench in the deep holes under the black shadow of the aspens. (Tench feed in the dark: if you wish to take a big one wait till it is necessary to fix a piece of white paper on the float.) Now put the empty cartridge in your pocket instead of throwing it aside; pull the hare's neck across your knee, and hurry off. But you may safely stay to harle him; for those very echoes that have been heard a mile round about are the best safeguard: not one man in a thousand could tell the true direction whence the sound of the explosion originated.

The pleasure of wandering in a wood was so great that it could never be resisted, and did not solely arise from the instinct of shooting. Many expeditions were made without a gun, or any implement of destruction, simply to enjoy the trees and thickets. There was one large wood very carefully preserved, and so situate in an open country as not to be easily entered. But a little observation showed that the keeper had a 'habit'. He used to come out across the wheatfields to a small wayside 'public', and his route passed by a lonely barn and rickyard. One warm summer day I saw him come as usual to the 'public', and while he was there quietly slipped as far as the barn and hid in it.

In July such a rickyard is very hot: heat radiates from every straw. The ground itself is dry and hard, each crevice choked with particles of white chaff; so that even the couch can hardly grow except close under the low hedge where the pink flower of the pimpernel opens to the sky. White stone staddles— short conical pillars with broad capitals—stand awaiting the load of sheaves that will shortly press on them. Every now and then a rustling in the heaps of straw indicates the presence of mice. From straw and stone and bare earth heat seems to rise up. The glare of the sunlight pours from above. The black pitched wooden walls of the barn and sheds prevent the circulation of air. There are no trees for shadow—nothing but a few bushes, which are crowded at intervals of a few minutes with sparrows rushing with a whirr of wings up from the standing corn.

But the high pitched roof of the barn and of the lesser sheds has a beauty of its own—the minute vegetation that has covered the tiles having changed the original dull red to an orange hue. From ridge to eaves, from end to end, it is a wide expanse of colour, only varying so much in shade as to save it from monotony. It stands out glowing, distinct against the deep blue of the sky. The 'cheep' of fledgeling sparrows comes from the crevices above; but swallows do not frequent solitary buildings so much as those by dwelling-houses, being especially fond of cattle-sheds where cows are milked.

The proximity of animals apparently attracts them: perhaps in the more exposed places there may be dangers from birds of prey. As for the sparrows, they are innumerable. Some are marked with white patches —a few so much so as to make quite a show when they fly. One handsome cock bird has a white ring half round his neck, and his wings are a beautiful partridge-brown. He looks larger than the common sort; and there are several more here that likewise appear to exceed in size, and to have the same peculiar brown.

After a while there came the sound of footsteps and a low but cheerful whistle. The keeper having slaked a thirst very natural on such a sultry day returned, and re-entered the wood. I had decided that it would be the best plan to follow in his rear, because then there would be little chance of crossing his course haphazard, and the dogs would not sniff any strange footsteps, since the footsteps would not be there till they had gone by. To hide from the eyes of a man is comparatively easy; but a dog will detect an unwonted presence in the thickest bush, and run in and set up a yelping, especially if it is a puppy.

It was not more than forty yards from the barn to the wood: there was no mound or hedge, but a narrow, deep, and dry watercourse, a surface drain, ran across. Stooping a little and taking off my hat, I walked in this, so that the wheat each side rose above me and gave a perfect shelter. This precaution was necessary, because on the right there rose a steep Down, from whose summit the level wheat-fields could be easily surveyed. So near was it that I could distinguish the tracks of the hares worn in the short grass. But if you take off your hat no one can distinguish you in a wheat-field, more particularly if your hair is light: nor even in a hedge.

Where the drain or furrow entered the wood was a wire-netting firmly fixed, and over it tall pitched palings, sharp at the top. The wood was enclosed with a thick hawthorn hedge that looked impassable; but the keeper's footsteps, treading down the hedge-parsley and brushing aside the 'gicks', guided me behind a bush where was a very convenient gap. These signs and the smooth-worn bark of an ash against which it was needful to push proved that this quiet path was used somewhat frequently.

Inside the wood the grass and the bluebell leaves —the bloom past and ripening to seed—so hung over the trail that it was difficult to follow. It wound about the ash stoles in the most circuitous manner—now to avoid the thistles, now a bramble thicket, or a hollow filled with nettles. Then the ash poles were clothed with the glory of the woodbine—one mass of white and yellow wax-like flowers to a height of eight or nine feet, and forming a curtain of bloom from branch to branch.

After awhile I became aware that the trail was approaching the hill. At the foot it branched; and the question arose whether to follow the fork that zigzagged up among the thickets or that which seemed to plunge into the recesses beneath. I had never been in this wood before—the time was selected because it was probable that the keeper would be extremely occupied with his pheasant chicks. Though the earth was so hard in the exposed rick-yard, here the clayey ground was still moist under the shadow of the leaves. Examining the path more closely, I easily distinguished the impression of the keeper's boot: the iron toe-plate had left an almost perfect impression, and there were the deep grooves formed by the claws of his dog as it had scrambled up the declivity and the pad slipped on the clay.

As he had taken the upward path, no doubt it led direct to the pheasants, which were sure to be on the hill itself, or a dry and healthy slope. I therefore took the other trail, since I must otherwise have overtaken him; for he would stay long among his chicks: just as an old-fashioned farmer lingers at a gate, gazing on his sheep. Advancing along the lower path, after some fifteen minutes it turned sharply to the right, and I stood under the precipitous cliff-like edge of the hill in a narrow coombe. The earth at the top hung over the verge, and beech trees stood as it seemed in the act to topple, their exposed roots twisting to and fro before they re-entered the face of the precipice. Large masses of chalky rubble had actually fallen, and others were all but detached. The coombe of course could be overlooked from thence; but a moment's reflection convinced me there was no risk, for who would dare to go near enough to the edge to look down?

The coombe was full of fir trees; and by them stood a long narrow shed—the roof ruinous, but the plank walls intact. It had originally been erected in a field, since planted for covers. This long shed, a greenish grey from age and mouldering wood, became a place of much interest. Along the back there were three rows of weasels and stoats nailed through the head or neck to the planks. There had been a hundred in each row—about three hundred altogether. The lapse of time had entirely dissipated the substance of many on the upper row; nothing remained but the grim and rusty nail. Further along there hung small strips without shape. Beyond these the nails supported something that had a rough outline still of the animal. In the second row the dried and shrivelled creatures were closely wrapped in nature's mummy-cloth of green; in the third, some of those last exposed still retained a dull brown colour. None were recent. Above, under the eaves, the spiders' webs had thickly gathered; beneath, the nettles flourished.

But the end of the shed was the place where the more distinguished offenders were gibbeted. A footpath, well worn and evidently much used, went by this end, and, as I afterwards ascertained, communicated with the mansion above and the keeper's cottage some distance below. Every passenger between must pass the gallows where the show of more nobler traitors gave proof of the keeper's loyal activity. Four shorter rows rose in tiers. To the nails at the top strong beaks and black feathers adhered, much bedraggled and ruffled by weather. These crows had long been dead: the keeper when he shot a crow did not trouble to have it carried home, unless a nail was conspicuously vacant. The ignoble bird was left where he fell.

On the next row the black and white of magpies and the blue of jays alternated. Many of the magpies had been despoiled of their tails, and some of their wings, the feathers being saleable. The jays were more numerous, and untouched; they were slain in such numbers that the market for their plumage was glutted. Though the bodies were shrunken, the feathers were in fair condition. Magpies' nests are so large that in winter, when the leaves are off the trees, they cannot but be seen, and, the spot being marked, in the summer old and young are easily destroyed. Hawks filled the third row. The kestrels were the most numerous, but there were many sparrow-hawks. These made a great show, and were stuck so closely that a feather could hardly be thrust between them. In the midst, quite smothered under their larger wings, were the remains of a smaller bird—probably a merlin. But the last and lowest row, that was also nearest, or on a level with the face of a person looking at the gallows, was the most striking.

This grand tier was crowded with owls—not arranged in any order, but haphazard, causing a fine mixture of colour. Clearly this gallery was constantly renewed. The white owl gave the prevalent tint, side by side with the brown wood owls, and scattered among the rest, a few long horned owls—a mingling of white, yellowish brown, and tawny feathers. Though numerous here, yet trap and gun have so reduced the wood owls that you may listen half the night by a cover and never hear the 'Who-hoo' that seems to demand your name.

The barn owls are more liable to be shot, because they are more conspicuous; but, on the other hand, as they often breed and reside away from covers, they seem to escape. For months past one of these has sailed by my window every evening uttering a hissing 'skir-r-r'. Here, some were nailed with their backs to the wall, that they might not hide their guilty faces.

The delicate texture of the owl's feathers is very remarkable: these birds remind me of a huge moth. The owls were more showy than the hawks, though it is commonly said that without sunlight there is no colour—as in the case of plants grown in darkness. Yet the hawks are day birds, while the owls fly by night. There came the sound of footsteps; and I retreated, casting one glance backward at the black and white, the blue and brown colours that streaked the wall, while the dull green weasels were in perpetual shadow. By night the bats would flit round and about that gloomy place. It would not do to return by the same path, lest another keeper might be coming up it; so I stepped into the wood itself.

To those who walk only in the roads, hawks and owls seem almost rare. But a wood is a place to which they all flock; and any wanderer from the north or west naturally tends thither. This wood is of large extent; but even to the smaller plantations of the Downs it is wonderful what a number come in the course of a year. Besides the shed just visited there would be certain to be another more or less ornamented near the keeper's cottage, and probably others scattered about, where the commoner vermin could be nailed without the trouble of carrying them far away. Only the owls and hawks, magpies, and such more striking evidences of slaughter were collected here, and almost daily renewed.

To get into the wood was much easier than to get out, on account of the thick hedge, palings, and high sharp-sparred gates; but I found a dry ditch where it was possible to creep under the bushes into a meadow where was a footpath.

CHAPTER VI

LURCHER-LAND: 'THE PARK'

THE time of the apple-bloom is the most delicious season in Sarsen village. It is scarcely possible to obtain a view of the place, although it is built on the last slope of the Downs, because just where the ground drops and the eye expects an open space plantations of fir and the tops of tall poplars and elms intercept the glance. In ascending from the level meadows of the vale thick double mounds, heavily timbered with elm, hide the houses until you are actually in their midst.

Those only know a country who are acquainted with its footpaths. By the roads, indeed, the outside may be seen; but the footpaths go through the heart of the land. There are routes by which mile after mile may be travelled without leaving the sward. So you may pass from village to village; now crossing green meads, now cornfields, over brooks, past woods, through farmyard and rick 'bar-ken'. But such tracks are not mapped, and a stranger misses them altogether unless under the guidance of an old inhabitant.

At Sarsen the dusty road enters the more modern part of the village at once, where the broad signs hang from the taverns at the crossways and where the loafers steadily gaze at the new comer. The Lower Path, after stile and hedge and elm, and grass that glows with golden buttercups, quietly leaves the side of the double mounds and goes straight through the orchards. There are fewer flowers under the trees, and the grass grows so long and rank that it has already fallen aslant of its own weight. It is choked, too, by masses of clogweed, that springs up profusely over the site of old foundations; so that here ancient masonry may be hidden under the earth. Indeed, these orchards are a survival from the days when the monks laboured in vineyard and garden, and mayhap even of earlier times. When once a locality has got into the habit of growing a certain crop it continues to produce it for century after century; and thus there are villages famous for apple or pear or cherry, while the district at large is not at all given to such culture.

The trunks of the trees succeed each other in endless ranks, like columns that support the most beautiful roof of pink and white. Here the bloom is rosy, there white prevails: the young green is hidden under the petals that are far more numerous than leaves, or even than leaves will be. Though the path really is in shadow as the branches shut out the sun, yet it seems brighter here than in the open, as if the place were illuminated by a million tiny lamps shedding the softest lustre. The light is reflected and apparently increased by the countless flowers overhead.

The forest of bloom extends acre after acre, and only ceases where hedges divide, to commence again beyond the boundary. A wicket gate, all green with a film of vegetation over the decaying wood, opens under the very eaves of a cottage, and the path goes by the door—across a narrow meadow where deep and broad trenches, green now, show where ancient stews or fishponds existed, and then through a farmyard into a lane. Tall poplars rise on either hand, but there seem to be no houses; they stand in fact a field's breadth back from the lane, and are approached by footpaths that every few yards necessitate a stile in the hedge.

When a low thatched farmhouse does abut upon the way, the blank white wall of the rear part faces the road, and the front door opens on precisely the other side. Hard by is a row of beehives. Though the modern hives are at once more economical and humane, they have not the old associations that cling about the straw domes topped with broken earthenware to shoot off the heavy downfall of a thunderstorm.

Everywhere the apple-bloom; the hum of bees; children sitting on the green beside the road, their laps full of flowers; the song of finches; and the low murmur of water that glides over flint and stone so shadowed by plants and grasses that the sunbeams cannot reach and glisten on it. Thus the straggling flower-strewn village stretches along beneath the hill and rises up the slope, and the swallows wheel and twitter over the gables where are their hereditary nesting-places. The lane ends on a broad dusty road, and, opposite, a quiet thatched house of the larger sort stands, endways to the street, with an open pitching before the windows. There, too, the swallows' nests are crowded under the eaves, flowers are trained against the wall, and in the garden stand the same beautiful apple trees. But within, the lower part of the windows—that have recess seats—are guarded by horizontal rods of iron, polished by the backs of many men. It is an inn, and the rods are to save the panes from the impact of an excited toper's arm.

The talk to-day, as the brown brandy, which the paler cognac has not yet superseded, is consumed and the fumes of coarse tobacco and the smell of spilt beer and the faint sickly odour of evaporating spirits overpower the flowers, is of horses. The stable lads from the training stables far up on the Downs drop in or call at the door without dismounting. Once or twice in the day a tout calls and takes his 'grub', and scribbles a report in the little back parlour. Sporting papers, beer-stained and thumb-marked, lie on the tables; framed portraits of racers hang on the walls. Burly men, who certainly cannot ride a race but who have horse in every feature, puff cigars and chat in jerky monosyllables that to an outsider are perfectly incomprehensible. But the glib way in which heavy sums of money are spoken of conveys the impression that they dabble in enormous wealth.

There are dogs under the tables and chairs; dogs in the window-seat; dogs panting on the stone flags of the passage, after a sharp trot behind a trap, choosing the coolest spot to loll their red tongues out; dogs outside in the road; dogs standing on hind legs, and painfully lapping the water in the horse-trough; and there is a yapping of puppies in the distance. The cushions of the sofa are strewn with dogs' hairs, and once now and then a dog leisurely hops up the staircase.

Customers are served by the landlady, a decent body enough in her way: her son, the man of the house, is up in the 'orchut' at the rear, feeding his dogs. Where the 'orchut' ends in a paddock stands a small shed: in places the thatch on the roof has fallen through in the course of years and revealed the bare rafters. The bottom part of the door has decayed, and the long nose of a greyhound is thrust out sniffing through a hole. Dickon, the said son, is delighted to undo the padlock for a visitor who is 'square'. In an instant the long hounds leap up, half a dozen at a time, and I stagger backwards, forced by the sheer vigour of their caresses against the doorpost. Dickon cannot quell the uproarious pack: he kicks the door open, and away they scamper round and round the paddock at headlong speed.

What a joy it is to them to stretch their limbs! I forget the squalor of the kennel in watching their happy gambols. I cannot drink more than one tumbler of brown brandy and water; but Dickon overlooks that weakness, feeling that I admire his greyhounds. It is arranged that I am to see them work in the autumn.

The months pass, and in his trap with the famous trotter in the shafts we roll up the village street. Applebloom and golden fruit too are gone, and the houses show more now among the bare trees; but as the rim of the ruddy November sun comes forth from the edge of a cloud there appears a buff tint everywhere in the background. When elm and ash are bare the oaks retain their leaves, and these are illumined by the autumn beams. Overtopped by tall elms and hidden by the orchards, the oaks were hardly seen in summer; now they are found to be numerous and give the prevailing hue to the place.

Dickon taps the dashboard as the mare at last tops the hill, and away she speeds along the level plateau for the Downs. Two greyhounds are with us; two more have gone on under charge of a boy. Skirting the hills a mile or two, we presently leave the road and drive over the turf: there is no track, but Dickon knows his way. The rendezvous is a small fir plantation, the young trees in which are but shoulder-high. Below is a plain entirely surrounded by the hills, and partly green with root crops: more than one flock of sheep is down there, and two teams ploughing the stubble. Neither the ploughmen nor the shepherds take the least heed of us, except to watch for the sport.

The spare couple are fastened in the trap; the boy jumps up and takes the reins. Dickon puts the slip on the couple that are to run first, and we begin to range.

Just at the foot of the hill the grass is tall and grey; there, too, are the dead dry stalks of many plants that cultivation has driven from the ploughed fields and that find a refuge at the edge. A hare starts from the very verge and makes up the Downs. Dickon slips the hounds, and a faint halloo comes from the shepherds and the ploughmen. It is a beautiful sight to see the hounds bound over the sward; the sinewy back bends like a bow, but a bow that, instead of an arrow, shoots itself; the deep chests drink the air. Is there any moment so joyful in life as the second when the chase begins? As we gaze, before we even step forward, the hare is over the ridge and out of sight. Then we race and tear up the slope; then the boy in the trap flaps the reins and away goes the mare out of sight too.

Dickon is long and rawboned, a powerful fellow, strong of limb, and twice my build; but he sips too often at the brown brandy, and after the first burst I can head him. But he knows the hills and the route the hare will take, so that I have but to keep pace. In five minutes as we cross a ridge we see the chase again; the hare is circling back—she passes under us not fifty yards away, as we stand panting on the hill. The youngest hound gains, and runs right over her; she doubles, the older hound picks up the running. By a furze-bush she doubles again; but the young one turns her—the next moment she is in the jaws of the old dog.

Again and again the hounds are slipped, now one

couple, now the other: we pant, and can scarcely speak with running, but the wild excitement of the hour and the sweet pure air of the Downs supply fresh strength. The little lad brings the mare anywhere: through the furze, among the flint-pits, jolting over the ruts, she rattles along with sure alacrity. There are five hares in the sack under the straw when at last we get up and slowly drive down to the highway, reaching it some two miles from where we left it. Dickon sends the dogs home by the boy on foot; we drive round and return to the village by a different route, entering it from the opposite direction.

The reason of these things is that Sarsen has no great landlord. There are fifty small proprietors, and not a single resident magistrate. Besides the small farmers, there are scores of cottage owners, every one of whom is perfectly independent. Nobody cares for anybody. It is a republic without even the semblance of a Government. It is liberty, equality, and swearing. As it is just within the limit of a borough, almost all the cottagers have votes, and are not to be trifled with. The proximity of horse-racing establishments adds to the general atmosphere of dissipation. Betting, card-playing, ferret-breeding and dog-fancying, poaching and politics, are the occupations of the populace. A little illicit badger-baiting is varied by a little vicar-baiting; the mass of the inhabitants are the reddest of Reds. Que voulez-vous?

The edges of some large estates come up near, but the owners would hardly like to institute a persecution of these turbulent folk. If they did where would be their influence at the next election? If a landlord makes himself unpopular his own personal value depreciates. He is a nonentity in the committee-room, and his help rather deprecated by the party than desired. The Sarsen fellows are not such fools as to break pheasant preserves in the vale; as they are resident, that would not answer. They keep outside the *sanctum sanctorum* of the pheasant coverts. But with ferret, dog, and gun, and now and then a partridge net along the edge of the standing barley they excel. So, too, with the wire; and the broad open Downs are their happy hunting grounds, especially in misty weather.

This is the village of the apple-bloom, the loveliest spot imaginable. After all, they are not such desperately bad fellows if you deduct their sins against the game laws. They are a jovial lot, and free with their money; they stand by one another—a great virtue in these cold-blooded days. If one gets in trouble with the law the rest subscribe the fine. They are full of knowledge of a certain sort, and you may learn anything, from the best way to hang a dog upwards.

When we reach the inn, and Dickon calls for the brown brandy, there in the bar sits a gamekeeper, whose rubicund countenance beams with good humour. He is never called upon to pay his score. Good fellow! in addition he is popular, and everyone asks him to drink: besides which, a tip for a race now and then makes this world wear a smiling aspect to him.

Dickon's 'unconscious education'—absorbed rather than learnt in boyhood—had not been acquired under conditions likely to lead him to admire scenery. But rough as he was, he was a good-natured fellow, and it was through him that I became acquainted with a very beautiful place.

The footpath to The Park went for about half a mile under the shadow of elm trees, and in spring time there was a continual noise of young rooks in the nests above.

Occasionally dead twigs, either dislodged from the nests or broken off by the motions of the old birds, came rustling down. One or two nests that had been blown out strewed the sward with half a bushel of dead sticks. After the rookery the path passed a lonely dairy, where the polished brazen vessels in the skilling glittered like gold in the sunshine. Farther on came wide open meadows with numerous oak-trees scattered in the midst—the outposts of the great wood at hand. The elms were flourishing and vigorous; but these detached oaks were decaying, and some dead, their hoar antiquity contrasting with the green grass and flowers of the mead.

The mansion was hidden by elm and chestnut, pines and sombre cedars. From the edge of the lawn the steep slope of the down rose, planted with all manner of shrubs, the walks through which were inches deep in dead leaves, needles, and fir-cones. Long neglect had permitted these to accumulate, and the yew hedges had almost grown together and covered the walk they bordered.

The woods and preserves extended along the downs, between the hills and the meadows beneath. There was one path through these woods that led into a narrow steep-sided coombe, one side of which was planted with firs. On the other was a little grass, but so thin as scarcely to cover the chalk. This side jutted out from the general line of the hills, and formed a bold bluff, whose white precipitous cliff was a landmark for many miles. In climbing the coombe it was sometimes necessary to grasp the bunches of grass; for it would have been impossible to recover from a slip till, bruised and shaken, you rolled to the bottom, and perhaps into the little streamlet flowing through the hollow.

The summit was of small extent, but the view beautiful. A low fence of withy had long since decayed, nothing but a few rotten stakes remaining at the very verge of the precipice. Steep as it was, there were some ledges that the rabbits frequented, making their homes in mid-air. Further along, the slope, a little less perpendicular, was covered with nut-tree bushes, where you could scramble down by holding to the boughs. There was a tradition of a foxhunter, in the excitement of the chase, forcing his horse to descend through these bushes and actually reaching the level meadows below in safety.

Impossible as it seemed, yet when the hounds were in full cry beneath it was easy to understand that in the eagerness of the moment a horseman at the top might feel tempted to join the stirring scene at any risk: for the fox frequently ran just below, making along the line of coverts; and from that narrow perch on the cliff the whole field came into sight at once. There was Reynard slipping ahead, and two or more fields behind the foremost of the pack, while the rest, rushing after, made the hills resound with their chiding. The leaders taking the hedges, the main squadron splashing through a marshy place, the outsiders straining to come up, and the last man behind, who rode harder than any—all could be seen at the same time.

It was a lovely spot, too, for dreaming on a summer's day, reclining on the turf, with the harebells swinging in the faint breeze. The extreme solitude was its charm: no lanes or tracks other than those purely pastoral came near. There were woods on either hand; in the fir plantations the jays chattered unceasingly. The broad landscape stretched out to the illimitable distance, till the power of the eye failed and could trace it no farther. But if the gaze was lifted it looked into blue space—the azure heaven not only overhead, but, as it seemed, all around.

Dickon was always to and fro the mansion here, and took me with him. His object was ostensibly business: now it was a horse to buy, now a fat bullock or sheep; now it was an acre or two of wood that was to be cut. The people of the mansion were so much from home that their existence was almost forgotten, and they were spoken of vaguely as 'on the Continent'. There was, in fact, a lack of ready-money, perhaps from the accumulation of settlements, that reduced the nominal income of the head to a tithe of what it should have been.

Yet they were too proud to have in the modern builder, the modern upholsterer, and, most dreadful of all, the modern 'gardener', to put in French sashes, gilding and mirrors, and to root up the fine old yew hedges and level the grand old trees. Such is the usual preparation before an advertisement appears that a mansion of 'historic association', and 'replete with every modern convenience', is to let, with some thousand acres of shooting, &c.

They still kept up an establishment of servants— after a fashion—who did much as they pleased. Dickon was a great favourite. As for myself, a mere dreamy lad, I could go into the woods and wander as I liked, which was sufficient. But I recollect the immense kitchen very well, and the polished relics of the ancient turnspit machinery. There was a door from it opening on a square stone-flagged court with a vertical sun-dial on the wall; and beyond that ranges of disused coach-houses—all cloudy, as it were, with cobwebs hanging on old-fashioned post-chaises. Dickon was in love with one of the maids, a remarkably handsome girl.

She showed me the famous mantelpiece, a vast carved work, under which you could stand upright. The legend was that once a year on a certain night a sable horse and cloaked horseman rode across that great apartment, flames snorting from the horse's nostrils, and into the fireplace, disappearing with a clap of thunder. She brought me, too, an owl from the coachhouses, holding the bird by the legs firmly, her hand defended by her apron from the claws.

The butler was a little merry fellow, extremely fond of a gun and expert in using it. He seemed to have nothing to do but tell tales and sing, except at the rare intervals when some of the family returned unexpectedly. The keeper was always up there in the kitchen; he was as pleasant and jovial as a man could well be, though full of oaths on occasion. He was a man of one tale—of a somewhat enigmatical character. He would ask a stranger if they had ever heard of such-and-such a village where water set fire to a barn, ducks were drowned, and pigs cut their own throats, all in a single day.

It seemed that some lime had been stored in the barn, when the brook rose and flooded the place; this slaked the lime and fired the straw, and so the barn. Something of the same kind happens occasionally on the river barges. The ducks were in a coop fastened down, so that they could not swim on the surface of the flood, which passed over and drowned them. The pigs were floated out of the sty, and in swimming their sharp-edged hoofs struck their fat jowls just behind the ear at every stroke till they cut into the artery, and so bled to death. Where he got this history from I do not know.

One bright October morning (towards the end of the month) Dickon drove me over to the old place with his fast trotter—our double-barrels hidden under some sacks in the trap. The keeper was already waiting in the kitchen, sipping a glass of hot purl; the butler was filling every pocket with cartridges. After some comparison of their betting-books, for Dickon, on account of his acquaintance with the training establishments, was up to most moves, we started. The keeper had to send a certain number of pheasants and other game to the absent family and their friends every now and then, and this duty was his pretext. There was plenty of shooting to be got elsewhere, but the spice of naughtiness about this was alluring. To reach that part of the wood where it was proposed to shoot the shortest way led across some arable fields.

Fieldfares and redwings rose out of the hedges and flew away in their peculiarly scattered manner—their flocks, though proceeding in the same direction, seeming all loose and disordered. Where the ploughs had been at work already the deep furrows were full of elm leaves, wafted as they fell from the trees in such quantities as to make the groove left by the share level with the ridges. A flock of lapwings were on the clods in an adjacent field, near enough to be seen, but far beyond gunshot. There might perhaps have been fifty birds, all facing one way and all perfectly motionless. They were, in fact, watching us intently, although not apparently looking towards us: they act so much in concert as to seem drilled. So soon as the possibility of danger had gone by each would begin to feed, moving ahead.

The path then passed through the little meadows
that joined the wood: and the sunlight glistened on
the dew, or rather on the hoar frost that had melted
and clung in heavy drops to the grass. Here one
flashed emerald; there ruby; another a pure brilliance
like a diamond. Under foot by the stiles the fallen
acorns crunched as they split into halves beneath the
sudden pressure.

The leaves still left on the sycamores were marked
with large black spots: the horse-chestnuts were quite
bare; and already the tips of the branches carried the
varnish-coloured sheaths of the buds that were to
appear the following spring. These stuck to the finger
if touched, as if they really had been varnished.
Through the long months of winter they would remain, till under April showers and sunshine the sheath
fell back and the green leaflets pushed up, the two
forming together a rude cross for a short time.

The day was perfectly still, and the colours of the
leaves still left glowed in the sunbeams. Beneath, the
dank bronzed fern that must soon shrivel was wet,
and hung with spiders' webs that like a slender netting
upheld the dew. The keeper swore a good deal about
a certain gentleman farmer whose lands adjoined the
estate, but who held under a different proprietor.
Between these two there was a constant bickering—
the tenant angry about the damage done to his crops
by the hares and rabbits, and the keeper bitterly re-
senting the tenant's watch on his movements, and
warnings to his employer that all was not quite as it
should be.

The tenant had the right to shoot, and he was
always about in the turnips—a terrible thorn in the
side of Dickon's friend. The tenant roundly declared

the keeper a rascal, and told his master so in written communications. The keeper declared the tenant set gins by the wood, in which the pheasants stepped and had their legs smashed. Then the tenant charged the keeper with trespassing; the other retorted that he decoyed the pheasants by leaving peas till they dropped out of the pods. In short, their hatred was always showing itself in some act of guerrilla warfare. As we approached the part of the woods fixed on, two of the keeper's assistants, carrying thick sticks, stepped from behind a hedge, and reported that they had kept a good watch, and the old fox (the tenant) had not been seen that morning. So these fellows went round to beat, and the guns were got ready.

Sometimes you could hear the pheasants running before they reached the low-cropped hawthorn hedge at the side of the plantation; sometimes they came so quietly as to appear suddenly out from the ditch, having crept through. Others came with a tremendous rush through the painted leaves, rising just before the hedge; and now and then one flew screaming high over the tops of the firs and ash-poles, his glossy neck glowing in the sunlight and his long tail floating behind. These last pleased me most, for when the shot struck the great bird going at that rate even death could not at once arrest his progress. The impetus carried him yards, gradually slanting downwards till he rolled in the green rush bunches.

Then a hare slipped out and ran the gauntlet, and filled the hollow with his cries when the shot broke his hindquarters, till the dog had him. Jays came in couples, and green woodpeckers singly: the magpies cunningly flew aside instead of straight ahead; they never could do anything straightforward. A stoat peeped out, but went back directly when a rabbit whose retreat had been cut off bolted over his most insidious enemy. Every now and then Dickon's shot when he fired high cut the twigs out of the ash by me. Then came the distant noise of the beaters' sticks, and the pheasants, at last thoroughly disturbed, flew out in twos and threes at a time. Now the firing grew fierce, and the roll of the volleys ceaseless. It was impossible to jam the cartridges fast enough in the breech.

A subtle flavour of sulphur filled the mouth, and the lips became dry. Sunshine and gleaming leaves and sky and grass seemed to all disappear in the fever of the moment. The gun burned the hands, all blackened by the powder; the metal got hotter and hotter; the sward was poached and trampled and dotted with cases; shot hissed through the air and pattered in showers on the opposite plantation; the eyes, bleared and bloodshot with the smoke, could scarce see to point the tube. Pheasants fell, and no one heeded; pheasants escaped, and none noticed it; pheasants were but just winged and ran wounded into the distant hedges; pheasants were blown out of all living shape and could hardly be gathered up. Not a word spoken: a breathless haste to load and blaze; a storm of shot and smoke and slaughter.

CHAPTER VII

OBY AND HIS SYSTEM: THE MOUCHER'S CALENDAR

One dark night, as I was walking on a lonely road, I kicked against something, and but just saved myself from a fall. It was an intoxicated man lying at full length. As a rule, it is best to let such people alone; but it occurred to me that the mail-cart was due: with two horses harnessed tandem-fashion, and travelling at full speed, the mail would probably go over him. So I seized the fellow by the collar and dragged him out of the way. Then he sat up, and asked in a very threatening tone who I was. I mentioned my name: he grunted, and fell back on the turf, where I left him.

The incident passed out of my mind, when one afternoon a labourer called, asking for me in a mysterious manner, and refusing to communicate his business to anyone else. When admitted, he produced a couple of cock pheasants from under his coat, the tail feathers much crumpled, but otherwise in fine condition. These he placed on the table, remarking, 'I ain't forgot as you drawed I out of the raud thuck night.' I made him understand that such presents were too embarrassing; but he seemed anxious to do 'summat', so I asked him to find me a few ferns and rare plants.

This he did from time to time; and thus a species of acquaintanceship grew up and I learned all about him. He was always called 'Oby' (*i.e.* Obadiah), and was the most determined poacher of a neighbouring district—a notorious fighting man—hardened against shame, an Ishmaelite openly contemning authority and yet not insensible to kindness. I give his history in his own language—softening only the pronunciation, that would otherwise be unintelligible.

'I lives with my granny in Thorney-lane: it be outside the village. My mother be married agen, you see, to the smith: her have got a cottage as belongs to her. My brother have got a van and travels the country; and sometimes I and my wife goes with him. I larned to set up a wire when I went to plough when I were a boy, but never took to it regular till I went a-navigating [navvying] and seed what a spree it were.

'There ain't no such chaps for poaching as they navigators in all England: I means where there be a railway a-making. I've knowed forty of 'em go out together on a Sunday, and every man had a dog, and some two; and good dogs too—lots of 'em as you wouldn't buy for ten quid. They used to spread out like, and sweep the fields as clean as the crownd of your hat. Keepers weren't no good at all, and besides they never knowed which place us was going to make for. One of the chaps gave I a puppy, and he growed into the finest greyhound as you'd find in a day's walk. The first time I was took up before the bench I had to go to gaol, because the contractor had broke and the works was stopped, so that my mates hadn't no money to pay the fine.

'The dog was took away home to granny by my butty [comrade], but one of the gentlemen as seed it in the court sent his groom over and got it off the old woman for five pound. She thought if I hadn't the hound I should give it up, and she come and paid me out of gaol. It was a wonder as I didn't break her neck; only her was a good woman, you see, to I. But

I wouldn't have parted with that hound for a quart-full of sovereigns. Many's a time I've seed his name—they changed his name, of course—in the papers for winning coursing matches. But we let that gent as bought him have it warm: we harried his pheasants and killed the most of 'em.

'After that I come home, and took to it regular. It ain't no use unless you do it regular. If a man goes out into the fields now and then chance-like he don't get much, and is most sure to be caught—very likely in the place of somebody else the keepers were waiting for and as didn't come. I goes to work every day the same as the rest, only I always take piece-work, which I can come to when I fancy, and stay as late in the evening as suits me with a good excuse. As I knows navigating, I do a main bit of draining and water-furrowing, and I gets good wages all the year round, and never wants for a job. You see, I knows more than the fellows as have never been at nothing but plough.

'The reason I gets on so well poaching is because I'm always at work out in the fields, except when I goes with the van. I watches everything as goes on, and marks the hares' tracks and the rabbit buries, and the double mounds and little copses as the pheasants wanders off to in the autumn. I keeps a 'nation good look out after the keeper and his men, and sees their dodges—which way they walks, and how they comes back sudden and unexpected on purpose. There's mostly one about with his eyes on me—when they sees me working on a farm they puts a man special to look after me. I never does nothing close round where I'm at work, so he waits about a main bit for nothing.

'You see by going out piece-work I visits every
farm in the parish. The other men they works for one
farmer for two or three or maybe twenty years; but I
goes very nigh all round the place—a fortnight here
and a week there, and then a month somewhere else.
So I knows every hare in the parish, and all his runs
and all the double mounds and copses, and the little
covers in the corners of the fields. When I be at work
on one place I sets my wires about half a mile away
on a farm as I ain't been working on for a month,
and where the keeper don't keep no special look out
now I be gone. As I goes all round, I knows the ways
of all the farmers, and them as bides out late at night
at their friends' and they as goes to bed early; and so
I knows what paths to follow and what fields I can
walk about in and never meet nobody.

'The dodge is to be always in the fields and to know
everybody's ways. Then you may do just as you be
a-mind. All of 'em knows I be a-poaching; but that
don't make no difference for work; I can use my tools,
and do it as well as any man in the country, and they
be glad to get me on for 'em. They farmers as have
got their shooting be sharper than the keepers, and you
can't do much there; but they as haven't got the
shooting don't take no notice. They sees my wires in
the grass, and just looks the other way. If they sees I
with a gun I puts un in the ditch till they be gone by,
and they don't look among the nettles.

'Some of them as got land by the wood would like
I to be there all day and night. You see, their clover
and corn feeds the hares and pheasants; and then
some day when they goes into the market and passes
the poultry-shop there be four or five score pheasants
a-hanging up with their long tails a-sweeping in the

faces of them as fed 'em. The same with the hares and the rabbits; and so they'd just as soon as I had 'em—and a dalled deal sooner—out of spite. Lord bless you! if I was to walk through their courtyards at night with a sack over my shoulders full of you knows what, and met one of 'em, he'd tell his dog to stop that yowling, and go indoors rather than see me. As for the rabbits, they hates they worse than poison. They knocks a hare over now and then themselves on the quiet—bless you! I could tell tales on a main few, but I bean't such a fellow as that.

'But you see I don't run no risk except from the keeper hisself, the men as helps un, and two or three lickspittles as be always messing round after a ferreting job or some wood-cutting, and the Christmas charities. It be enough to make a man sick to see they. This yer parish be a very big un, and a be preserved very high, and I can do three times as much in he as in the next one, as ain't much preserved. So I sticks to this un.

'Of course they tried to drive I out of un, and wanted the cottage; but granny had all the receipts for the quit-rent, and my lard and all the lawyers couldn't shove us out, and there we means to bide. You have seed that row of oaks as grows in the hedge behind our house. One of 'em leaned over the roof, and one of the limbs was like to fall; but they wouldn't cut him, just to spite us, and the rain dripping spoilt the thatch. So I just had another chimney built at that end for an oven, and kept up the smoke till all the tree that side died. I've had more than one pheasant through them oaks, as draws 'em: I had one in a gin as I put in the ditch by my garden.

'They started a tale as 'twas I as stole the lambs a

year or two ago, and they had me up for it; but they couldn't prove nothing agen me. Then they had me for unhinging the gates and drowning 'em in the water, but when they was going to try the case they two young farmers as you know of come and said as they did it when they was tight, and so I got off. They said as 'twas I that put the poison for the hounds when three on 'em took it and died while the hunt was on. It were the dalledest lie! I wouldn't hurt a dog not for nothing. The keeper hisself put that poison, I knows, 'cause he couldn't bear the pack coming to upset the pheasants. Yes, they been down upon I a main bit, but I means to bide. All the farmers knows as I never touched no lamb, nor even pulled a turmot, and they never couldn't get no witnesses.

'After a bit I catched the keeper hisself and the policeman at it; and there be another as knows it, and who do you think that be? It be the man in town as got the licence to sell game as haves most of my hares: the keeper selled he a lot as the money never got to my lard's pocket and the steward never knowed of. Look at that now! So now he shuts his eye and axes me to drink, and give me the ferreting job in Longlands Mound; but, Lord bless 'ee, I bean't so soft as he thinks for.

'They used to try and get me to fight the keeper when they did catch me with a wire, but I knowed as hitting is transporting, and just put my hands in my pockets and let 'em do as they liked. *They* knows I bean't afraid of 'em in the road; I've threshed more than one of 'em, but I ain't going to jump into *that* trap. I've been before the bench, at one place and t'other, heaps of times, and paid the fine for trespass.

Last time the chairman said to I, "So you be here again, Oby; we hear a good deal about you." I says, "Yes, my lard, I be here agen, but people never don't hear nothing about *you*." That shut the old duffer up. Nobody never heard nothing of he, except at rent-audit.

'However, they all knows me now—my lard and the steward, and the keeper and the bailies, and the farmers; and they don't take half the notice of I as they used to. The keeper he don't dare nor the policeman as I told you, and the rest be got used to me and my ways. And I does very well one week with t'other. One week I don't take nothing, and the next I haves a good haul, chiefly hares and rabbits: 'cause of course I never goes into the wood, nor the plantations. It wants eight or ten with crape masks on for that job.

'I sets up about four wires, sometimes only two: if you haves so many it is a job to look after 'em. I stops the hare's other runs, so that she is sure to come along mine where I've got the turnpike up: the trick is to rub your hand along the runs as you want to stop, or spit on 'em, or summat like that; for a hare won't pass nothing of that sort. So pussy goes back and comes by the run as I've chose: if she comes quick she don't holler; if she comes slow she squeals a bit sometimes before the wire hangs her. Very often I bean't fur off and stops the squealing. That's why I can't 'ise a gin—it makes 'em holler so. I ferrets a goodish few rabbits on bright nights in winter.

'As for the pheasants, I gets them mostly about acorn-time; they comes out of the plantations then. I keeps clear of the plantations, because, besides the men a-watching, they have got dogs chained up and alarm-guns as goes off if you steps on the spring; and some have got a string stretched along as you be pretty sure to kick against, and then, bang! and all the dogs sets up a yowling. Of course it's only powder, but it brings the keepers along. But when the acorns and the berries be ripe, the pheasants comes out along the hedges after 'em, and gets up at the haws and such like. They wanders for miles, and as they don't care to go all the way back to roost they bides in the little copses as I told you of. They come to the same copses every year, which is curious, as most of them as will come this year will be shot before next.

'If I can't get 'em the fust night, I just throws a handful or two of peas about the place, and they'll be sure to stay, and likely enough bring two or three more. I mostly shoots 'em with just a little puff of powder as you wouldn't hear across one field, especially if it's a windy night. I had a air-gun as was took from me, but he weren't much go: I likes a gun as throws the shot wide, but I never shoots any but roosters, unless I can catch 'em standing still.

'All as I can tell you is as the dodge is this: you watch everybody, and be always in the fields, and always work one parish till you knows every hare in un, and always work by yourself and don't have no mates.'

There were several other curious characters whom we frequently saw at work. The mouchers were about all the year round, and seemed to live in, or by the hedges, as much as the mice. These men probably see more than the most careful observer, without giving it a thought.

In January the ice that freezes in the ditches appears of a dark colour, because it lies without intervening water on the dead brown leaves. Their tint shows through the translucent crystal, but near the edge of

the ice three white lines or bands run round. If by
any chance the ice gets broken or upturned, these
white bands are seen to be caused by flanges projecting from the under surface, almost like stands. They
are sometimes connected in such a way that the
parallel flanges appear like the letter 'h' with the
two down-strokes much prolonged. In the morning
the chalky rubble brought from the pits upon the
Downs and used for mending gateways leading into
the fields glistens brightly. Upon the surface of each
piece of rubble there adheres a thin coating of ice:
if this be lightly struck it falls off, and with it a flake
of the chalk. As it melts, too, the chalk splits and
crumbles; and thus in an ordinary gateway the same
process may be seen that disintegrates the most majestic
cliff.

The stubbles—those that still remain—are full of
linnets, upon which the mouching fowler preys in the
late autumn. And when at the end of January the
occasional sunbeams give some faint hope of spring,
he wanders through the lanes carrying a decoy bird
in a darkened cage, and a few boughs of privet studded
with black berries and bound round with rushes for
the convenience of handling.

The female yellow-hammers, whose hues are not so
brilliant as those of the male birds, seem as winter
approaches to flock together, and roam the hedges
and stubble fields in bevies. Where loads of corn have
passed through gates the bushes often catch some
straws, and the tops of the gateposts, being decayed
and ragged, hold others. These are neglected while
the seeds among the stubble, the charlock, and the
autumn dandelion are plentiful and while the ears
left by the gleaners may still be found. But in the

shadowless winter days, hard and cold, each scattered straw is sought for.

A few days before the new year [1879] opened I saw a yellow-hammer attacking, in a very ingenious manner, a straw that hung pendent, the ear downwards, from the post of a windy gateway. She fluttered up from the ground, clung to the ear, and outspread her wings, keeping them rigid. The draught acted on the wings just as the breeze does on a paper kite, and there the bird remained supported without an effort while the ear was picked. Now and then the balance was lost, but she was soon up again, and again used the wind to maintain her position. The brilliant cock-birds return in the early spring, or at least appear to do so, for the habits of birds are sometimes quite local.

It is probable that in severe and continued frost many hedgehogs die. On January 19 [1879], in the midst of the sharp weather, a hedgehog came to the door opening on the garden at night, and was taken in. Though carefully tended, the poor creature died next day: it was so weak it could scarcely roll itself into a ball. As the vital heat declined the fleas deserted their host and issued from among the spines. In February, unless it be a mild season, the mounds are still bare; and then under the bushes the ground may be sometimes seen strewn with bulbous roots, apparently of the blue-bell, lying thickly together and entirely exposed.

The moucher now carries a bill-hook, and as he shambles along the road keeps a sharp look-out for briars. When he sees one the roots of which are not difficult to get at, and whose tall upright stem is green —if dark it is too old—he hacks it off with as much of the root as possible. The lesser branches are cut, and, the stem generally trimmed; it is then sold to the gardeners as the stock on which to graft standard roses. In a few hours as he travels he will get together quite a bundle of such briars. He also collects moss, which is sold for the purpose of placing in flowerpots to hide the earth. The moss preferred is that growing on and round stoles.

The melting of the snow and the rains in February cause the ditches to overflow and form shallow pools in the level meadows. Into these sometimes the rooks wade as far as the length of their legs allows them, till the discoloured yellow water almost touches the lower part of the breast. The moucher searches for small shell snails, of which quantities are sold as food for cage birds, and cuts small 'turfs' a few inches square from the green by the roadside. These are in great request for larks, especially at this time of the year, when they begin to sing with all their might.

Large flocks of woodpigeons are now in every field where the tender swede and turnip tops are sprouting green and succulent. These 'tops' are the moucher's first great crop of the year. The time that they appear varies with the weather: in a mild winter some may be found early in January; if the frost has been severe there may be none till March. These the moucher gathers by stealth; he speedily fills a sack, and goes off with it to the nearest town. Turnip-tops are much more in demand now than formerly, and the stealing of them a more serious matter. This trade lasts some time, till the tops become too large and garden greens take their place.

In going to and fro the fields the moucher searches the banks and digs out primrose 'mars', and ferns with

the root attached, which he hawks from door to door in
the town. He also gathers quantities of spring flowers,
as violets. This spring [1879], owing to the severity of
the season, there were practically none to gather, and
when the weather moderated the garden flowers preceded those of the hedge. Till the 10th of March not
a spot of colour was to be seen. About that time bright
yellow flowers appeared suddenly on the clayey banks
and waste places, and among the hard clay lumps of
fields ploughed but not sown.

The brilliant yellow formed a striking contrast to
the dull brown of the clods, there being no green leaf
to moderate the extremes of tint. These were the blos-
soms of the coltsfoot, that sends up a stalk surrounded
with faintly rosy scales. Several such stalks often
spring from a single clod: lift the heavy clod, and you
have half a dozen flowers, a whole bunch, without a
single leaf. Usually the young grasses and the seed-
leaves of plants have risen up and supply a general
green; but this year the coltsfoot bloomed unsup-
ported, studding the dark ground with gold.

Now the frogs are busy, and the land lizards come
forth. Even these the moucher sometimes captures;
for there is nothing so strange but that someone selects
it for a pet. The mad March hares scamper about in
broad daylight over the corn, whose pale green blades
rise in straight lines a few inches above the soil. They
are chasing their skittish loves, instead of soberly
dreaming the day away in a bunch of grass. The
ploughman walks in the furrow his share has made,
and presently stops to measure the 'lands' with the
spud. His horses halt dead in the tenth of a second at
the sound of his voice, glad to rest for a minute from
their toil. Work there is in plenty now, for stone-

picking, hoeing, and other matters must be attended to; but the moucher lounges in the road decoying chaffinches, or perhaps earns a shilling by driving some dealer's cattle home from fair and market.

By April his second great crop is ready—the watercress; the precise time of course varies very much, and at first the quantities are small. The hedges are now fast putting on the robe of green that gradually hides the wreck of last year's growth. The withered head of the teazle, black from the rain, falls and disappears. Great burdock stems lie prostrate. Thick and hard as they are while the sap is still in them, in winter the wet ground rots the lower part till the blast overthrows the stalk. The hollow 'gicks' too, that lately stood almost to the shoulder, is down, or slanting, temporarily supported by some branch. Just between the root and the stalk it has decayed till nothing but a narrow strip connects the dry upper part with the earth. The moucher sells the nests and eggs of small birds to townsfolk who cannot themselves wander among the fields, but who love to see something that reminds them of the green meadows.

As the season advances and the summer comes he gathers vast quantities of dandelion leaves, parsley, sowthistle, clover, and so forth, as food for the tame rabbits kept in towns. If his haunt be not far from a river, he spends hours collecting bait—worm and grub and fly—for the boatmen, who sell them again to the anglers.

Again there is work in the meadows—the haymaking is about, and the farmers are anxious for men. But the moucher passes by and looks for quaking grass, bunches of which have a ready sale. Fledgeling goldfinches and linnets, young rabbits, young squirrels, even the nest of the harvest-trow mouse, and occasionally a snake, bring him in a little money. He picks the forget-me-nots from the streams and the 'bluebottle' from the corn: bunches of the latter are sometimes sold in London at a price that seems extravagant to those who have seen whole fields tinted with its beautiful azure. By-and-by the golden wheat calls for an army of workers; but the moucher passes on and gathers groundsel.

Then come the mushrooms: he knows the best places, and soon fills a basket full of 'buttons,' picking them very early in the morning. These are then put in 'punnets' by the greengrocers and retailed at a high price. Later the blackberries ripen and form his third great crop; the quantity he brings in to the towns is astonishing, and still there is always a customer. The blackberry harvest lasts for several weeks, as the berries do not all ripen at once, but successively, and is supplemented by elderberries and sloes. The moucher sometimes sleeps on the heaps of disused tan in a tanyard: tanyards are generally on the banks of small rivers. The tan is said to possess the property of preserving those who sleep on it from chills and cold, though they may lie quite exposed to the weather.

There is generally at least one such a man as this about the outskirts of market towns, and he is an 'original' best defined by negatives. He is not a tramp, for he never enters the casual wards and never begs—that is, of strangers; though there are certain farmhouses where he calls once now and then and gets a slice of bread and cheese and a pint of ale. He brings to the farmhouse a duck's egg that has been dropped in the brook by some negligent bird, or carries intelligence of the nest made by some roaming goose in a distant withy-bed. Or once, perhaps, he found a sheep on its back in a narrow furrow, unable to get up and likely to die if not assisted, and by helping the animal to gain its legs earned a title to the owner's gratitude.

He is not a thief; apples and plums and so on are quite safe, though the turnip-tops are not: there is a subtle casuistry involved here—the distinction between the quasi-wild and the garden product. He is not a poacher in the sense of entering coverts, or even snaring a rabbit. If the pheasants are so numerous and so tame that passing carters have to whip them out of the way of the horses it is hardly wonderful if one should disappear now and then. Nor is he like the Running Jack that used to accompany the more famous packs of foxhounds, opening gates, holding horses, and a hundred other little services, and who kept up with the hunt by sheer fleetness of foot.

Yet he is fleet of foot in his way, though never seen to run; he *pads* along on naked feet like an animal, never straightening the leg, but always keeping the knee a little bent. With a basket of watercress slung at his back by a piece of tar-cord, he travels rapidly in this way; his feet go 'pad, pad' on the thick white dust, and he easily overtakes a good walker and keeps up the pace for miles without exertion. The watercress is a great staple, because it lasts for so many months. Seeing the nimble way in which he gathers it, thrusting aside the brook-lime, breaking off the coarser sprays, snipping away pieces of root, sorting and washing, and thinking of the amount of work to be got through before a shilling is earned, one would imagine that the slow, idling life of the labourer, with his regular wages, would be far more enticing.

Near the stream the ground is perhaps peaty; little black pools appear between tufts of grass, some of them streaked with a reddish or yellowish slime that glistens on the surface of the dark water; and as you step there is a hissing sound as the spongy earth yields, and a tiny spout is forced forth several yards distant. Some of the drier part of the soil the moucher takes to sell for use in gardens and flowerpots as peat.

The years roll on, and he grows old. But no feebleness of body or mind can induce him to enter the workhouse: he cannot quit his old haunts. Let it rain or sleet, or let the furious gale drive broken boughs across the road, he still sleeps in some shed or under a straw-rick. In sheer pity he is committed every now and then to prison for vagabondage—not for punishment, but in order to save him from himself. It is in vain: the moment he is out he returns to his habits. All he wants is a little beer—he is not a drunkard—and a little tobacco, and the hedges. Some chilly evening, as the shadows thicken, he shambles out of the town, and seeks the limekiln in the ploughed field, where, the substratum being limestone, the farmer burns it. Near the top of the kiln the ground is warm; there he reclines and sleeps.

The night goes on. Out from the broken blocks of stone now and again there rises a lambent flame, to shine like a meteor for a moment and then disappear. The rain fails. The moucher moves uneasily in his sleep; instinctively he rolls or crawls towards the warmth, and presently lies extended on the top of the kiln. The wings of the water-fowl hurtle in the air as they go over; by-and-by the heron utters his loud call.

Very early in the morning the quarryman comes to

tend his fire, and starts to see on the now redhot and glowing stones, sunk below the rim, the presentment of a skeleton formed of the purest white ashes—a ghastly spectacle in the grey of the dawn, as the mist rises and the peewit plaintively whistles over the marshy meadow.

CHAPTER VIII

CHURCHYARD PHEASANTS: BEFORE THE BENCH

THE tower of the church at Essant Hill was so low that it scarcely seemed to rise above the maples in the hedges. It could not be seen until the last stile in the footpath across the meadows was passed. Church and tower then came into view together on the opposite side of a large open field. A few aged hawthorn trees dotted the sward, and beyond the church the outskirts of a wood were visible, but no dwellings could be seen. Upon a second and more careful glance, however, the chimney of a cottage appeared above a hedge, so covered with ivy as hardly to be separated from the green of the boughs.

There were houses of course somewhere in Essant, but they were so scattered that a stranger might doubt the existence of the village. A few farmsteads long distances apart, and some cottages standing in green lanes and at the corners of the fields, were nearly all; there was nothing resembling a 'street'—not so much as a row. The church was in effect the village, and the church was simply the mausoleum of the Dessant family, the owners of the place. Essant Hill as a name had been rather a problem to the archaeologists, there being no hill: the ground was quite level. The explanation at last admitted was that Essant Hill was a corruption of D'Essant-ville.

It seemed probable that the population had greatly diminished; because, although the church was of great antiquity, there was space still for interments in the yard. A yew tree of immense size stood in one corner, and was by tradition associated with the fortunes of the family. Though the old trunk was much decayed, yet there were still green and flourishing shoots; so that the superstitious elders said the luck of the house was returning.

Within, the walls of the church were covered with marble slabs, and the space was reduced by the tombs of the Dessants, one with a recumbent figure; there were two brasses level with the pavement, and in the chancel hung the faded hatchments of the dead. For the pedigree went back to the battle by Hastings, and there was scarce room for more heraldry. From week's end to week's end the silent nave and aisles remained empty; the chirp of the sparrows was the only sound to be heard there. There being no house attached to the living, the holder could not reside; so the old church slumbered in the midst of the meadows, the hedges, and woods, day after day, year after year.

You could sit on the low churchyard wall in early summer under the shade of the elms in the hedge, whose bushes and briars came right over, and listen to the whistling of the blackbirds or the varied note of the thrush; you might see the whitethroat rise and sing just over the hedge, or look upwards and watch the swallows and swifts wheeling, wheeling, wheeling in the sky. No one would pass to disturb your meditations, whether simply dreaming of nothing in the genial summer warmth or thinking over the course of history since the prows of the Norman ships grounded on the beach. If we suppose the time, instead of June, to be August or September, there would not even be the singing of the birds. But as you sat on the wall, by-and-by the pheasants, tame as chickens, would come up the hedge and over into the churchyard.

Leaving the church to stroll by the footpath across the meadow towards the wood, at the first gateway half-a-dozen more pheasants scatter aside, just far enough to let you pass. In the short dusty lane more pheasants; and again at the edge of the cornfield. None of these show any signs of alarm, and only move just far enough to avoid being trodden on. Approaching the wood there are yet more pheasants, especially near the fir plantations that come up to the keeper's cottage and form one side of the enclosure of his garden. The pheasants come up to the door to pick up what they can—not long since they were fed there—and then wander away between the slender fir trunks, and beyond them out into the fields.

The path leads presently into a beautiful park, the only defect of which is that it is without undulation. It is quite level; but still the clumps of noble timber are pleasant to gaze upon. In one spot there still stands the grey wall and buttress of some ancient building, doubtless the relic of an ecclesiastical foundation. The present mansion is not far distant; it is of large size, but lacks elegance. Inside, nothing that modern skill can supply to render a residence comfortable, convenient, and (as art is understood in furniture) artistic has been neglected.

Behind the fir plantations there is an extensive range of stabling, recently erected, with all the latest improvements. A telegraph wire connects the house with the stable, so that carriage or horse may be instantly summoned. Another wire has been carried to the nearest junction with the general telegraphic system; so that the resident in this retired spot may communicate his wishes without a moment's delay to any part of the world.

In the gardens and pleasure-grounds near the house all manner of ornamental shrubs are planted. There are conservatories, vineries, pineries; all the refinements of horticulture. The pheasants stray about the gravel walks and across the close-mown lawn where no daisy dares to lift its head. Yet, with all this precision of luxury, one thing is lacking—*the* one thing, the keystone of English country life—*i.e.* a master whose heart is in the land.

The estate is in process of 'nursing' for a minor. The revenues had become practically sequestrated to a considerable extent in consequence of careless living when the minor nominally succeeded. It happened that the steward appointed was not only a lawyer of keen intelligence, but a conscientious man. He did his duty thoroughly. Every penny was got out of the estate that could be got, and every penny was saved.

First, the rents were raised to the modern standard, many of them not having been increased for years. Then the tenants were in effect ordered to farm to the highest pitch, and to improve the soil itself by liberal investment. Buildings, drains, and so forth were provided for them; they only had to pay a small percentage upon the money expended in construction. In this there was nothing that could be complained of; but the hard, mechanical, unbending spirit in which it was done—the absence of all kind of sympathy—caused a certain amount of discontent. The steward next proceeded to turn the mansion, the park, home farm, and preserves into revenue.

Everything was prepared to attract the wealthy man who wanted the temporary use of a good country house, first-class shooting, and hunting. He succeeded in doing what few gentlemen have accomplished: he made the pheasants pay. One reason, of course, was that gentlemen have expenses outside and beyond breeding and keeping: the shooting party itself is expensive; whereas here the shooting party paid hard cash for their amusement. The steward had no knowledge of pheasants; but he had a wide experience of one side of human nature, and he understood accounts.

The keepers were checked by figures at every turn, finding it impossible to elude the businesslike arrangements that were made. In revenue the result was highly successful. The mansion with the first-class shooting, hunting, and lovely woodlands—every modern convenience and comfort in the midst of the most rural scenery—let at a high price to good tenants. There was an income from what had previously been profitless. Under this shrewd management the estate was fast recovering.

At the same time the whole parish groaned in spirit. The farmers grumbled at the moral pressure which forced them to progress in spite of themselves. They grumbled at the strange people who took up their residence in their midst and suddenly claimed all the loyalty which was the due of the old family. These people hunted over their fields, jumped over the hedges, glanced at them superciliously, and seemed astonished if every hat was not raised when they came in sight. The farmers felt that they were regarded as ignorant barbarians, and resented the town-bred insolence of people who aped the country gentleman.

They grumbled about the over-preservation of game, and they grumbled about the rabbits. The hunt had its grumble too because some of the finest coverts were closed to the hounds, and because they wanted to know what became of the foxes that formerly lived in those coverts. Here was a beautiful place—a place that one might dream life away in—filled with all manner of discontent.

Everything was done with the best intention. But the keystone was wanting—the landlord, the master, who had grown up in the traditions of the spot, and between whom and the people there would have been, even despite of grievances, a certain amount of sympathy. So true is it that in England, under the existing system of land tenure, an estate cannot be worked like the machinery of a factory.

At first, when the pheasant-preserving began to reach such a height, there was a great deal of poaching by the resident labourers. The temptation was thrust so closely before their faces they could not resist it. When pheasants came wandering into the cottage gardens, and could even be enticed into the sheds and so secured by simply shutting the door, men who would not have gone out of their way to poach were led to commit themselves.

There followed a succession of prosecutions and fines, till the place began to get a reputation for that sort of thing. It was at last intimated to the steward by certain gentlemen that this course of prosecution was extremely injudicious. For it is a fact—a fact carefully ignored sometimes—that resident gentlemen object to prosecutions, and, so far from being anxious to fine or imprison poachers, would very much rather not. The steward took the hint, and instead increased his watchers. But by this time the novelty of pheasants roaming about like fowls had begun to wear off, and their services were hardly needed. Men went by pheasants with as much indifference as they would pass a tame duck by the roadside.

Such poachers as visited the woods came from a distance. Two determined raids were carried out by strangers, who escaped. Every now and then wires were found that had been abandoned, but the poaching ceased to be more than is usual on most properties. So far as the inhabitants of the parish were concerned it almost ceased altogether; but every now and then the strollers, gipsies, and similar characters carried off a pheasant or a hare, or half a dozen rabbits. These offenders when detected were usually charged before the bench at a market town not many miles distant. Let us follow one there.

The little town of L——, which has not even a branch railway, mainly consists of a long street. In one part this street widens out, so that the houses are some forty yards or more apart, and it then again contracts. This irregularly shaped opening is the marketplace, and here in the centre stands a rude-looking building. It is supported upon thick short pillars, and was perhaps preceded by a wooden structure. Under these pillars there is usually a shabby chaise or two run in for cover, and the spot is the general rendezvous of all the dogs in the town.

This morning there are a few loafers hanging round the place; and the tame town pigeons have fluttered down, and walk with nodding heads almost up to them. These pigeons always come to the edge of a group of people, mindful of the stray grain and peas that fall from the hands of farmers and dealers examining samples on market days. Presently two constables come across, carrying a heavy, clumsy box between them. They unlock a door, and take the box upstairs into the hall over the pillars. After them saunters a seedy man, evidently a clerk, with a rusty black bag;

and after him again—for the magistrates' Clerk's clerk must have *his* clerk—a boy with some leather-bound books.

Some of the loafers touch their hats as a gentleman —a magistrate—rides up the street. But although the church clock is striking the hour fixed for the sessions to begin he does not come over to the hall upon dismounting in the inn-yard, but quietly strolls away to transact some business with the wine-merchant or the saddler. There really is not the least hurry. The Clerk stands in the inn porch calmly enjoying the September sunshine, and chatting with the landlord. Two or three more magistrates drive up; presently the chairman strolls over on foot from his house, which is almost in the town, to the inn and joins in the pleasant gossip going on there, of course in a private apartment.

Up in the justice-room the seedy Clerk's clerk is leaning out of the window and conversing with a man below who has come along with a barrow-load of vegetables from his allotment. Some boys are spinning tops under the pillars. On the stone steps that lead up to the hall a young mother sits nursing her infant; she is waiting to 'swear' the child. In the room itself several gipsy-looking men and women lounge in a corner. At one end is a broad table and some comfortable chairs behind it. In front of each chair, on the table, two sheets of clean foolscap have been placed on a sheet of blotting-paper. These and a variety of printed forms were taken from the clumsy box that is now open.

At last there is a slight stir as a group is seen to emerge from the inn, and the magistrates take their seats. An elderly man who sits by the chair cocks his felt hat on the back of his head: the clerical magistrate very tenderly places his beaver in safety on the broad mantelpiece, that no irreverent sleeve may ruffle its gloss: several others who rarely do more than nod assent range themselves on the flanks; one younger man who looks as if he understood horses pulls out his toothpick. The chairman, stout and gouty, seizes a quill and sternly looks over the list of cases.

Half a dozen summonses for non-payment of rates come first; then a dispute between a farmer and his man. After this the young mother 'swears' her child; and, indeed, there is some very hard swearing here on both sides. A wrangle between two women—neighbours—who accuse each other of assault, and scream and chatter their loudest, comes next. Before they decide it, the bench retire, and are absent a long time.

By degrees a buzz arises, till the justice-room is as noisy as a market. Suddenly the door of the private room opens, and the Clerk comes out; instantly the buzz subsides, and in the silence those who are nearest catch something about the odds and the St. Leger, and an anything but magisterial roar of laughter. The chairman appears, rigidly compressing his features, and begins to deliver his sentence before he can sit down, but the solemn effect is much marred by the passing of a steam ploughing engine. The audience, too, tend away towards the windows to see whose engine it is.

'Silence!' cries the Clerk, who has himself been looking out of window; the shuffling of feet ceases, and it is found that after this long consultation the bench have dismissed both charges. The next case on the list is poaching; and at the call of his name one of the gipsy-looking men advances and is ordered to stand before that part of the table which by consent represents the bar.

'Oby Bottleton,' says the Clerk, half reading, half extemporizing, and shuffling his papers to conceal certain slips of technicality; 'you are charged with trespassing in pursuit of game at Essant Hill—that you did use a wire on the estate—on land in the occupation of Johnson.'—'It's a lie!' cries a good-looking, dark-complexioned woman, who has come up behind the defendant (the whilome navvy), and carries a child so wrapped in a shawl as to be invisible. 'Silence! or you'll have to go outside the court. Mr. Dalton Dessant will leave the bench during the hearing of this case.' Mr. Dalton Dessant, one of the silent magistrates already alluded to, bows to the chairman, and wriggles his chair back about two feet from the table. There he gazes at the ceiling. He is one of the trustees of the Essant Hill property; and the bench are very careful to consult public opinion in L——borough.

The first witness is an assistant keeper: the head keeper stands behind him—a fine man, still upright and hearty-looking, but evidently at the beginning of the vale of years; he holds his hat in his hand; the sunlight falls through the casement on his worn velveteen jacket. The assistant, with the aid of a few questions from the Clerk, gives his evidence very clear and fairly. 'I saw the defendant's van go down the lane,' he says:

'It bean't my van,' interrupts the defendant; 'it's my brother's.'

'You'll have an opportunity of speaking presently,' says the Clerk. 'Go on' (to the witness).

'After the van went down the lane, it stopped by

the highway-road, and the horse was taken out. The women left the van with baskets, and went towards the village.'

'Yes, yes; come to the point. Did you hide yourself by order of the head keeper?'

'I did—in the nutwood hedge by Three Corner Piece; after a bit I saw the defendant.'

'Had you any reason for watching there?'

'There was a wire and a rabbit in it.'

'Well, what happened?

'I waited a long time, and presently the defendant got over the gate. He was very particular not to step on the soft mud by the gate—he kind of leaped over it, not to leave the mark of his boots. He had a lurcher with him, and I was afraid the dog would scent me in the hedge.'

'You rascal!' (from the defendant's wife).

'But he didn't, and, after looking carefully round, the defendant picked up the rabbit, and put it and the wire in his pocket.'

'What did you do then?'

'I got out of the hedge and came towards him. Directly he saw me he ran across the field; I whistled as loud as I could, and he' (jerking a thumb back towards the head keeper) 'came out of the firs into the lane and stopped him. We found the wire and the rabbit in his pocket, and two more wires. I produce the wires.'

This was the sum of the evidence; the head keeper simply confirmed the latter part of it. Oby replied that it was all false from beginning to end. He had not got corduroy trousers on that day, as stated. He was not there at all: he was in the village, and he could call witnesses to prove it. The Clerk reminded the audience that there was such a thing as imprisonment for perjury.

Then the defendant turned savagely on the first witness, and admitted the truth of his statement by asking what he said when collared in the lane. 'You said you had had a good lot lately, and didn't care if you was nailed this time.'

'Oh, what awful lies!' cried the wife. 'It's a wonder you don't fall dead!'

'You were not there,' the Clerk remarked quietly. 'Now, Oby, what is your defence? Have you got any witnesses?'

'No; I ain't got no witnesses. All as I did, I know I walked up the hedge to look for mushrooms. I saw one of them things'—meaning the wires on the table— 'and I just stooped down to see what it was, 'cos I didn't know. I never seed one afore; and I was just going to pick it up and look at it' (the magistrates glance at each other, and cannot suppress a smile at this profound innocence), 'when this fellow jumped out and frightened me. I never seed no rabbit.'

'Why, you put the rabbit in your pocket,' interrupts the first witness.

'Never mind,' said the Clerk to the witness; 'let him go on.'

'That's all as I got to say,' continues the defendant, 'I never seed no such things afore; and if he hadn't come I should have put it down again.'

'But you were trespassing,' said the Clerk.

'I didn't know it. There wasn't no notice-board.'

'Now, Oby,' cried the head keeper, 'you know you've been along that lane this ten years.'

'That will do' (from the chairman); 'is there any more evidence?'

As none was forthcoming, the bench turned a little aside and spoke in low tones. The defendant's wife immediately set up a sobbing, varied occasionally by a shriek; the infant woke up and cried, and two or three women of the same party behind began to talk in excited tones about 'Shame.' The sentence was 2*l.* and costs—an announcement that caused a perfect storm of howling and crying.

The defendant put his hands in his pockets with the complacent expression of a martyr. 'I must go to gaol a' spose; none of ourn ever went thur afore: a' spose *I* must go.' 'Come,' said the Clerk, 'why, you or your brother bought a piece of land and a cottage not long ago,'—then to the bench, 'They're not real gipsies: he is a grandson of old Bottleton who had the tollgate; you recollect, Sir.'

But the defendant declares he has no money; his friends shake their heads gloomily; and amid the shrieking of his wife and the crying of the child he is removed in the custody of two constables, to be presently conveyed to gaol. With ferocious glances at the bench, as if they would like to tear the chairman's eyes out, the women leave the court.

'Next case,' calls the Clerk. The court sits about two hours longer, having taken some five hours to get through six cases. Just as the chairman rises the poacher's wife returns to the table, without her child, angrily pulls out a dirty canvas bag, and throws down three or four sovereigns before the seedy Clerk's clerk. The canvas bag is evidently half-full of money—the gleam of silver and gold is visible within it. The bench stay to note this proceeding with an amused expression on their features. The woman looks at them as bold as brass, and stalks off with her man.

Half an hour afterwards, two of the magistrates riding away from the town pass a small tavern on the outskirts. A travelling van is outside, and from the chimney on its roof thin smoke arises. There is a little group at the doorway, and among them stands the late prisoner. Oby holds a foaming tankard in one hand, and touches his battered hat, as the magistrates go by, with a gesture of sly humility.

CHAPTER IX

LUKE, THE RABBIT CONTRACTOR:
THE BROOK-PATH

THE waggon-track leading to the Upper Woods almost always presented something of interest, and often of beauty. The solitude of the place seemed to have attracted flowers and ferns as well as wild animals and birds. For though flowers have no power of motion, yet seeds have a negative choice and lie dormant where they do not find a kindly welcome. But those carried hither by the birds or winds took root and flourished, secure from the rude ploughshare or the sharp scythe.

The slow rumble of waggon-wheels seldom disturbed the dreamy silence, or interrupted the song of the birds; so seldom that large docks and thistles grew calmly beside the ruts untouched by hoofs. From the thick hedges on either side trailing brambles and briars stretched far out, and here and there was a fallen branch, broken off by the winds, whose leaves had turned brown and withered while all else was green. Round sarsen stones had been laid down in the marshy places to form a firm road, but the turf had long since covered most of them. Where the smooth brown surfaces did project mosses had lined the base, and rushes leaned over and hid the rest.

In the ditches, under the shade of the brambles, the hart's-tongue fern extended its long blade of dark glossy green. By the decaying stoles the hardy fern flourished, under the trees on the mounds the lady fern could be found, and farther up nearer the wood the tall brake almost supplanted the bushes. Oak and ash boughs reached across: in the ash the wood-pigeons lingered. Every now and then the bright colours of the green woodpeckers flashed to and fro their nest in a tree hard by. They would not have chosen it had not the place been nearly as quiet as the wood itself.

Blackthorn bushes jealously encroached on the narrow stile that entered the lane from a meadow— a mere rail thrust across a gap. The gates, set in deep recesses—short lanes themselves cut through the mounds—were rotten and decayed, so as to scarcely hold together, and not to be moved without care. Hawthorn branches on each side pushed forward and lessened the opening; on the ground, where the gate- posts had rotted nearly off, fungi came up in thick bunches.

The little meadows to which they led were rich in oaks, growing on the 'shore' of the ditches, tree after tree. The grass in them was not plentiful, but the flowers were many; in the spring the orchis sent up its beautiful purple, and in the heat of summer the bird's-foot lotus flourished in the sunny places. Far- ther up, nearer the wood, the lane became hollow— worn down between high banks, at first clothed with fern, and then, as the hill got steeper, with fir trees.

Where firs are tall and thick together the sunbeams that fall aslant between them seem to be made more visible than under other trees, by the motes or wood dust in the air. Still farther the banks became even steeper, till nothing but scanty ash stoles could grow upon them, the fir plantations skirting along the sum- mit. Then suddenly, at a turn, the ground sank into a deep hollow, where in spring the eye rested with relief and pleasure on the tops of young firs, acre after acre, just freshly tinted with the most delicate green. From thence the track went into the wood.

By day all through the summer months there was always something to be seen in the lane—a squirrel, a stoat; always a song-bird to listen to, a flower or fern to gather. By night the goatsucker visited it, and the bat, and the white owl gliding down the slope. In winter when the clouds hung low the darkness in the hollow between the high banks, where the light was shut out by the fir trees, was like that of a cavern. It was then that night after night a strange procession wended down it.

First came an old man, walking stiffly—not so much from age as rheumatism—and helping his unsteady steps on the slippery sarsen stones with a stout ground-ash staff. Behind him followed a younger man, and in the rear a boy. Sometimes there was an extra assistant, making four; sometimes there was only the old man and one companion. Each had a long and strong ash stick across his shoulder, on which a load of rabbits was slung, an equal number in front and behind, to balance. The old fellow, who was dressed shabbily even for a labourer, was the contractor for the rabbits shot or ferreted in these woods.

He took the whole number at a certain fixed price all round, and made what he could out of them. Every evening in the season he went to the woods to fetch those that had been captured during the day, conveying them to his cottage on the outskirts of the village. From thence they went by carrier's cart to the railway. Old Luke's books, such as they were, were quite beyond the understanding of anyone but himself and his wife; nor could even they themselves tell you exactly how many dozen he purchased in the year. But in his cups the wicked old hypocrite had often been known to boast that he paid the lord of the manor as much money as the rent of a small farm.

One of Luke's eyes was closed with a kind of watery rheum, and was never opened except when he thought a rabbit was about to jump into a net. The other was but half open, and so overhung with a thick grey eyebrow as to be barely visible. His cheeks were the hue of clay, his chin scrubby, and a lanky black forelock depended over one temple. A battered felt hat, a ragged discoloured slop, and corduroys stained with the clay of the banks completed his squalid costume.

A more miserable object or one apparently more deserving of pity it would be hard to imagine. To see him crawl with slow and feeble steps across the fields in winter, gradually working his way in the teeth of a driving rain, was enough to arouse compassion in the hardest heart: there was something so utterly woebegone in his whole aspect—so weather-beaten, as if he had been rained upon ever since childhood. He seemed humbled to the ground—crushed and spiritless.

Now and then Luke was employed by some of the farmers to do their ferreting for them and to catch the rabbits in the banks by the roadside. More than once benevolent people driving by in their cosy cushioned carriages, and seeing this lonely wretch in the bitter wind watching a rabbit's hole as if he were a dog well beaten and thrashed, had been known to stop and call the poor old fellow to the carriage door. Then Luke would lay his hand on his knee, shake his head, and sorrowfully state his pains and miseries: 'Aw, I be terrable bad, I be,' he would say; 'I be most terrible bad: I can't but just drag my leg out of this yer ditch. It be a dull job, bless 'ee, this yer.' The tone, the look of the man, the dreary winter landscape all so thoroughly agreed together that a few small silver coins would drop into his hand, and Luke, with a deep groaning sigh of thankfulness, would bow and scrape and go back to his 'dull job'.

Luke, indeed, somehow or other was always in favour with the 'quality'. He was as firmly fixed in his business as if he had been the most clever courtier. It was not of the least use for any one else to offer to take the rabbits, even if they would give more money. No, Luke was the trusty man; Luke, and nobody else, was worthy. So he grovelled on from year to year, blinking about the place. When some tenant found a gin in the turnip field, or a wire by the clover, and quietly waited till Luke came fumbling by, and picked up the hare or rabbit, it did not make the slightest difference, though he went straight to the keeper and made a formal statement.

Luke had an answer always ready: he had not set the wire, but had stumbled on it unawares, and was going to take it to the keeper; or he had noticed a colony of rats about, and had put the gin for them. Now, the same excuse might have been made by any other poacher; the difference lay in this—that Luke was believed. At all events, such little trifles were forgotten, and Luke went on as before. He did a good deal of the ferreting in the hedges outside the woods himself: if he took home three dozen from the mound and only paid for two dozen, that scarcely concerned the world at large.

If in coming down the dark and slippery lane at night somebody with a heavy sack stepped out from the shadow at the stile, and if the contents of the sack were rapidly transferred to the shoulder-sticks, or the bag itself bodily taken along—why, there was nobody there to see. As for the young man and the boy who helped, those discreet persons had always a rabbit for their own pot, or even for a friend; and indeed it was often remarked that old Luke could always get plenty of men to work for him. No one ever hinted at searching the dirty shed at the side of his cottage that was always locked by day or looking inside the disused oven that it covered. But if fur or feathers had been found there, was not he the contractor? And clearly if a pheasant *was* there he could not be held responsible for the unauthorized acts of his assistants.

The truth was that Luke was the most thorough-paced poacher in the place—or, rather, he was a wholesale receiver. His success lay in making it pleasant for everybody all round. It was pleasant for the keeper, who could always dispose of a few hares or pheasants if he wanted a little money. The keeper, in ways known to himself, made it pleasant for the bailiff. It was equally pleasant for the under-keepers, who had what they wanted (in reason) and enjoyed a little by-play on their own account. It was pleasant for his men; and it was pleasant—specially pleasant— at a little wayside inn kept by Luke's nephew, and, as was believed, with Luke's money. Everybody concerned in the business could always procure refreshment there, including the policeman.

There was only one class of persons whom Luke could not conciliate; and they were the tenants. These very inconsiderate folk argued that it was the keepers' and Luke's interest to maintain a very large stock of rabbits, which meant great inroads on their crops. There seemed to be even something like truth in their complaints; and once or twice the more independent carried their grievances to headquarters so effectually as to elicit an order for the destruction of the rabbits forthwith on their farms. But of what avail was such an order when the execution of it was entrusted to Luke himself?

In time the tenants got to put up with Luke; and the wiser of them turned round and tried to make it still more pleasant for *him*: they spoke a good word for him; they gave him a quart of ale, and put little things in his way, such as a chance to buy and sell faggots at a small profit. Not to be ungrateful, Luke kept their rabbits within reasonable bounds; and he had this great recommendation—that whether they bullied him or whether they gave him ale and bread-and-cheese, Luke was always humble and always touched his hat.

His wife kept a small shop for the sale of the coarser groceries and a little bacon. He had also rather extensive gardens, from which he sold quantities of vegetables. It was more than suspected that the carrier's cart was really Luke's—that is, he found the money for horsing it, and could take possession if he liked. The carrier's cart took his rabbits, and the game he purchased of poachers, to the railway, and the vegetables from the gardens to the customers in town.

At least one cottage besides his own belonged to him; and some would have it that this was one of the reasons of his success with the 'quality'. The people at the great house, anxious to increase their influence, wished to buy every cottage and spare piece of land. This was well known, and many small owners prided themselves upon spiting the big people at the great house by refusing to sell, or selling to another person. The great house was believed to have secured the first 'refuse' of Luke's property, if ever he thought of selling. Luke, in fact, among the lower classes was looked upon as a capitalist—a miser with an unknown hoard. The old man used to sit of a winter's evening, after he had brought down the rabbits, by the hearth, making rabbit-nets of twine. Almost everybody who came along the road, home from the market town, stopped, lifted the latch without knocking, and looked in to tell the news or hear it. But Luke's favourite manœuvre was to take out his snuff-box, tap it, and offer it to the person addressing him. This he would do to a farmer, even though it were the largest tenant of all. For this snuff-box was a present from the lady at the great house, who took an interest in poor old Luke's infirmities, and gave him the snuff-box, a really good piece of workmanship, well filled with the finest snuff, to console his wretchedness.

Of this box Luke was as proud as if it had been the insignia of the Legion of Honour, and never lost an opportunity of showing it to everyone of standing. When the village heard of this kindly present it ran over in its mind all that it knew about the stile, and the sacks, and the disused oven. Then the village very quietly shrugged its shoulders, and though it knew not the word irony, well understood what that term conveys.

At the foot of the hill on which the Upper Woods were situate there extended a level tract of meadows with some cornfields. Through these there flowed a large slow brook, often flooded in winter by the water rushing down from the higher lands. It was pleasant in the early year to walk now and then along the footpath that followed the brook, noting the gradual changes in the hedges.

When the first swallow of the spring wheels over the watery places the dry sedges of last year still stand as they grew. They are supported by the bushes beside the meadow ditch where it widens to join the brook, and the water it brings down from the furrows scarcely moves through the belt of willow lining the larger stream. As the soft west wind runs along the hedge it draws a sigh from the dead dry stalks and leaves that will no more feel the rising sap.

By the wet furrows the ground has still a brownish tint, for there the floods lingered and discoloured the grass. Near the ditch pointed flags are springing up, and the thick stems of the marsh marigold. From bunches of dark green leaves slender stalks arise and bear the golden petals of the marsh buttercups, the lesser celandine. If the wind blows cold and rainy they will close, and open again to the sunshine.

At the outside of the withies, where the earth is drier, stand tall horse-chestnut trees, aspen, and beech. The leaflets of the horse-chestnut are already opening; but on the ground, half-hidden under beech leaves not yet decayed, and sycamore leaves reduced to imperfect grey skeletons, there lies a chestnut shell. It is sodden, and has lost its original green—the prickles, too, have decayed and disappeared; yet at a touch it falls apart, and discloses two chestnuts, still of a rich, deep polished brown.

On the very bank of the brook there grows a beech whose bare boughs droop over, almost dipping in the water, where it comes with a swift rush from the narrow arches of a small bridge whose bricks are green with moss. The current is still slightly turbid, for the floods have not long subsided, and the soaked meadows and ploughed fields send their rills to swell the brook and stain it with sand and earth. On the surface float down twigs and small branches forced from the trees by the gales: sometimes an entangled mass of aquatic weeds—long, slender green filaments twisted and matted together—comes more slowly because heavy and deep in the water.

A little bird comes flitting silently from the willows and perches on the drooping beech branch. It is a delicate little creature, the breast of a faint and dull yellowy green, the wings the lightest brown, and there is a pencilled streak over the eye. The beak is so slender it scarce seems capable of the work it should do, the legs and feet so tiny that they are barely visible. Hardly has he perched than the keen eyes detect a small black speck that has just issued from the arch, floating fast on the surface of the stream and borne round and round in a tiny whirlpool.

He darts from the branch, hovers just above the water, and in a second has seized the black speck and returned to the branch. A moment or two passes, and again he darts down and takes something—this time invisible—from the water. A third time he hovers, and on this occasion just brushes the surface. Then suddenly finding that these movements are watched, he flits—all too soon—up high into the beech and away into the narrow copse. The general tint and shape of the bird are those of the willow wren, but it is difficult to identify the species in so brief a glance and without hearing its note.

The path now trends somewhat away from the stream and skirts a ploughed field, where the hedges are cropped close and the elms stripped of the lesser boughs about the trunks, that the sparrows may not find shelter. But all the same there are birds here

too—one in the thick low hedge, two or three farther
on, another in the ditch perching on the dead white
stems of last year's plants that can hardly support
an ounce weight, and all calling to each other. It is
six marsh tits, as busy as they can well be.

One rises from the ditch to the trunk of an elm
where the thick bark is green with lichen: he goes up
the tree like a woodpecker, and peers into every
crevice. His little beak strikes, peck, peck, at a place
where something is hidden: then he proceeds farther
up the trunk; next he descends a few steps in a sidelong way, and finally hops down some three inches
head foremost, and alights again on the all but perpendicular bark. But his tail does not touch the tree,
and in another minute down he flies again to the
ditch.

A shrill and yet low note that sounds something like
'skeek-skeek' comes from a birch, and another 'skeek-
skeek' answers from an elm. It is like the friction of
iron against iron without oil on the bearings. This is
the tree-climber calling to his mate. He creeps over
the boles of the birch, and where the larger limbs
join the trunk, trailing his tail along the bark, and
clinging so closely that but for the sharp note he would
be passed. Even when that has called attention the
colour of his back so little differs from the colour of
bark that if he is some height up the tree it is not easy
to detect him.

The days go on and the hedges become green—
the sun shines, and the blackbirds whistle in the trees.
They leave the hedge, and mount into the elm or ash
to deliver their song; then, after a pause, dive down
again to the bushes. Up from the pale green corn
that is yet but a few inches high rises a little brown

bird, mounting till he has attained to the elevation of the adjacent oak. Then, beginning his song, he extends his wings, lifts his tail, and gradually descends slanting forward—slowly, like a parachute—sing, sing, singing all the while till the little legs, that can be seen against the sky somewhat depending, touch the earth and the wheat hides him. Still from the clod comes the finishing bar of his music.

In a short time up he rises again, and this time from the summit of his flight sinks in a similar manner singing to a branch of the oak. There he sings again; and, again rising, comes back almost to the same bough singing as he descends. But he is not alone: from an elm hard by come the same notes, and from yet another tree they are also repeated. They cannot rest— now one flits from the topmost bough of an elm to another topmost bough; now a second comes up from feeding, and cries from the branches. They are titlarks [tree-pipits]; and though the call is monotonous, yet it is so cheerful and pleasing that one cannot choose but stay and listen.

Suddenly, two that have been vigorously calling start forward together and meet in mid-air. They buffet each other with their wings; their little beaks fiercely strike; their necks are extended; they man-œuvre round each other, trying for an advantage. They descend, heedless in the rage of their tiny hearts, within a few yards of the watcher, and then in alarm separate. But one flies to the oak branch and defiantly calls immediately.

Over the meadows comes the distant note of the cuckoo. When he first calls his voice is short and somewhat rough, but in a few days it gains power. Then the second syllable has a mellow ring; and as he cries from the tree, the note, swiftly repeated and echoed by the wood, dwells on the ear something like the 'hum' or vibration of a beautiful bell.

As the hedges become green the ivy leaves turn brown at the edge and fall; the wild ivy is often curiously variegated. At the foot of the tree up which it climbs the leaves are five-angled, higher up they lose the angles and become rounded, though growing on the same plant. Sometimes they have a grey tint, especially those that trail along the bank; sometimes the leaves are a reddish brown with pale green ribs.

By the brook now the meadow has become of a rich bright green, the stream has sunk and is clear, and the sunlight dances on the ripples. The grasses at the edge—the turf—curl over and begin to grow down the steep side that a little while since was washed by the current. Where there is a ledge of mud and sand the yellow wagtail runs; he stands on a stone and jerks his tail.

The ploughed field that comes down almost to the brook—a mere strip of meadow between—is green too with rising wheat, high enough now to hide the partridges. Before it got so tall it was pleasant to watch the pair that frequent it: they were so confident that they did not even trouble to cower. At any other time of year they would have run, or flown; but then, though scarcely forty yards away and perfectly visible, they simply ceased feeding but showed no further alarm.

Upon the plough birds in general should look as their best friend, for it provides them with the staff of life as much as it does man. The earth turned up under the share yields them grubs and insects and worms: the seed is sown and the clods harrowed, and they take a second toll; the weeds are hoed or pulled up, and at their roots there are more insects; from the stalk and ears and the bloom of the rising corn they seize caterpillars; when it is ripe they enjoy the grain; when it is cut and carried there are ears in the stubble, and they can then feast on the seeds of the innumerable plants that flowered among it; finally comes the plough again. It is as if the men and horses worked for the birds.

The horse-chestnut trees in the narrow copse bloom; the bees are humming everywhere, and summer is at hand. Presently the brown cockchafers will come almost like an army of locusts, as suddenly appearing without a sign. They seem to be particularly numerous where there is much maple in the hedges.

Resting now on the sward by the stream—contracted in seeming by the weeds and flags and fresh sedges— there comes the distant murmur of voices and the musical laugh of girls. The ear tries to distinguish the words and gather the meaning; but the syllables are intertangled—it is like listening to a low sweet song in a language all unknown. This is the water falling gently over the mossy hatch and splashing faintly on the stones beneath: the blue dragon-flies dart over the smooth surface or alight on a broad leaf—these blue dragon-flies when thus resting curl the tail upwards.

Farther up above the mere there is a spot where the pool itself ends, or rather imperceptibly disappears among a vast mass of aquatic weeds. To these on the soft oozy mud succeed acres of sedge and rush and great tufts of greyish grass. Low willows are scattered about, and alder at the edge and where the ground is firmer. This is the home of the dragon-flies, of the coots, whose white bald foreheads distinguish them at a distance, and of the moorhens.

A narrow lane crosses it on a low bank or causeway but just raised above the level of the floods. It is bordered on either side by thick hawthorn hedges, and these again are further rendered more impassable by the rankest growth of hemlocks, 'gicks', nettles, hedge-parsley, and similar coarse plants. In these the nettle-creeper (white-throat) hides her nest, and they have so encroached that the footpath is almost threatened. This lane leads from the Upper Woods across the marshy level to the cornfields, being a branch from that down which Luke the contractor carried his rabbits.

Now a hare coming from the uplands beyond the woods, or from the woods, and desirous of visiting the cornfields of the level grounds below, found it difficult to pass the water. For besides the marsh itself, the mere, and the brook, another slow, stagnant stream, quite choked with sedges and flags, uncut for years, ran into it, or rather joined it, and before doing so meandered along the very foot of the hill-side over which the woods grew. To a hare or a rabbit, therefore, there was but one path or exit without taking to the water in this direction for nearly a mile, and that was across this narrow raised causeway. The pheasants frequently used it, as if preferring to walk than to fly. Partridges came, too to seat themselves in the dry dust—a thing they do daily in warm weather.

Hares were constantly passing from the cornfields to the wood, and the wood to the cornfields; and they had another reason for using this track, because so many herbs and plants, whose leaves they like better than grass, flourished at the sides of the hedges. No scythe cuts them down, as it does by the hedges in the meadows; nor was a man sent round with a reaping-hook to chop them off, as is often done round the arable fields. There was, therefore, always a feast here, to which, also, the rabbits came.

The poachers were perfectly well aware of all this, and as a consequence this narrow lane became a most favourite haunt of theirs. A wire set in the runs that led to the causeway, or in the causeway itself, was almost certain to be thrown. At one time it was occasionally netted; and now and then a bolder fellow hid himself in the bushes with a gun, and took his choice of pheasant, partridge, hare, or rabbit. These practices were possible, because, although so secluded, there was a public right-of-way along the lane.

But of recent years, as game became more valued and the keepers were increased, a check was put upon it, though even now wires are frequently found which poachers have been obliged to abandon. They are loth to give up a place that has a kind of poaching reputation. As if in revenge for the interference, they have so ransacked the marsh every spring for the eggs of the waterfowl that the wild duck will not lay there, but seek spots safer from such enemies. The marsh is left to the coots and moorhens that from thence stock the brooks.

CHAPTER X

ONE October morning towards the end of the month, Orion and I started to beat over Redcote Farm upon the standing invitation of the occupier. There was a certainty of sport of some kind, because the place had remained almost unchanged for the last century. It is 'improvement' that drives away game and necessitates the pheasant preserve.

The low whitewashed walls of the house were of a dull yellowish hue from the beating of the weather. They supported a vast breadth of thatched roof drilled by sparrows and starlings. Under the eaves the swallows' nests adhered, and projecting shelves were fixed to prevent any inconvenience from them. Some of the narrow windows were still darkened with the black boarding put up in the days of the window tax.

In the courtyard a number of stout forked stakes were used for putting the dairy buckets on, after being cleaned, to dry. No attempt was made to separate the business from the inner life of the house. Here in front these oaken buckets, scoured till nearly white, their iron handles polished like silver, were close under the eyes of anyone looking out. By the front door a besom leaned against the wall that every comer might clean the mud from his boots; and you stepped at once from the threshold into the sitting-room. A lane led past the garden, if that could be called a lane which widened into a field and after rain was flooded so deeply as to be impassable to foot passengers.

The morning we had chosen was fine; and, after

shaking hands with old Farmer 'Willum', whose shooting days were over, we entered the lane, and by it the fields. The meadows were small, enclosed with double mounds, and thickly timbered, so that as the ground was level you could not see beyond the field in which you stood, and upon looking over the gate might surprise a flock of pigeons, a covey of partridges, or a rabbit out feeding. Though the tinted leaves were fast falling, the hedges were still full of plants and vegetation that prevented seeing through them. The 'kuck-kuck' of the redwings came from the bushes—the first note of approaching winter—and the tips of the rushes were dead. Red haws on the hawthorn and hips on the briar sprinkled the hedge with bright spots of colour.

The two spaniels went with such an eager rush into a thick double-mound, dashing heedlessly through the nettles and under the brambles, that we hastened to get one on each side of the hedge. A rustling—a short bark; another, then a movement among the rushes in the ditch, evidently not made by the dogs; then a silence. But the dogs come back, and as they give tongue the rabbit rushes past a bare spot on the slope of the bank. I fire—a snap shot—and cut out some fur, but do no further harm; the pellets bury themselves in the earth. But, startled and perhaps just stung by a stray shot, the rabbit bolts fairly at last twenty yards in front of Orion, the spaniel tearing at his heels.

Up goes the double-barrel with a bright gleam as the sunlight glances on it. A second of suspense: then from the black muzzle darts a cylinder of tawny flame and an opening cone of white smoke: a sharp report rings on the ear. The rabbit rolls over and over, and is dead before the dog can seize him. After harling the rabbit, Orion hangs him high on a projecting branch, so that the man who is following us at a distance may easily find the game. He is a labourer, and we object to have him with us, as we know he would be certain to get in the way.

We then tried a corner where two of these large mounds, meeting, formed a small copse in which grew a quantity of withy and the thick grasses that always border the stoles. A hare bolted almost directly the dogs went in: hares trust in their speed, rabbits in doubling for cover. I fired right and left, and missed: fairly missed with both barrels. Orion jumped upon the mound from the other side, and from that elevation sent a third cartridge after her.

It was a long, a very long shot, but the hare perceptibly winced. Still, she drew easily away from the dogs, going straight for a distant gateway. But before it was reached the pace slackened: she made ineffectual attempts to double as the slow spaniels overtook her, but her strength was ebbing, and they quickly ran in. Reloading, and in none of the best of tempers, I followed the mound. The miss was of course the gun's fault—it was foul; or the cartridges, or the bad quality of the powder.

We passed the well-remembered hollow ash pollard, whence, years before, we had taken the young owls, and in which we had hidden the old single-barrel gun one sultry afternoon when it suddenly came on to thunder. The flashes were so vivid and the discharges seemingly so near that we became afraid to hold the gun, knowing that metal attracted electricity. So it was put in the hollow tree out of the wet, and with it the powder-flask, while we crouched under an adjacent hawthorn till the storm ceased.

Then by the much-patched and heavy gate where I shot my first snipe, that rose out of the little stream and went straight up over the top bar. The emotion, for it was more than excitement, of that moment will never pass from memory. It was the bird of all others that I longed to kill, and certainly to a lad the most difficult. Day after day I went down into the water-meadows; first thinking over the problem of the snipe's peculiar twisting flight. At one time I determined that I would control the almost irresistible desire to fire till the bird had completed his burst of zig-zag and settled to something like a straight line. At another I as firmly resolved to shoot the moment the snipe rose before he could begin to twist. But some unforeseen circumstance always interfered with the execution of these resolutions.

Now the snipe got up unexpectedly right under foot; now one rose thirty yards ahead; now he towered straight up, forced to do so by the tall willows; and occasionally four or five rising together and calling 'sceap, sceap' in as many different directions, made me hesitate at which to aim. The continual dwelling upon the problem rendered me nervous, so that I scarcely knew when I pulled the trigger.

But one day, in passing this gateway, which was a long distance from the particular water-meadows where I had practised, and not thinking of snipes, suddenly one got up, and with a loud 'sceap' darted over the gate. The long slender gun—the old single-barrel—came to the shoulder instinctively, without premeditation, and the snipe fell.

Coming now to the brook, which was broad and bordered by a hedge on the opposite side, I held Orion's gun while he leaped over. The bank was steep and awkward, but he had planned his leap so as to alight just where he could at once grasp an ash branch and so save himself from falling back into the water. He could not, however, stay suspended there, but had to scramble over the hedge, and then called for his gun. I leaned mine against a hollow withy pollard, and called 'ready'.

Taking his gun a few inches above the trigger guard (and with the guard towards his side), holding it lightly just where it seemed to balance in a perpendicular position, I gave it a slow heave rather than a throw, and it rose into the air. This peculiar *feeling* hoist, as it were, caused it to retain the perpendicular position as it passed over brook and hedge in a low curve. As it descended it did indeed slope a little, and Orion caught it with one hand easily. The hedge being low he could see it coming; but guns are sometimes heaved in this way over hedges that have not been cropped for years. Then the gun suddenly appears in the air, perhaps fifteen feet high, while the catch depends not only upon the dexterity of the hand but the ear—to judge correctly where the person who throws it is standing, as he is invisible.

The spaniels plunged in the brook among the flags, but though they made a great splashing nothing came of it till we approached a marshy place where was a pond. A moorhen then rose and scuttled down the brook, her legs dragging along the surface some distance before she could get up, and the sunshine sparkling on the water that dropped from her. I fired and knocked her over: at the sound of the discharge a bird rose from the low mound by the pond some forty yards ahead. My second barrel was empty in an instant.

Both Orion's followed; but the distance, the intervening pollard willows, or our excitement spoilt the aim. The woodcock flew off untouched, and made straight away from the territories we could beat into those that were jealously guarded by a certain keeper with whom Farmer 'Willum' had waged war for years. 'Come on!' shouted Orion as soon as he had marked the cock down in a mound two fields away. Throwing him my gun, I leaped the brook; and we at first raced, but on second thoughts walked slowly, for the mound. Running disturbs accuracy of fire, and a woodcock was much too rare a visitor for the slightest chance to be lost.

As we approached we considered that very probably the cock would either lie close till we had walked past, and get up behind, or he would rise out of gunshot. What we were afraid of was his making for the preserves, which were not far off. So we tossed for the best position, and I lost. I had therefore to get over on the side of the hedge towards the preserves and to walk down somewhat faster than Orion, who was to keep (on his side) about thirty yards behind. The object was to flush the cock on his side, so that if missed the bird might return towards our territories. In a double-mound like this it is impossible to tell what a woodcock will do, but this was the best thing we could think of.

About half-way down the hedge I heard Orion fire both barrels in quick succession—the mound was so thick I could not see through. The next instant the cock came over the top of the hedge just above my head. Startled at seeing me so close, he flew straight down along the summit of the bushes—a splendid chance to look at from a distance; but in throwing up the gun a projecting briar caught the barrels, and before I could recover it the bird came down at the side of the hedge.

It was another magnificent chance; but again three pollard willows interfered, and as I fired the bark flew off one of them in small strips. Quickened by the whistling pellets, the cock suddenly lifted himself again to the top of the hedge to go over, and for a moment came full in view, and quite fifty yards away. I fired a snap shot as a forlorn hope, and lost sight of him; but the next instant I heard Orion call, 'He's down!' One single chance pellet had dropped the cock—he fell on the other side just under the hedge.

We hastened back to the brook, thinking that the shooting would attract the keepers, and did not stay to look at the bird till safe over the water. The long beak, the plumage that seems painted almost in the exact tints of the dead brown leaves he loves so well, the eyes large by comparison and so curiously placed towards the poll of the head as if to see behind him —there was not a point that did not receive its share of admiration. We shot about half a dozen rabbits, two more hares, and a woodpigeon afterwards; but all these were nothing compared with the woodcock.

How Farmer 'Willum' chuckled over it—especially to think that we had cut out the game from the very batteries of the enemy! It was the one speck of bitterness in the old man's character—his hatred of this keeper. Disabled himself by age and rheumatism from walking far, he heard daily reports from his men of this fellow coming over the boundary to shoot, or drive pheasant or partridge away. It was a sight to see Farmer 'Willum' stretch his bulky length in his old armchair, right before the middle of the great fire of logs on the hearth, twiddling his huge thumbs, and

every now and then indulging in a hearty laugh, followed by a sip at the 'straight-cup'.

There was a stag's horn over the staircase: 'Willum'
loved to tell how it came there. One severe winter
long since, the deer in the forest many miles away
broke cover, forced by hunger, and came into the
rickyards and even the gardens. Most of them were
got back, but one or two wandered beyond trace.
Those who had guns were naturally on the look-out;
indeed, a regular hunt was got up—'Willum', then
young and active, in it of course. This chase was not
successful; but early one morning, going to look for
wild geese in the water-meadow with his long-barrelled
gun, he saw something in a lonely rickyard. Creeping
cautiously up, he rested the heavy gun on an ash stole,
and the big duck-shot tore its way into the stag's
shoulder. Those days were gone, but still his interest
in shooting was unabated.

Nothing had been altered on the place since he was
a boy: the rent even was the same. But all that is
now changed—swept away before modern improvements; and the rare old man is gone too, and I think
his only enemy also.

There was nothing I used to look forward to, as the
summer waned, with so much delight as the snipe
shooting. Regularly as the swallow to the eaves in
spring, the snipe comes back with the early frosts of
autumn to the same well-known spots—to the bend of
the brook or the boggy corner in the ploughed field—
but in most uncertain numbers. Sometimes flocks of
ten or twenty, sometimes only twos and threes are
seen, but always haunting particular places.

They have a special affection for peaty ground,
black and spongy, where every footstep seems to

squeeze water out of the soil with a slight hissing sound, and the boot cuts through the soft turf. There, where a slow stream winds in and out, unmarked by willow or bush, but fringed with green aquatic grasses growing on a margin of ooze, the snipe finds tempting food; or in the meadows where a little spring breaks forth in the ditch and does not freeze—for water which has just bubbled out of the earth possesses this peculiarity, and is therefore favourable to low forms of insect or slug life in winter—the snipe may be found when the ponds are bound with ice.

Some of the old country folk used to make as much mystery about this bird as the cuckoo. Because it was seldom seen till the first fogs the belief was that it had lost its way in the mist at sea, and come inland by mistake.

Just as in the early part of the year green buds and opening flowers welcome swallow and cuckoo, so the colours of the dying leaf prepare the way for the second feathered immigration in autumn. Once now and then the tints of autumn are so beautiful that the artist can hardly convey what he sees to canvas. The maples are aglow with orange, the oaks one mass of buff, the limes light gold, the elms a soft yellow. In the hawthorn thickets bronze spots abound; here and there a bramble leaf has turned a brilliant crimson (though many bramble leaves will remain a dull green all the winter through); the edible chestnut sheds leaves of a dark fawn hue, but all, scattered by the winds, presently resolve into a black pulp upon the earth. Noting these signs the sportsman gets out his dust-shot for the snipe, and the farmer, as he sees the fieldfare flying over after a voyage from Norway, congratulates himself that last month was reasonably dry, and enabled him to sow his winter seed.

'Sceap—sceap!' and very often the snipe successfully carries out the intention expressed in his odd-
sounding cry, and does escape in reality. Although
I could not at first put my theory into practice, yet I
found by experience that it was correct. He is the
exception to the golden rule that the safest way lies
in the middle, and that therefore you should fire not
too soon nor too late, but half-way between. But the
snipe must either be knocked over the instant he rises
from the ground, and before he has time to commence
his puzzling zig-zag flight, or else you must wait till
he has finished his corkscrew burst.

Then there is a moment just before he passes out
of range when he glides in a straight line and may be
hit. This singular zig-zag flight so deceives the eye
as almost to produce the idea of a spiral movement.
No barrel can ever be jerked from side to side swiftly
enough, no hair-trigger is fine enough, to catch him
then, except by the chance of a vast scattering over-
charge, which has nothing to do with sport. If he
rises at some little distance, then fire instantly, because
by the time the zigzag is done the range will be too
great; if he starts up under your feet, out of a bunch
of rushes, as is often the case, then give him law till
his eccentric twist is finished.

When the smoke has cleared away in the crisp air,
there he lies, the yet warm breast on the frozen ground,
to be lifted up not without a passing pity and admiration. The brown feathers are exquisitely shaded, and
so exactly resemble the hue of the rough dead aquatic
grass out of which he sprang that if you cast the bird
among it you will have some trouble to find it again.
To discover a living snipe on the ground is indeed a
test of good eyesight; for as he slips in and out among

the brown withered flags and the grey grass it requires not only a quick eye but the in-bred sportsman's instinct of perception (if such a phrase is permissible) to mark him out.

If your shot has missed and merely splashed up the water or rattled against bare branches, then step swiftly behind a tree-trunk, and stay in ambuscade, keeping a sharp watch on him as he circles round high up in the air. Very often in a few minutes he will come back in a wide sweep, and drop scarcely a gun-shot distant in the same watercourse, when a second shot may be obtained. The little jack snipe, when flushed, will never fly far, if shot at several times in succession, still settling fifty or sixty yards farther on, and is easily bagged.

Coming silently as possible round a corner, treading gently on the grass still white with hoar-frost in the shadow of the bushes, you may chance to spring a stray woodcock, which bird, if you lose a moment, will put the hedge between him and you. Artists used to seek for certain feathers which he carries, one in each wing, thinking to make of them a more delicate brush than the finest camel's hair.

In the evening I used to hide in the osier-beds on the edge of a great water-meadow; for now that the marshes are drained, and the black earth of the fens yields a harvest of yellow corn, the broad level meads which are irrigated to fertilize them are among the chief inland resorts of wild fowl. When the bright moon is rising, you walk in among the tapering osier-wands, the rustling sedges, and dead dry hemlock stems, and wait behind an aspen tree.

In the thick blackthorn bush a round dark ball indicates the blackbird, who has puffed out his feathers to shield him from the frost, and who will sit so close and quiet that you may see the moonlight glitter on his eye. Presently comes a whistling noise of wings, and a loud 'quack, quack!' as a string of ducks, their long necks stretched out, pass over not twenty yards high, slowly slanting downwards to the water. This is the favourable moment for the gun, because their big bodies are well defined against the sky, and aim can be taken; but to shoot anything on the ground at night, even a rabbit, whose white tail as he hops away is fairly visible, is most difficult.

The baffling shadows and the moonbeams on the barrel, and the faint reflection from the dew or hoar frost on the grass, prevent more than a general direction being given to the gun, even with the tiny piece of white paper which some affix to the muzzle-sight as a guide. From a punt with a swivel gun it is different, because the game is swimming and visible as black dots on the surface, and half a pound of shot is sure to hit something. But in the water-meadows the ducks get among the grass, and the larger water carriers where they can swim usually have small raised banks, so that at a distance only the heads of the birds appear above them.

So that the best time to shoot a duck is just as he slopes down to settle—first, because he is distinctly visible against the sky; next, because he is within easy range; and, lastly, his flight is steady. If you attempt to have ducks driven towards you, though they may go right overhead, yet it will often be too high—for they rise at a sharp angle when frightened; and men who are excellent judges of distance when it is a hare running across the fallow, find themselves all at fault trying to shoot at any elevation. Perhaps this arises from the peculiarity of the human eye which draughts-men are fond of illustrating by asking a tyro to cor-rectly bisect a vertical line: a thing that looks easy, and is really only to be done by long practice.

To make certain of selecting the right spot in the osiers over which the ducks will pass, for one or two evenings previously a look-out should be kept and their usual course observed; for all birds and animals, even the wildest wild fowl, are creatures of habit and custom, and having once followed a particular path will continue to use it until seriously disturbed. Even-ing after evening the ducks will rise above the horizon at the same place and almost at the same time, and fly straight to their favourite feeding-place.

If hit, the mallard falls with a thud on the earth, for he is a heavy bird; and few are more worthy of powder and shot either for his savoury flavour, far surpassing the tame duck, or the beauty of his burn-ished neck. With the ducks come teal and widgeon and moorhen, till the swampy meadow resounds with their strange cries. When ponds and lakes are frozen hard is the best time for sport in these irrigated fields. All day long the ducks will stand or waddle to and fro on the ice in the centre of the lake or mere, far out of reach and ready to rise at the slightest alarm. But at night they seek the meadow where the water, running swiftly in the carriers, never entirely freezes, and where, if the shallow spots become ice, the rising cur-rent flows over it and floods another place.

There is, moreover, never any difficulty in getting the game when hit, because the water, except in the main carriers, which you can leap across, hardly rises to the ankle, and ordinary water-tight boots will enable you to wade wherever necessary. This is a great advantage with wild fowl, which are sometimes shot and lost in deep ooze and strong currents and eddies, and on thin ice where men cannot go and even good dogs are puzzled.

CHAPTER XI

THE ferreting season commences when the frosts have caused the leaves to drop, and the rabbits grow fat from feeding on bark. Early one December morning, Orion and I started, with our man Little John, to ferret a double-mound for our old friend Farmer 'Willum' at Redcote.

Little John was a labourer—one of those frequently working at odd times for Luke, the Rabbit-Contractor. We had nicknamed him Little John because of his great size and unwieldy proportions. He was the most useful man we knew for such work; his heart was so thoroughly in it.

He was waiting for us before we had finished breakfast, with his tools and implements, having carefully prepared these while yet it was dark at home in his cottage. The nets require looking to before starting, as they are apt to get into a tangle, and there is nothing so annoying as to have to unravel strings with chilled fingers in a ditch. Some have to be mended, having been torn; some are cast aside altogether because weak and rotten. The twine having been frequently saturated with water has decayed. All the nets are of a light yellow colour from the clay and sand that has worked into the string.

These nets almost filled a sack, into which he also cast a pair of 'owl-catchers', gloves of stout white leather, thick enough to turn a thorn while handling bushes, or to withstand the claws of an owl furiously resisting capture. His ferrets cost him much thought,

which to take and which to leave behind. He had
also to be particular how he fed them—they must be
eager for prey, and yet they must not be starved, else
they would gorge on the blood of the first rabbit, and
become useless for hunting.

Two had to be muzzled—an operation of some
difficulty that generally results in a scratched hand.
A small piece of small but strong twine is passed
through the jaws behind the tusk-like teeth, and
tightly tied round, so tightly as almost to cut into
the skin. This is the old way of muzzling a ferret,
handed down from generations: Little John scorns
the muzzles that can be bought at shops, and still
more despises the tiny bells to hang round the neck.
The first he says often come off, and the second em-
barrass the ferret and sometimes catch in projecting
rootlets and hold it fast. He has, too, a line—many
yards of stout twine wound about a short stick—to
line a ferret if necessary.

The ferrets are placed in a smaller bag, tightly
tied at the top—for they will work through and get
out if any aperture be left. Inside the bag is a little
hay for them to lie on. He prefers the fitchew ferret
as he calls it: that is the sort that are coloured like a
polecat. He says they are fiercer, larger of make and
more powerful. But he has also a couple of white ones
with pink eyes. Besides the sack of nets, the bag of
ferrets, and a small bundle in a knotted handkerchief—his 'nuncheon'—which in themselves make a
tolerable load, he has brought a billhook, and a 'navigator', or draining-tool.

This is a narrow spade of specially stout make; the
blade is hollow and resembles an exaggerated gouge,
and the advantage is that in digging out a rabbit the

tool is very apt to catch under a root, when an ordinary spade may bend and become useless. The 'navigator' will stand anything, and being narrow is also more handy. All these implements Little John has prepared by the dim light of a horn lantern in the shed at the back of his cottage. A mug of ale while we get our guns greatly cheers him, and unlooses his tongue.

All the way to Redcote he impresses on us the absolute necessity for silence while ferreting, and congratulates us on having a nearly still day. He is a little doubtful about Orion's spaniel and whether it will keep quiet or not.

When we reach the double-mound, his talk entirely ceases: he is as silent and as rugged as a pollard oak. By the top of the mound the sack of nets is thrown down on the sward and opened. As there are more holes on the other side of the hedge Orion goes over with Little John, and I proceed to set up the nets on mine.

I found some difficulty in getting at the bank, the bushes being so thick, and had to use the billhook and chop a way in: I heard Little John growling about this in a whisper to Orion. Very often before going with the ferrets people send a man or two a few hours previously to chop and clear the bushes. The effect is that the rabbits will not bolt freely. They hear the men chopping, and the vibration of the earth as they clumsily climb over the banks, and will not come out till absolutely forced. If it is done at all, it should be done a week beforehand. This was why Little John grumbled at my chopping though he knew it was necessary.

To set up a rabbit net you must arrange it so that it covers the whole of the mouth of the hole, for if there is any opening between it and the bank the rabbit will slip through. He will not face the net unless obliged to. Along the upper part, if the bank is steep, so that the net will not lie on it of itself, two or three little twigs should be thrust through the meshes into the earth to suspend it.

These twigs should be no larger than are used by birds in constructing their nests: just strong enough to hold the net in place and no more. On the other hand, care must be taken that no stout projecting root catches a corner of the net, else it will not draw up properly and the rabbit will escape.

Little John, not satisfied with my assurance that I had netted all the holes my side, now came over—crawling on hands and knees that he might not jar the bank—to examine for himself. His practised eye detected two holes that I had missed: one on the top of the mound much overhung by dead grass, and one under a stole. These he attended to. He then crawled up on the mound two or three yards below the end of the bury, and with his own hands stretched a larger net right across the top of the bank, so that if a rabbit did escape he would run into this. To be still more sure he stretched another similar net across the whole width of the mound at the other end of the bury.

He then undid the mouth of the ferret bag, holding it between his knees—the ferrets immediately attempted to struggle out: he selected two and then tied it up again. With both these in his own hands, for he would trust nothing to another, he slipped quietly back to Orion's side, and so soon as he saw I was standing well back placed them in different holes.

Almost the next instant one came out my side disarranging a net. I got into the ditch, hastily reset the

net, and put the ferret to an adjacent hole, lifting up
the corner of the net there for it to creep in. Unlike
the weasel a ferret once outside a hole, seems at a loss,
and wanders slowly about, till chance brings him to
a second. The weasel used to hunting is no sooner out
of one hole than he darts away to the next. But this
power the ferret has partially lost from confinement.

For a moment the ferret hesitated inside the hole,
as if undecided which of two passages to take: then he
started, and I lost sight of his tail. Hardly had I got
back to my stand than I heard Little John leap into
the ditch his side: the next minute I saw the body of
the rabbit which he had killed thrown out into the
field.

I stood behind a somewhat advanced bush that
came out into the meadow like a buttress, and kept
an eye on the holes along the bank. It is essential to
stand well back from the holes and, if possible, out of
sight. In a few moments something moved, and I
saw the head of a rabbit at the mouth of a hole just
behind the net. He looked through the meshes as
through a lattice, and I could see his nostrils work, as
he considered within himself how to pass this thing.
It was but for a moment; the ferret came behind,
and wild with hereditary fear, the rabbit leaped into
the net.

The force of the spring not only drew the net together, but dragged out the peg, and rabbit and net
inextricably entangled rolled down the bank to the
bottom of the ditch. I jumped into the ditch and
seized the net; when there came a hoarse whisper:
'Look sharp you, measter: put up another net fust—
he can't get out; hould un under your arm, *or in your
teeth.*'

I looked up, and saw Little John's face peering over the mound. He had thrust himself up under the bushes; his hat was off; his weather-beaten face bleeding from a briar, but he could not feel the scratch so anxious was he that nothing should escape. I pulled another net from my pocket, and spread it roughly over the hole; then more slowly took the rabbit from the other net.

You should never hold a rabbit up till you have got fast hold of his hind legs; he will so twist and work himself as to get free from any other grasp. But when held by the hind legs and lifted from the ground he can do nothing. I now returned to my buttress of bushes and waited. The rabbits did not bolt my side again for awhile. Every now and then I saw, or heard, Orion or Little John leap into their ditch, and well knew what it meant before the dead rabbit was cast out to fall with a helpless thud upon the sward.

Once I saw a rabbit's head at the mouth of a hole, and momentarily expected him to dart forth driven by the same panic fear. But either the ferret passed, or there was another side-tunnel—the rabbit went back. Some few minutes afterwards Little John exclaimed: 'Look out, you: ferret's out!' One of the ferrets had come out of a hole and was aimlessly—as it appeared—roaming along the bank.

As he came nearest my side, I got quietly into the ditch and seized him, and put him into a hole. To my surprise he refused to go in—I pushed him: he returned and continued to try to come out till I gave him a sharp fillip with the finger, when he shook the dust and particles of dry earth from his fur with a shiver, as if in protest, and slowly disappeared inside the hole.

As I was creeping out of the deep ditch on hands and knees, I heard Orion call angrily to the spaniel to come to heel. Hitherto the spaniel had sat on his haunches behind Orion fairly quiet and still, though not without an occasional restless movement. But now he broke suddenly from all control, and disregarding Orion's anger—though with hanging tail—rushed into the hedge, and along the top of the mound where there was a thick mass of dead grass. Little John hurled a clod of clay at him, but before I was quite out of the ditch the spaniel gave tongue, and at the same moment I saw a rabbit come from the ditch and run like mad across the field.

The dog gave chase—I rushed for my gun, which was some yards off, placed against a hollow withy tree. The haste disconcerted the aim—the rabbit too was almost fifty yards away when I fired. But the shot broke one hind leg—it trailed behind—and the spaniel had him instantly. 'Look at yer nets,' said Little John in a tone of suppressed indignation, for he disliked the noise of a gun, as all other noises.

I did look, and found that one net had been partly pushed aside: yet to so small an extent that I should hardly have believed it possible for the rabbit to have crept through. He must have slipped out without the slightest sound and quietly got on the top of the mound without being seen. But there, alas! he found a wide net stretched right across the bank so that to slip down the mound on the top was impossible. That would certainly have been his course had not the net been there.

It was now doubtless that the spaniel caught wind of him, and the scent was so strong that it overcame his obedience. The moment the dog got on the bank, the rabbit slipped down into the rushes in the ditch —I did not see him because my back was turned in the act to scramble out. Then, directly the spaniel gave tongue the rabbit darted for the open, hoping to reach the buries in the hedge on the opposite side of the meadow.

This incident explained why the ferret seemed so loth to go back into the hole. He had crept out some few moments behind the rabbit and in his aimless uncertain manner was trying to follow the scent along the bank. He did not like being compelled to give up this scent and to search again for another. 'Us must be main careful how us fixes our nets, you,' said Little John, going as far as he could in reproof of my negligence.

The noise of the gun, the barking, and talking was of course heard by the rabbits still in the bury, and as if to show that Little John was right, for a while they ceased to bolt. Standing behind the bushes—against which I now placed the gun to be nearer at hand—I watched the nets till my eye was caught by the motions of the ferret bag. It lay on the grass and had hitherto been inert. But now the bag reared itself up, and then rolled over, to again rise and again tumble. The ferrets left in it in reserve were eager to get out—sharp set on account of a scanty breakfast—and their motions caused the bag to roll along a short distance.

I could see Orion on the other side of the mound tolerably well because he was standing up and the leaves had fallen from the upper part of the bushes. Little John was crouched in the ditch: the dead grasses, 'gicks', withered vines of bryony, the thistles, and dark shrivelled fern concealed him.

There was a round black sloe on the blackthorn beside me, the beautiful gloss, or bloom, on it made it look like a tiny plum. It tasted not only sour, but seemed to positively fill the mouth with a rough acid. Overhead light grey clouds, closely packed but not rainy, drifted very slowly before a N.E. upper current. Occasionally a brief puff of wind came through the bushes rustling the dead leaves that still remained on the oaks.

Despite the cold, something of Little John's intense concentration communicated itself to us: we waited and watched with eager patience. After a while he got out of the ditch where he had been listening with his ear close against the bank, and asked me to pass him the ferret-bag. He took out another ferret and lined it—that is, attached one end of a long string to its neck, and then sent it in.

He watched which way the ferret turned, and then again placed his head upon the hard clay to listen. Orion had to come and hold the line, while he went two or three yards farther down, got into the ditch and once more listened carefully. 'He be about the middle of the mound you,' he said to me; 'he be between you and I. Lor! look out.'

There was a low rumbling sound—I expected to see a rabbit bolt into one of my nets. I heard Little John moving some leaves, and then he shouted, 'Give I a net, you—quick. Lor! here be another hole: he's coming!' I looked over the mound and saw Little John, his teeth set and staring at a hole which had no net, his great hands open ready to pounce instantly like some wild animal on its prey. In an instant the rabbit bolted—he clutched it and clasped it tight to his chest. There was a moment of struggling, the next the rabbit was held up for a moment and then cast across his knee.

It was always a sight to see Little John's keen delight in 'wristing' their necks. He affected utter unconsciousness of what he was doing, looked you in the face, and spoke about some indifferent subject. But all the while he was feeling the rabbit's muscles stretch before the terrible grasp of his hands, and an expression of complacent satisfaction flitted over his features as the neck gave with a sudden looseness, and in a moment what had been a living straining creature became limp.

The ferret came out after the rabbit; he immediately caught it and thrust it into his pocket. There were still two ferrets in—one that was suspected to be gorging on a rabbit in a *cul de sac*, and the other lined, and which had gone to join that sanguinary feast. The use of the line was to trace where the loose ferret lay. 'Chuck I the show'l, measter,' said Little John.

I gave the 'navigator' tool a heave over the hedge; it fell and stuck upright in the sward. Orion handed it to him. He first filled up the hole from which a rabbit had just bolted with a couple of 'spits', *i.e.* spadefuls, and then began to dig on the top of the mound.

This digging was very tedious. The roots of the thorn bushes and trees constantly impeded it, and had to be cut. Then upon at last getting down to the hole, it was found that the right place had not been hit by several feet. Here was the line and the lined ferret— he had got hitched in a projecting root, and was furiously struggling to go forward to the feast of blood.

Another spell of digging—this time still slower because Little John was afraid lest the edge of his tool should suddenly slip through and cut his ferret on the head, and perhaps kill it. At last the place was reached and the ferret drawn forth still clinging to its victim. The rabbit was almost beyond recognition as a rabbit. The poor creature had been stopped by a *cul de sac*, and the ferret came upon him from behind.

As the hole was small the rabbit's body completely filled it, and the ferret could not scramble past to get at the spot behind the ear where it usually seizes. The ferret had therefore deliberately gnawn away the hind-quarters and so bored a passage. The ferret being so gorged was useless for further hunting and was replaced in the bag. But Little John gave him a drink of water first from the bottom of the ditch.

Orion and I, wearied with the digging, now insisted on removing to the next bury, for we felt sure that the remaining rabbits in this one would not bolt. Little John had no choice but to comply, but he did so with much reluctance and many rueful glances back at the holes from which he took the nets. He was sure, he said, that there were at least half-a-dozen still in the bury: he only wished he might have all that he could get out of it. But we imperiously ordered a removal.

We went some thirty yards down the mound, passing many smaller buries, and chose a spot perfectly drilled with holes. While Little John was in the ditch putting up nets, we slily undid the ferret bag and turned three ferrets at once loose into the holes. 'Lor! measter, measter, what be you at!' cried Little John, quite beside himself. 'You'll spoil all on it. Lor!'

A sharp report as Orion fired at a rabbit that bolted almost under Little John's fingers drowned his remonstrances, and he had to scramble out of the way quick. Bang! bang! right and left: the firing became rapid. There being no nets to alarm the rabbits and three ferrets hunting them, they tumbled out in all directions as fast as we could load. Now the cartridges struck branches and shattered them. Now the shot flattened itself against sarsen stones imbedded in the mound. The rabbits had scarce a yard to bolt from one hole to another, so that it was sharp work.

Little John now gave up all hope, and only pleaded piteously for his ferrets. 'Mind as you doan't hit 'em, measter; doant'ee shoot into a hole, you.' For half an hour we had some really good shooting; then it began to slacken, and we told him to catch his ferrets and go on to the next bury. I am not sure that he would not have rebelled outright but just then a boy came up carrying a basket of provisions, and a large earthenware jar with a bung cork, full of humming ale. Farmer Willum had sent this, and the strong liquor quite restored Little John's good humour. It really was ale—such as is not to be got for money.

The boy said that he had seen Farmer Willum's hereditary enemy, the keeper, watching us from his side of the boundary, doubtless attracted by the sound of the firing. He said also that there was a pheasant in a little copse beside the brook. We sent him out again to reconnoitre: he returned and repeated that the keeper had gone, and that he thought he saw him enter the distant fir plantations. So we left the boy to help Little John at the next bury—a commission that made him grin with delight, and suited the other very well, since the noisy guns were going away, and he could use his nets.

We took the lined ferret with us, and started after the pheasant. Just as we approached the copse, the spaniel gave tongue on the other side of the hedge.

Orion had tied him up to a bush, wishing to leave him with Little John. But the spaniel tore and twisted till he got loose and had followed us—keeping out of sight—till now crossing the scent of a rabbit he set up his bark. We called him to heel, and I am afraid he got a kick. But the pheasant was alarmed and rose before we could properly enfilade the little copse, where we should most certainly have had him. He flew high and straight for the fir plantations where it was useless to follow.

However, we leaped the brook and entered the keeper's territory under shelter of a thick double-mound. We slipped the lined ferret into a small bury, and succeeded in knocking over a couple of rabbits. The object of using the lined ferret was because we could easily recover it. This was pure mischief, for there were scores of rabbits on our own side. But then there was just a little spice of risk in this, and we knew Willum would gloat over it.

After firing these two shots we got back again as speedily as possible, and once more assisted Little John. We could not, however, quite resist the pleasure of shooting a rabbit occasionally and so tormenting him. We left one hole each side without a net, and insisted on the removal of the net that stretched across the top of the bank. This gave us a shot now and then, and the removal of the cross net allowed the rabbit some little law.

Notwithstanding these drawbacks—to him—Little John succeeded in making a good bag. He stayed till it was quite dark to dig out a ferret that had killed a rabbit in the hole. He took his money for his day's work with indifference: but when we presented him with two couple of clean rabbits his gratitude was too much for him to express. The gnawn and 'blown' rabbits [by shot] were his perquisite, the clean rabbits an unexpected gift. It was not their monetary value: it was the fact that they were rabbits.

The man's instinct for hunting was so strong that it seemed to overcome everything else. He would walk miles—after a long day's farm work—just to help old Luke, the rabbit contractor, bring home the rabbits in the evening from the Upper Woods. He worked regularly for one farmer, and did his work well; he was a sober man too as men go, that is, he did not get drunk more than once a month. A strong man must drink now and then: but he was not a sot, and took nine tenths of his money faithfully home to his wife and children.

In the winter when farm work is not so pressing he was allowed a week off now and then, which he spent in ferreting for the farmers, and sometimes for Luke, and of course he was only too glad to get such an engagement as we gave him. Sometimes he made a good thing of his ferreting: sometimes when the weather was bad it was a failure. But although a few shillings were of consequence to him, it really did not seem to be the money-value but the sport that he loved. To him that sport was all-absorbing.

His ferrets were well looked after, and he sometimes sold one for a good price to keepers. As a rule a man who keeps ferrets is suspected: but Little John was too well understood, and he had no difficulty in begging a little milk for them.

His tenacity in pursuit of a rabbit was always a source of wonder to me. In rain, in wind, in frost; his feet up to the ankle in the ice-cold slush at the bottom of a ditch: no matter what the weather or how rough,

he patiently stood to his nets. I have known him stand
the whole day long in a snowstorm—the snow on the
ground and in the holes, the flakes drifting against his
face—and never once show impatience. All he disliked was wind—not on account of discomfort, but
because the creaking of the branches and the howling
of the blast made such a noise that it was impossible to
tell where the rabbit would bolt.

He congratulated himself that evening because he
had recovered all his ferrets. Sometimes one will lie in
and defy all efforts to bring it out. One plan is to
place a dead fresh rabbit at the mouth of the hole
which may tempt the ferret to come and seize it. In
large woods there are generally one or more ferrets
wandering loose in the season, that have escaped from
the keepers or poachers.

If the keeper sees one he tries to catch it, failing that
he puts a charge of shot into it. Some keepers think
nothing of shooting their own ferrets if they will not
come when called by the chirrup with the lips, or dis-
please them in other ways. They do not care because
they can have as many as they like. Little John made
pets of his: they obeyed him very well as a rule.

Poaching men are sometimes charged with stealing
ferrets, *i.e.* with picking up and carrying off those that
keepers have lost. A ferret is, however, a difficult
thing to identify and swear to.

Those who go poaching with ferrets choose a moonlight night: if it is dark it is difficult to find the holes.
Small buries are best because so much more easily
managed, and the ferret is usually lined. If a large
bury is attempted, they take the first half-dozen that
bolt and then move on to another. The first rabbits
come out rapidly; the rest linger as if warned by the

fate of their companions. Instead of wasting time over them it is best to move to another place.

Unless a keeper should chance to pass up the hedge-row there is comparatively little risk, for the men are in the ditch and invisible ten yards away under the bushes and make no noise. It is more difficult to get home with the game: but it is managed. Very small buries with not more than four or five holes may be ferreted even on the darkest nights by carefully observing beforehand where the holes are situate.

CHAPTER XII

W<small>HEN</small> the moon is full and nearly at the zenith it
seems to move so slowly that the shadows scarcely
change their position. In winter, when the branches
are bare, a light that is nearly vertical over a tree can
cast but little shadow, and that falls immediately
around the trunk. So that the smallness of the shadow
itself and the slowness of its motion together tend to
conceal it.

The snow on the ground increases the sense of light,
and in approaching the wood the scene is even more
distinct than during the gloomy day. The tips of the
short stubble that has not yet been ploughed in places
just protrude above the surface, and the snow, frozen
hard, crunches with a low sound under foot. But for
that all is perfectly still. The level upland cornfields
stretch away white and vacant to the hills—white,
too, and clear against the sky. The plain is silent, and
nothing that can be seen moves upon its surface.

On the verge of the wood which occupies the sloping ground there stands a great oak tree, and down
one side of its trunk is a narrow white streak of snow.
Leaning against the oak and looking upwards, every
branch and twig is visible, lit up by the moon. Overhead the stars are dimmed, but they shine more
brightly yonder above the hills. Such leaves as have
not yet fallen hang motionless: those that are lying
on the ground are covered by the snow, and thus held
fast from rustling even were the wind to blow. But
there is not the least breath—a great frost is always

quiet, profoundly quiet—and the silence is undisturbed even by the fall of a leaf. The frost that kills them holds the leaves till it melts, and then they drop.

The tall ash poles behind in the wood stand stark and straight, pointing upwards, and it is possible to see for some distance between them. No lesser bats flit to and fro outside the fence under the branches; no larger ones pass above the tops of the trees. There seems, indeed, a total absence of life. The pheasants are at roost in the warmer covers; and the wood-pigeons are also perched—some in the detached oaks of the hedgerows, particularly those that are thickly grown with ivy about the upper branches. Up in the great beeches the rooks are still and silent: sometimes the boughs are encrusted with rime about their very claws.

Leaving the oak now and skirting the wood, after a while the meadows on the lower ground are reached; and here perhaps the slight scampering sound of a rabbit may be heard. But as they can see and hear you so far in the bright light and silence, they will most likely be gone before you can get near. They are restless—very restless; first because of the snow, and next because of the moonlight. The hares, unable to find anything on the hills or the level white plain above, have come down here and search along the sheltered hedgerows for leaf and blade. To-night the rabbits will run almost like the hares, to and fro, hither and thither.

In the thickest hawthorns the blackbirds and lesser feathered creatures are roosting, preferring the hedgerow to the more open wood. Some of the lesser birds have crept into the ivy around the elms, and which crowns the tops of the withy pollards. Wrens and sparrows have gone to the hayricks, roosting in little holes in the sides under the slightly projecting thatch. They have taken refuge too in the nest-holes made in the thatched eaves of the sheds: tits are there also; and sometimes two or three of the latter are captured at once in such holes.

A dark line across the lower meadows marks the course of the brook; it is dark because the snow falling on the water melted. Even now there is a narrow stream unfrozen; though the banks against which it chafes are hard, and will not take the impression of the moorhen's foot. The water-rats that in summer-time played and fed along the margin among the flags are rarely seen in winter. In walking in daylight by the brook now their plunge into the water will not be heard, nor can they be seen travelling at the bottom.

They lay up a store of food in a hole away from the stream, generally choosing the banks or higher ground in the withy-beds—places that are not often flooded. Their ordinary holes, which are half, and sometimes quite, under water, will not do for winter; they would be frozen in them, and perhaps their store of food would be spoiled: besides which the floods cause the stream to rise above its banks, and they could not exist under water for weeks together.

Still further down, where the wood ends in scattered bushes and withy-beds, the level shore of the shallow mere succeeds. The once soft, oozy ground is now firm; the rushes are frozen stiff, and the ice for some distance out is darkened by the aquatic weeds frozen in it. From here the wood, rising up the slope, comes into view at once—the dark trees, the ash poles, the distant beeches, the white crest of the hill—all still and calm under the moonlight. The level white plain of ice behind stretches away, its real extent concealed by the islands of withy and the dark pines along the distant shore: while elsewhere the ice is not distinguishable from the almost equally level fields that join it. Looking now more closely on the snow, the tracks of hares and rabbits that have crossed and recrossed the ice are visible.

In passing close to the withy-beds to return to the wood some branches have to be pushed aside and cause a slight noise. Immediately a crowd of birds rise out of the withies, where they have been roosting, and scatter into the night. They are redwings and thrushes; every withy-bed is full of them. After wheeling about in the air they will presently return—first one, then three or four, and finally the flock, to their roosting-place.

It is easy now to walk through the wood without making a noise: there is room to pass between the stoles of ash; and the dead sticks that would have cracked under foot are covered with snow. But be careful how you step; for in some places the snow has fallen upon a mass of leaves filling a swampy hollow. Above there is a thin crust of snow, but under the leaves the oozy ground is still soft.

Upon the dark pines the snow has lodged, making the boughs bend downwards. Where the slope becomes a hill the ash stoles and nut-tree bushes are far apart and thinner, so that there are wide white spaces around them. Regaining now the top of the hill where the plain comes to the verge of the wood, there is a clear view down across the ash poles to the withies, the white mere, and the meadows below. Everywhere silence, stillness, sleep.

In the high trees slumbering creatures; in the hedge-rows, in the bushes, and the withies birds with feathers puffed out, slumbering; in the banks, under the very ground, dormant animals. A quiet cold that at first does not seem cold because it is so quiet, but which gradually seizes on and stills the sap of plants and the blood of living things. A ruthless frost, still, subtle, and irresistible, that will slay the bird on its perch and weaken the swift hare.

The most cruel of all things this snow and frost, because of the torture of hunger which the birds must feel even in their sleep. But how beautiful the round full moon, the brilliant light, the white landscape, the graceful lines of the pine brought out by the snow, the hills yonder, and the stars rising above them!

It was on just such a night as this that some years since a most successful raid was made upon this wood by a band of poachers coming from a distance. The pheasants had been kept later than usual to be shot by a Christmas party, and perhaps this had caused a relaxation of vigilance. The band came in a cart of some kind; the marks of the wheels were found on the snow where it had been driven off the highway and across a field to some ricks. There, no doubt, the horse and cart were kept out of sight behind the ricks, while the men, who were believed to have worn smock-frocks, entered the wood.

The bright moonlight made it easy to find the pheasants, and they were potted in plenty. Finding that there was no opposition, the gang crossed from the wood to some outlying plantations and continued their work there. The keeper never heard a sound. He was an old man—a man who had been on the estate all his life—and had come in late in the evening after a long round. He sat by the fire of split logs and enjoyed the warmth after the bitter cold and frost; and as he himself confessed, took an extra glass in consideration of the severity of the weather.

His wife was old and deaf. Neither of them heard the guns nor the dogs. Those in the kennels close to the cottage, and very likely one or more indoors, must have barked at the noise of the shooting. But if any dim sense of the uproar did reach the keeper's ear he put it down to the moon, at which dogs will bay. As for his assistants, they had quietly gone home, so soon as they felt sure that the keeper was housed for the night. Long immunity from attack had bred over-confidence; the staff also was too small for the extent of the place, and this had doubtless become known. No one sleeps so soundly as an agricultural labourer; and as the nearest hamlet was at some distance it is not surprising that they did not wake.

In the early morning a fogger going to fodder his cattle came across a pheasant lying dead on the path, the snow stained with its blood. He picked it up, and put it under his smock-frock, and carried it to the pen, where he hid it under some litter, intending to take it home. But afterwards, as he crossed the fields towards the farm, he passed near the wood and observed the tracks of many feet and a gap in the fence. He looked through the gap and saw that the track went into the preserves. On second thoughts he went back for the pheasant and took it to his master.

The farmer, who was sitting down to table, quietly ate his breakfast, and then strolled over to the keeper's cottage with the bird. This was the first intimation: the keeper could hardly believe it, till he himself went down and followed the trail of foot-marks. There was not the least difficulty in tracing the course of the poachers through the wood; the feathers were lying about; the scorched paper (for they used muzzle loaders), broken boughs, and shot-marks were all too plain. But by this time the gang were well away, and none were captured or identified.

The extreme severity of the frost naturally caused people to stay indoors, so that no one noticed the cart going through the village; nor could the track of its wheels be discerned from others on the snow of the highway beaten down firm. Even had the poachers been disturbed, it is doubtful if so small a staff of keepers could have done anything to stop them. As it was, they not only made a good haul—the largest made for years in that locality—but quite spoiled the shooting.

There are no white figures passing through the peaceful wood to-night and firing up into the trees. It is perfectly still. The broad moon moves slow, and the bright rays light up tree and bush, so that it is easy to see through, except where the brambles retain their leaves and are fringed with the dead ferns.

The poaching of the present day is carried on with a few appliances only. An old-fashioned poacher could employ a variety of 'engines', but the modern has scarcely any choice. There was, for instance, a very effective mode of setting a wire with a springe or bow. A stout stick was thrust into the ground, and then bent over into an arch. When the wire was thrown it instantly released the springe, which sprang up and drew it fast round the neck of the hare or rabbit, whose fore feet were lifted from the earth. Sometimes a growing sapling was bent down for the bow if it chanced to stand conveniently near a run.

The hare no sooner put her head into the noose than she was suspended and strangled.

I tried the springe several times for rabbits, and found it answer; but the poacher cannot use it because it is so conspicuous. The stick itself, rising above the grass, is visible at some distance, and when thrown it holds the hare or rabbit up for any one to see that passes by. With a wire set in the present manner the captured animal lies extended, and often rolls into a furrow and is further hidden.

The springe was probably last employed by the mole-catchers. Their wooden traps were in the shape of a small tunnel, with a wire in the middle, which, when the mole passed through, set free a bent stick. This stick pulled the wire and hung the mole. Such mole-catchers' bows or springes used to be seen in every meadow, but are now superseded by the iron trap.

Springes with horsehair nooses on the ground were also set for woodcocks and for wild ducks. It is said that a springe of somewhat similar construction was used for pheasants. Horsehair nooses are still applied for capturing woodpeckers and the owls that spend the day in hollow trees, being set round the hole by which they leave the tree. A more delicate horsehair noose is sometimes set for finches and small birds. I tried it for bullfinches, but did not succeed from lack of the dexterity required. The modes of using bird-lime were numerous, and many of them are in use for taking song-birds.

But the enclosure of open lands, the strict definition of footpaths, closer cultivation, and the increased value of game have so checked the poacher's operations with nets that in many districts the net may be said to be extinct. It is no longer necessary to bush the stubbles immediately after reaping. Brambles are said to have been the best for hindering the net, which frequently swept away an entire covey, old birds and young together. Stubbles are now so short that no birds will lie in them, and the net would not be successful there if it were tried.

The net used to be so favourite an 'engine' because partridges and pheasants will run rather than fly. In the case of partridges the poacher had first to ascertain the haunt of the covey, which he could do by looking for where they roost at night: the spot is often worn almost bare of grass and easily found. Or he could listen in the evening for the calling of the birds as they run together. The net being set, he walked very slowly down the wind towards the covey. It could not be done too quietly or gently, because if one got up all the rest would immediately take wing; for partridges act in concert. If he took his time and let them run in front of him he secured the whole number.

That was the principle; but the nets were of many kinds: the partridges were sometimes driven in by a dog. The partridges that appear in the market on the morning of the 1st of September are said to be netted, though probably by those who have a right to do so. These birds by nature lend themselves to such tricks, being so timid. It is said that if continually driven to and fro they will at last cower, and can be taken by hand or knocked over with a stick.

The sight of a paper kite in the air makes them motionless till forced to rise; and there was an old dodge of ringing a bell at night, which so alarmed the covey that they remained still till the net was ready, when a sudden flash of light drove them into it. Im-

agine a poacher ringing a bell nowadays! Then,
partridges were peculiarly liable to be taken; now,
perhaps, they escape better than any other kind of
game. Except with a gun the poacher can hardly
touch them, and after the coveys have been broken up
it is not worth his while to risk a shot very often. If
only their eggs could be protected there should be
little difficulty with partridges.

Pheasants are more individual in their ways, and
act less together; but they have the same habit of
running instead of flying, and if a poacher did but
dare he could take them with nets as easily as possible.
They form runs through the woods—just as fowls will
wander day after day down a hedge, till they have
made quite a path. So that, having found the run
and knowing the position of the birds, the rest is sim-
plicity itself. The net being stretched, the pheasants
were driven in. A cur dog was sometimes sent round
to disturb the birds. Being a cur, he did not bark, for
which reason a strain of cur is preferred to this day by
the mouchers who keep dogs. Now that the woods are
regularly watched such a plan has become impractic-
able. It might indeed be done once, but surely not
twice where competent keepers were about.

Nets were also used for hares and rabbits, which
were driven in by a dog; but, the scent of these animals
being so good, it was necessary to work in such a manner that the wind might not blow from the net, meeting them as they approached it. Pheasants, as every
one knows, roost on trees, but often do not ascend very
high; and, indeed, before the leaves are off they are
said to be sometimes taken by hand—sliding it along the
bough till the legs are grasped, just as you might fowls
perched at night on a rail across the beams of a shed.

The spot where they roost is easily found out, because of the peculiar noise they make upon flying up; and with a little precaution the trees may be approached without startling them. Years ago the poacher carried a sulphur match and lit it under the tree, when the fumes, ascending, stupefied the birds, which fell to the ground. The process strongly resembled the way in which old-fashioned folk stifled their bees by placing the hive at night, when the insects were still, over a piece of brown paper dipped in molten brimstone and ignited. The apparently dead bees were afterwards shaken out and buried; but upon moving the earth with a spade some of them would crawl out, even after two or three days.

Sulphur fumes were likewise used for compelling rabbits to bolt from their buries without a ferret. I tried an experiment in a bury once with a mixture the chief component of which was gunpowder, so managed as to burn slowly and give a great smoke. The rabbits did, indeed, just hop out and hop in again; but it is a most clumsy expedient, because the fire must be lit on the windward side, and the rabbits will only come out to leeward. The smoke hangs, and does not penetrate into half the tunnels; or else it blows through quickly, when you must stop half the holes with a spade. It is a wretched substitute for a ferret.

When cock-fighting was common the bellicose inclinations of the cock-pheasants were sometimes excited to their destruction. A game-cock was first armed with the sharp spur made from the best razors, and then put down near where a pheasant-cock had been observed to crow. The pheasant-cock is so thoroughly game that he will not allow any rival crowing in his

locality, and the two quickly met in battle. Like a
keen poniard the game-cock's spur either slew the
pheasant outright or got fixed in the pheasant's
feathers, when he was captured.

A pheasant, too, as he ran deeper into the wood
upon an alarm, occasionally found his neck in a noose
suspended across his path. For rabbiting, the lurcher
was and is the dog of all others. He is as cunning
and wily in approaching his game as if he had a cross
of feline nature in his character. Other dogs trust to
speed; but the lurcher steals on his prey without a
sound. He enters into the purpose of his master, and
if any one appears in sight remains quietly in the
hedge with the rabbit or leveret in his mouth till a
sign bids him approach. If half the stories told of the
docility and intelligence of the lurcher are true, the
poacher needs no other help than one of these dogs for
ground game. But the dogs called lurchers nowadays
are mostly of degenerate and impure breed; still, even
these are capable of a good deal.

There is a way of fishing with rod and line, but
without a bait. The rod should be in one piece, or
else a stout one—the line also very strong and short,
the hook of large size. When the fish is discovered the
hook is quietly dropped into the water and allowed
to float, in seeming, along, till close under it. The rod
is then jerked up, and the barb enters the body of the
fish and drags it out.

This plan requires, of course, that the fish should be
visible, and if stationary is more easily practised; but
it is also effective even against small fish that swim
together in large shoals, for if the hook misses one it
strikes another. The most fatal time for fish is when
they spawn: roach, jack, and trout alike are then

within reach, and if the poacher dares to visit the water he is certain of a haul.

Even in the present day and in the south a fawn is now and then stolen from parks and forests where deer are kept. Being small, it is not much more difficult to hide than a couple of hares; and once in the carrier's cart and at a little distance no one asks any questions. Such game always finds a ready sale; and when a savoury dish is on the table those who are about to eat it do not inquire whence it came any more than the old folk did centuries ago. A nod and a wink are the best sauce. As the keepers are allowed to sell a certain number of fawns (or say they are), it is not possible for anyone at a distance to know whether the game was poached or not. An ordinary single-barrel muzzle-loader of the commonest kind with a charge of common shot will kill a fawn.

I once started to stalk a pheasant that was feeding in the corner of a meadow. Beyond the meadow there was a cornfield which extended across to a preserved wood. But the open stubble afforded no cover —anyone walking in it could be seen—so that the pheasant had to be got at from one side only. It was necessary also that he should be shot dead without fluttering of wings, the wood being so near.

The afternoon sun, shining in a cloudless sky—it was a still October day—beat hot against the western side of the hedge as I noiselessly walked beside it. In the aftermath, green but flowerless, a small flock of sheep were feeding—one with a long briar clinging to his wool. They moved slowly before me; a thing I wanted; for behind sheep almost any game can be approached.

I have also frequently shot rabbits that were out

feeding, by the aid of a herd of cows. It does not seem to be so much the actual cover as the scent of the animals; for a man of course can be seen over sheep, and under the legs of cattle. But the breath and odour of sheep or cows prevent the game from scenting him, and, what is equally effective, the cattle, to which they are accustomed, throw them off their guard.

The cart-horses in the fields do not answer so well: if you try to use one for stalking, unless he knows you he will sheer off and set up a clumsy gallop, being afraid of capture and a return to work. But cows will feed steadily in front; and a flock of sheep, very slowly driven, move on with a gentle 'tinkle, tinkle'. Wild creatures show no fear of what they are accustomed to, and the use of which they understand.

If a solitary hurdle be set up in a meadow as a hiding-place from behind which to shoot the rabbits of a burrow, not one will come out within gun-shot that evening. They know that it is something strange, the use of which they do not understand and therefore avoid. When I first began to shoot, the difficulty was to judge the distances, and to know how far a rabbit was from a favourite hiding-place. I once carefully dropped small green boughs, just broken off, at twenty, thirty, and forty yards, measuring by paces. This was in the morning.

In the evening not a rabbit would come out anywhere near these boughs; they were shy of them even when the leaves had withered and turned brown; so that I took them away. Yet of the green boughs blown off by a gale, or the dead grey branches that fall of their own weight, they take no notice.

First, then, they must have heard me in their burrows pacing by; secondly, they scented the boughs as

having been handled, and connected the two circumstances together; and, thirdly, though aware that the
boughs themselves were harmless, they felt that harm
was intended. The pheasant had been walking about
in the corner where the hedges met, but now he went
in; still, as he entered the hedge in a quiet way, he did
not appear to be alarmed. The sheep, tired of being
constantly driven from their food, now sheered out
from the hedge, and allowed me to go by.

As I passed I gathered a few haws and ate them.
The reason why birds do not care much for berries
before they are forced to take to them by frost is
because of the stone within, so that the food afforded
by the berries is really small. Yew-berries are an
exception; they have a stone, but the covering to it is
sweet, succulent, and thick, and dearly loved by
thrushes. In the ditch the tall grasses, having escaped
the scythe, bowed low with the weight of their own
awn-like seeds.

The corner was not far off now; and I waited awhile
behind a large hawthorn bush growing on the 'shore'
of the ditch, thinking that I might see the pheasant on
the mound, or that at least he would recover confidence if he had previously heard anything. Inside
the bush was a nest already partly filled with fallen
leaves, like a little basket.

A rabbit had been feeding on the other side, but
now, suspicious, came over the bank, and, seeing me,
suddenly stopped and lifted himself up. In that
moment I could have shot him, being so near, without putting the gun to the shoulder, by the sense of
direction in the hands; the next he dived into a burrow. Looking round the bush, I now saw the pheasant
in the hedge that crossed at right angles in front; this

was fortunate, because through that hedge there was another meadow. It was full of nut-tree bushes, very tall and thick at the top, but lower down thin, as is usually the case when poles grow high. To fill the space a fence had been made of stakes and bushes woven between them, and on this the pheasant stood.

It was too far for a safe shot; in a minute he went down into the meadow on the other side. I then crept on hands and knees towards the nut-bushes: as I got nearer there was a slight rustle and a low hiss in the grass, and I had to pause while a snake went by hastening for the ditch. A few moments afterwards, being close to the hedge, I rose partly up, and looked carefully over the fence between the hazel wands. There was the pheasant not fifteen yards away! his back somewhat towards me, and quietly questing about.

In lifting the gun I had to push aside a bough— the empty hoods from which a bunch of brown nuts had fallen rested against the barrel as I looked along it. I aimed at the head—knowing that it would mean instant death, and would also avoid shattering the bird at so short a range; besides which there would be fewer scattered feathers to collect and thrust out of sight into a rabbit bury. A reason why people frequently miss pheasants in cover-shooting, despite of their size, is because they look at the body, the wings, and the tail. But if they looked only at the head, and thought of that, very few would escape. My finger felt the trigger, and the least increase of pressure would have been fatal; but in the act I hesitated, dropped the barrel, and watched the beautiful bird.

That watching so often stayed the shot that at last

it grew to be a habit: the mere simple pleasure of seeing birds and animals, when they were quite unconscious that they were observed, being too great to be spoiled by the discharge. After carefully getting a wire over a jack; after waiting in a tree till a hare came along; after sitting in a mound till the partridges began to run together to roost: in the end the wire or gun remained unused. The same feeling has equally checked my hand in legitimate shooting: time after time I have flushed partridges without firing, and have let the hare bound over the furrow free.

I have entered many woods just for the pleasure of creeping through the brake and the thickets. Destruction in itself was not the motive; it was an overpowering instinct for woods and fields. Yet woods and fields lose half their interest without a gun—I like the power to shoot, even though I may not use it. The very perfection of our modern guns is to me one of their drawbacks: the use of them is so easy and so certain of effect that it takes away the romance of sport.

There could be no greater pleasure to me than to wander with a matchlock through one of the great forests or wild tracts that still remain in England. A hare a day, a brace of partridges, or a wild duck would be ample in the way of actual shooting. The weapon itself, whether matchlock, wheel-lock, or even a crossbow, would be a delight. Some of the antique wheel-lock guns are really beautiful specimens of design. The old powder-horns are often gems of workmanship —hunting scenes cut out in ivory, and the minutest detail of hoof or antler rendered with life-like accuracy. How pleasant these carvings feel to the fingers! It is delightful to handle such weapons and such implements.

The matchlocks, too, are inlaid or the stocks carved. There is slaughter in every line of our modern guns—mechanical slaughter. But were I offered participation in the bloodiest battue ever arranged, or the freedom of an English forest or mountain tract, to go forth at any time untrammelled by attendant, but only to shoot with matchlock, wheel-lock, or crossbow, my choice would be unhesitating.

There would be pleasure in winding up the lock with the spanner; pleasure in adjusting the priming; or with the matchlock in lighting the match. To wander out into the brake, to creep from tree to tree so noiselessly that the woodpecker should not cease to tap—in that there is joy. The consciousness that everything depends upon your own personal skill, and that you have no second resource if that fails you, gives the real zest to sport.

If the wheel did not knock a spark out quickly; if the priming had not been kept dry or the match not properly blown, or the crossbow set exactly accurate, then the care of approach would be lost. You must hold the gun steady, too, while the slow priming ignites the charge.

An imperfect weapon—yes; but the imperfect weapon would accord with the great oaks, the beech trees full of knot-holes, the mysterious thickets, the tall fern, the silence and the solitude. The chase would become a real chase: not, as now, a foregone conclusion. And there would be time for pondering and dreaming.

Let us be always out of doors among trees and grass, and rain and wind and sun. There the breeze comes and strikes the cheek and sets it aglow: the gale increases and the trees creak and roar, but it is only a ruder music. A calm follows, the sun shines in the sky, and it is the time to sit under an oak, leaning against the bark, while the birds sing and the air is soft and sweet. By night the stars shine, and there is no fathoming the dark spaces between those brilliant points, nor the thoughts that come as it were between the fixed stars and landmarks of the mind.

Or it is the morning on the hills, when hope is as wide as the world; or it is the evening on the shore. A red sun sinks, and the foam-tipped waves are crested with crimson; the booming surge breaks, and the spray flies afar, sprinkling the face watching under the pale cliffs. Let us get out of these indoor narrow modern days, whose twelve hours somehow have become shortened, into the sunlight and the pure wind. A something that the ancients called divine can be found and felt there still.